D0190637

Lots of good advice makes living a life with Christ less risky. Kent and Davidene Humphreys in Show and Then Tell *have clarified Biblical principles for living "real life" in the marketplace. This is a "soul nurturing" book that provides practical help with spiritual insight for lay men and women in the various stages of life. All who read this work will relate better to society, appreciate life more, and have an increased ministry to those around them.*

Tom Phillips
President/CEO, International Students, Inc.

What a refreshing and challenging presentation from Kent and Davidene Humphreys, ordinary folks with an extraordinary vision of what you can do for God! Biblical principles are fleshed out through personal testimonies and inspirational vignettes and punctuated with brief words of wisdom. The Humphreys challenge us to both "show" through lifestyle and "tell" with verbal witness the Good News of the Gospel to unbelievers and then to nurture and disciple believers in order to continue the cycle!

Dorothy Kelley Patterson
Southeastern Baptist Theological Seminary

It is a pleasure to commend Show and Then Tell *by Kent and Davidene Humphreys. I've known them both for years. No one I have ever met exemplifies what they teach better than Kent and Davidene. What they teach, they have practiced. You can apply their insights with confidence that they are biblical and that they fit life as it really is. I hope this book gets a wide circulation.*

Lorne Sanny
The Navigators

Show and Then Tell *captures spiritual realities that will encourage you to live the life of Jesus Christ so people will listen. Kent and Davidene have had a tremendous influence on those around them; and with their help, you can too.*

John Nieder
Art of Family Living

Show and Then Tell *is one of the simplest yet most profound Christian books written in the last one hundred years. It is not only inspirational, but the contents of this husband-and-wife team collaboration is spiritually motivational. No one can read this book without being impressed with its sincerity, simplicity, and insights into the Christian walk and the Christian witness. I recommend it to every believer who wants to live the life and then share it with others.*

Gilford A. Stricklin, Sr.
Founder and President
Marketplace Ministries

SHOW
and then
TELL

PRESENTING
THE GOSPEL
THROUGH
DAILY
ENCOUNTERS

Kent & Davidene
HUMPHREYS

MOODY PRESS
CHICAGO

© 2000 by
KENT AND DAVIDENE HUMPHREYS

All rights reserved. No part of this book may be reproduced in any form without permission in writing from the publisher, except in the case of brief quotations embodied in critical articles or reviews.

All Scripture quotations, unless indicated, are taken from the *Holy Bible: New International Version*®. NIV®. Copyright © 1973, 1978, 1984 by International Bible Society. Used by permission of Zondervan Publishing House. All rights reserved.

The "NIV" and "New International Version" trademarks are registered in the United States Patent and Trademark Office by International Bible Society. Use of either trademark requires permission of International Bible Society.

Scripture quotations marked (KJV) are taken from the King James Version.

Scripture quotations marked (TLB) are taken from *The Living Bible,* © 1971. Used by permission of Tyndale House Publishers, Inc., Wheaton, IL 60189. All rights reserved.

Scripture quotations marked (NKJV) are taken from the New King James Version. Copyright © 1979, 1980, 1982 by Thomas Nelson, Inc. Used by permission. All rights reserved.

Scripture quotations marked (Phillips) are taken from *The New Testament in Modern English,* J.B. Phillips, 1958. Used by permission.

Library of Congress Cataloging-in-Publication Data

Humphreys, Kent.
    Show and then tell : presenting the Gospel through daily encounters / by Kent and Davidene Humphreys.
        p. cm.
    ISBN 0-8024-8538-3
    1. Evangelistic work. I. Humphreys, Davidene. II. Title.

BV3790 .H885 2000
269'.2--dc21

00-055425

3 5 7 9 10 8 6 4 2

Printed in the United States of America

To W. David Stuart, M.D.,
whose life exemplified
the principles presented
in this book

CONTENTS

FOREWORD

In reading this story-rich book I was struck by many things. First, I couldn't help but notice how easy it is to relate to the authors, Kent and Davidene Humphreys. They write with a comfortable-to-follow, conversational style. Like you and me, they are really quite ordinary people—except for this one thing: They've been emboldened to do great things for God.

And that was the second thing I noticed. However, I wasn't surprised to learn they started many years ago by doing *little* things for God. The lesson is quite clear: If you and I want to do something great for God, we can start now by doing whatever little thing lies before us. The Humphreys have written an inspiring account of how to go about it.

I also noticed they have a unique facility to explain the much-discussed, little-described concept of lifestyle evangelism in a way my mind could grasp. You'll find it extremely visual—full of word pictures of ordinary people whose lives are making a difference. When you've finished reading you will have a clear picture in your mind of what you might add to the work of building God's kingdom.

A fourth thing I couldn't help but notice were their hearts. You cannot help but love, dare I say envy, their heartfelt passion to share Christ. It was striking to observe their focus on knowing God as the foundation for everything.

Finally, I noticed this is not only an inspirational book, but a handbook of concrete, practical ideas. They have spent years scratching around to find the best resources and ideas available.

What makes Kent and Davidene different from the rest of us? Hopefully a year from now, nothing.

PATRICK MORLEY
Author and Speaker

ACKNOWLEDGMENTS

There are a number of people without whose help and encouragement this project would not have been completed.

We wish to extend heartfelt gratitude to Tracy Rader, who spent an untold number of hours transcribing interviews and research, even while in the hospital. She showed tremendous dedication, and her efforts gave us success at reaching our deadlines.

Thank you to our manuscript readers, Chris and Janet Parrington, David Stewart, and John Burris. Your work was invaluable and saved us many costly errors. Special thanks goes to Glenda Steves, who not only read our manuscripts, but spent afternoons helping with all the tedious behind-the-scenes tasks. Much appreciation goes to Bruce and Paul, who rescued us when computer problems were making our effort seem fruitless.

Blessings to all of you who allowed us to use your stories. You brought heart to this book.

We have made new friends among the Moody Press staff. They have given us huge amounts of support and encouragement. We are grateful that you have made this project such a positive experience for us. Special thanks goes to James Vincent, our tireless teacher/editor.

We would not have completed this book without the support of family and friends who encouraged us to write, and then prayed with us throughout the process. Most of all, great love to our children and their spouses, Lance and Stacy, Kenda and Jason, and Kami and Mark, who believe in us and rejoice with us. They are our treasure and our blessing.

INTRODUCTION: SHOW AND THEN TELL

She knocked tentatively on the doorframe to my office and peered around the corner of the open doorway.

"May I talk to you for a minute?"

I sensed that something was very wrong. Mary was a perky young woman with bouncy blonde curls that usually matched her stride and personality. One could hear her giggles all the way down the hall as she told her latest story in the break room, and all the ladies considered her a friend. But today there were no giggles, or even a smile. She had a serious manner about her and the look on her face; what was it? Maybe *resigned* was the word my mind was searching for.

"Sure, Mary. Come on in," I replied as I set down the papers I had been working on, prepared to give her my total attention. As she slowly progressed toward the only extra chair in my small office, I could not help but wonder.

Months before, I had told God of my desire to learn how to minister in my workplace. I cared about my employees and their families, and I knew without a doubt that they all needed Christ's love, encouragement, hope, and peace in their lives. I also had been taught that God wants me to be a "light in the world," showing Him to those around me, at work and at home, indeed, wherever my world is. I was willing, but how? How would I know an open door of opportunity if it were there? And how would I know what to do if I did recognize it? Thus began the greatest adventure of my life, an adventure that makes me wake every morning with the excitement of seeing what new thing God will do today.

But on this particular day, I sat with my insides trembling and a feeling of trepidation growing as Mary walked closer.

"Mr. Humphreys, I just came to tell you good-bye and to say thank you. You have been a good employer, and I didn't feel like I could leave without telling that to you. It isn't your fault, but my life is not happy. In fact, there is no one who will care or notice that I am gone . . ." The pause and silence were deafening. "I am going to take my life this afternoon; I have it all planned. I'm sorry. Good-bye."

As she stood up to leave, my mind raced and my heart prayed like never before. If I had had time to think, I'm sure my prayers would have gone something like this, "God, do You have to begin with *this* open door?" Instead, my heart sent a plea to God to show me what to do, and I felt a great sense of relief and thankfulness that in Mary's greatest crisis she did feel that one person cared enough that she would seek him out. It was what I had desired, that as an employer I would find the secret of caring for the people I worked with in ways that would demonstrate God's love.

During my thirty years in business, I have met hundreds of other Christians who feel the same way. They have a heart for people, but do not know where to begin to have a ministry in their own spheres of influence. You may be one of them, and your thoughts may say to you, "Open door? How can I have an open door; I don't even *have* a door! I work in the back room, rarely seeing other workers except at break. Besides, the management and CEO of my company are not exactly tolerant of the whole Christian thing."

I have heard variations of that theme over and over, and I must confess to wondering the same things in my early years in business. But as I prayed and studied God's Word, I was reminded of the Christians who labored in their marketplaces to God's glory.

Joseph and Daniel were both in places where people were antagonistic to God. Joseph worked in prison and later in Pharaoh's court. During his work years he was both a laborer (in prison) and part of upper management (in Pharaoh's court). It is interesting that his position did not alter or affect his ministry; God used him greatly in both places to meet people's needs and to glorify Himself. Daniel lived in a totally pagan land, having been kidnaped by the Babylonians during his teenage years. He labored as a trainee in Babylon, and later he was in high level leadership for four kings in succession. Because of Daniel's faithfulness in serving both God and his CEOs, God was able to change an entire culture to His glory through him. This is what I want, to see my corporate culture or my neighborhood changed because I live for God in it. God has shown us that it can be done; *He* will do it through us if we are available, like Daniel.

The apostle Paul wrote, "So, naturally, we proclaim Christ! We warn everyone we meet, and we teach everyone we can, all that we know about him, so that, we may bring every man up to his full maturity in Christ Jesus. This is what I am working and struggling at, with all the strength that God puts into me" (Colossians 1:28 Phillips).

"So, *naturally*, we proclaim Christ." I had found that most of what I did as a Christian, particularly out in my world, I did religiously, not naturally. But Paul said "naturally," as a normal part of our day. We are to do it in our natural sphere of influence. By our daily actions, by our daily words, we are to show and then tell the good news of God's love through Christ. "We proclaim Christ." That's our message. If our message is one of religion or church or anything other than Christ, it's the wrong message.

And Paul said that we are to do a couple of things. First, we "warn everyone we meet"; that is evangelism. We are also admonished to "teach everyone we can"; that is discipleship. To bring men and women to Christ and then to help bring them to maturity in Christ, what a challenge and honor! We are to do this with "everyone we meet." The verse does not say, "I challenge you to share Christ two or three times during the next twelve months." No! The verse says "everyone we meet," meaning that tomorrow in our families, in our neighborhoods, on our jobs, as we play, live, and work, we are to radiate the person of Jesus Christ to everyone we meet.

Then it says to tell everyone we meet "all that we know about Him." I was meditating on this verse yesterday as I was jogging around the gym. It made me wonder, "How much do I know about Him?" Tomorrow morning most of us will read the morning paper more than we will read the Bible. Tomorrow evening most of us will spend more time watching TV in one sitting than we will spend studying the Bible in a week. Perhaps the reason we are not telling others about Jesus is that we do not know Jesus. How do we get to know Him? Through spending time in His Word and by talking and listening to Him. And then the Colossians were told to "bring every man up to his full maturity in Christ." That is the goal of the Christian life, sanctification—to become more like Jesus.

"This is what I am working at all the time, with all the strength God gives me." The Christian life is not to be lived for a few hours each week on Sunday; the Christian life is to be lived all of the time. It's radical . . . and it's biblical. It is not an activity in our life; it is a moment by moment relationship with the living Lord. And we not only do this all of the time, but we do it with all of the strength that God gives us. At this point, we fail many times, because we do it with all the strength that is in us, rather than with the strength that God gives. I struggled for years as a layman trying to figure out how to live the Christian life, and I learned that I can't. I just can't. The way to live the Christian life is to let Jesus Christ live through me.

This book is about the gospel but it's about much more. Remember, "the gospel" means "good news"—good news about salvation, yes, but also about a life of freedom, hope, and peace. Thus, *this book is not simply about evangelism. It's about allowing Christ in us, His love and goodness, to affect those around us in our normal spheres of life, believers and nonbelievers alike.* As was true with Jesus, we find that words, actions, a listening ear, a touch, or an attitude can be powerful tools to channel God's compassion. The process of demonstrating such love results in evangelizing the unsaved, discipling and mentoring believers, and encouraging both. And, in our desire to love, we look for and find opportunities to proclaim the greatest message of all—that Christ gives the promise of hope and a new life in Him.

It's really about the basics of a transformed life that will naturally show and tell others of Jesus' love and power within. It is much like the story of the man healed of demons who wanted to follow the Savior from place to place. Jesus said to him, "Return home and tell how much God has done for you" (Luke 8:39). People who knew him before saw a difference. What he did and what he said showed and told onlookers that he had been with Jesus.

We are to show and then tell in similar fashion, naturally and regularly. That's why Paul wrote, "So, naturally, we proclaim Christ! We warn every man we meet, and we teach everyone we can, all that we know about him, so that if possible we may bring every man up to his full maturity in Christ Jesus. This is what I'm working and struggling at, with all the strength that God puts into me" Colossians 1:28 Phillips).

And this is where I was when Mary entered my office. In the midst of my clamoring thoughts, a still small voice gave me direction. Into my mind came the thought that although I could not effectively counsel Mary in her situation, she needed a sensitive helper immediately, and I knew whom I could call. I asked Mary if she would go to visit Davidene, my wife, before she did anything, and I phoned my wife to see if she was home and would do this. She was willing and shocked; things like this did not happen every day!

As Mary drove away, I prayed earnestly. I had unknowingly made a big mistake by sending Mary alone, an error I never made again.

On the way to our home, Mary reached her worst despair, and in a moment of desperation, caused an automobile accident that could have killed her and the two elderly women in another car. But God did not intend for Satan to have victory that day, and He protected all of the people involved from harm. Mary was totally shaken by the fact that she could have killed other people along with herself. When she finally arrived at our front door, she was trembling and sobbing. The trip had obviously taken too long, and both Davidene and I had been on our knees, bombarding heaven with our requests for her.

Mary found Jesus as her Lord that day, and slowly grew in her Christian life as the weeks progressed. She came to know His joy and peace, and others also responded to Him as Mary told her story and became a changed person before their eyes.

In this book we will learn how to distribute God's goodness in our workplaces, homes, neighborhoods, and social arenas. Doors of opportunity swing open not just from nine to five, but at various times and in all parts of our lives in which we contact other people. Letting Jesus Christ live through us is not simply a Sunday activity; it is part of living day by day. This book will look at a life of love that makes us sensitive to opportunities to show Christ's love everywhere, everyday.

We will give examples from many areas of life. We are a CEO and a homemaker. You'll also read about businesspeople, lawyers, moms, fishermen, a sports official, athletes, a small town mechanic, teenagers, and others. They represent just a few of the many ways that God chooses to work out His plans. And you'll be reminded of how God used ordinary people in Bible times too, as each chapter looks at how believers from times past responded to God's call to tell others about His care for them.

All of these are true stories, but they are not your life story. We cannot give enough stories to represent the uniqueness of your life, and the truth is that God wants to use you uniquely. Do not compare yourself to those whose stories are told herein. God created you with unique talents and personality to show His love in a way that only you can.

So take these examples into your heart with a prayer that God will transform them into ideas that will work for you—different from the lives revealed in these pages, but important and viable nonetheless. Then, as you distribute God's goodness you will *show* God's love, and, as you speak when opportunities arise, you will *tell* of God's love. It becomes simply show and tell.

God has uniquely called and prepared you to represent Him in your own world.

Chapter One

CALLED TO REPRESENT HIM

We live by faith, not by sight.

2 CORINTHIANS 5:7

At age seventeen, I walked purposefully down to the front of my church and informed the congregation that I felt God calling me into vocational Christian ministry. It was a very serious decision for me; I wanted nothing more than to spend my life bringing people to know and love God. I had given my heart and life to Jesus at age nine and had spent the next eight years developing a deeper and deeper relationship with Him.

At the same time, I was forming a picture of what life would look like to those who truly have their lives committed to God. I saw the Christian life as a type of ladder. On the top and best rung of this ladder, the rung reserved for the most committed, were the missionaries, and God sent them overseas. On the next rung were the preachers and pastors of this world, followed closely on the next rung by vocational church staff. Farther down the ladder came workers in Christian organizations, and somewhere down near the bottom was a businessperson.

FINDING MY PLACE ON THE LADDER

I did not think that I could attain to the lofty top rung, but I sincerely hoped I could succeed at becoming a pastor because I strongly felt "called" to be a minister for Christ. Since it was time to formulate plans regarding how to achieve this goal, I approached several friends with the question of whether I should attend a secular university or a Christian university before attending seminary. They were split fifty/fifty, so I decided to attend my parents' alma mater, the University of Oklahoma. I entered those hallowed halls and declared, "I want to major in preministry."

The registrars were confused. "In what?"

"Preministry," I replied.

They looked at each other. "Do we have such a major?" One clerk thought that such a thing existed, so they looked into back files, found one that had not been used in several years, dusted it off, handed it to me, and I was on my way.

Then they said, "Here's what you are supposed to do. Take English, history, science, and Greek."

Greek? Three semesters later, I had taken thirteen hours of Greek, and I was literally "suffering for Jesus." I could barely earn a C with my best effort, and I felt like a failure. To make matters worse, my dad phoned me at six o'clock one morning, with strong frustration in his voice, to question how much I was studying. After trying to tell him I was working as hard as I could, he informed me that I would not be studying for much longer if the best I could manage were these grades.

I was so confused. *What is happening?* I asked myself. *How can I become a minister if I can't even pass the classes that I needed to get into seminary?* My girlfriend, Davidene, asked me, "Kent, are you sure that God wants you to be a pastor? Would He give you a talent for numbers and a love of business stuff, if He didn't intend for you to use them?" I sought much counsel and prayed fervently, and finally decided to change my major to business. Although I did not fully understand how to be a minister if I was going to be a business-man, I felt a great sense of reprieve and relief that I was going to do what God had gifted me to do.

An interesting thing started to happen almost immediately. The student friends with whom I had previously shared my faith now seemed to take me more seriously than before. It was strange, but when I had tried to witness to them about Jesus' love as a pre-ministry student, they had reacted like, "Well, of course you talk like that. You are going to be a pastor; you have to practice." Now I could actually talk to students that I couldn't reach before! It was amazing, and I was enjoying it. I was also making good grades.

I was beginning to learn two aspects about God's call upon Christians' lives: First, God has uniquely prepared us with gifts we are to use in our vocation. My interests and aptitude in business were given by God to glorify Him and give me fulfillment in the workplace. Second, those gifts are to be used to make us effective representatives of Him as we model and present God's love to those we meet in our daily encounters. Notice that God's call to serve Him is rarely a voice or a specific Scripture (although God can work that way); it is His asking us to serve Him as representa-tives in a particular arena. He calls us to go to our corner of a lost world and bring His light by our actions and our declaration of His "good news."

Now I was only beginning to learn these truths; I had not yet fully accepted them. More discontent awaited until God used events and a kind Sunday school teacher to drive the point home.

FEELING LIKE A FAILURE

Davidene and I were married during our junior year at the university. We finished school, we had our first child, I went into the army, we had another child, and I served in Vietnam. Then I came back to Oklahoma City to settle down. I was twenty-six years old and, again, I felt like a failure. When I had left my home church to go to college, I had left as a youth leader who was planning a career as a pastor. I returned to the home folks, who had expressed high hopes for me, and I had not succeeded. I was just a regular guy, a family man with two kids and a regular job, not a pastor. My heart's desire to bring people to Christ had not changed, but I thought I had lost the platform to do it full time. My brother and I took over my father's business and lost all of it in seventeen months.

Even at church, my efforts seemed not good enough. I compared myself to other young men who seemed to have far greater talents than I had, and I fell short. One guy was a born evangelist. It seemed that everywhere he went, people were coming to know Jesus, but I was not having the same experience. Another man was a great disciple-maker. He met with individual men to help them grow in their Christian life and led Bible studies for groups. He lived on four hours of sleep a night and was still energetic. I thought he must be a spiritual superman, and I surely wasn't. My sense of inadequacy did not abate until I read 2 Corinthians 10:12, which says, "For we dare not class ourselves or compare ourselves with those who commend themselves. But they, measuring themselves by themselves, comparing themselves by themselves, are not wise" (KJV).

At about the same time, I met Gene Warr, an Oklahoma City businessman in his early forties who was also my Sunday school teacher. He modeled to me that a man could be in the business world and still minister for Jesus Christ. He even challenged me with the thought that I had been "called" to the ministry; I simply would not get paid by the church. I have never recovered from the sense of freedom that God has called me to be a minister for Him. He has placed me in this world with unique gifts and talents, not to minister as other people are gifted to minister, but as the person He made only me to be. What a thought! What an unspeakable privilege!

Now I was beginning to understand better that truth that God has uniquely prepared and gifted each of us to represent Him in our own world. My friend Bob Foster illustrates that truth in the following animal story. A duck, a rabbit, and an eagle were at school. The duck had to practice running, at which he was not very good. The rabbit broke his leg trying to fly, and the eagle became waterlogged in swimming class. By the end of the semester none of the animals was very good at anything. They had all tried to be something they were not and failed to develop their own God-given abilities. It's important not to weaken our areas of strength in our zeal to strengthen our areas of weakness. How true.

BEING LIGHT WHERE WE LIVE

Over the next twenty years, God used three men to mold my life. All three were businessmen who modeled to me that God planned for me to be a full-time minister while I am participating full time in the business world. Indeed, everyone reading this book has been called to full-time ministry wherever their world exists, whether downtown at an office, on campus in the classroom, at home as a telecommuter, as an operator of a personal business, or a homemaker with children.

The Bible's "Hall of Faith" in Hebrews 11 describes God's servants from all walks of life. We notice Moses and David right away (of course, we say), followed by Moses' parents (what were their names?), and other men and women of the Bible. But look at their occupations: politicians, ranchers, homemakers, carpenters, kings, and businesspeople. Of the people whom God listed and honored for their faith, all but two were laypeople, just like you and me.

God never intended for us to sit in pews and pay our church staff to do the ministry. God intended them to equip us to go out and do the work of the ministry, to be salt and light where God has placed us, where we live. The God of the universe has called you to a unique role that only you can fulfill.

Richard Halverson, chaplain of the United States Senate for fifteen years, put it this way:

> There is a difference between church work and the work of the church. When church work is being done, the church is gathered and visible, as on Sunday morning. When the work of the church is being done, the church is scattered and invisible like Monday morning. . . . The work of the church is what the members of the church do between Sundays—business, industry, homemaking, education, sales, agriculture. Like salt, the church is doing its work when scattered, when penetrating and becoming invisible. Salt confined in a

shaker is useless. But salt scattered with a purpose has limitless uses, flavoring food, softening meat, or healing a wound. In Matthew 5:13 Jesus declared, "You are the salt of the earth."[1]

We once had a bookmark that had printed on it a quotation from Francis Scott Key, author of "The Star Spangled Banner." He explained the phenomenon this way: "But let a Christian spirit be mingled into the mass of our population, till it pervades every neighborhood, and then where is the danger from within or without that can harm us? . . . When our people thus walk with God, God Himself will be with them, and He will be their God, and they shall be His people."

WALKING THROUGH OPEN DOORS

As followers of Jesus Christ, we are called to walk through open doors of opportunity. Walking through open doors means caring for the people in our everyday world in ways that demonstrate God's love and draw them to Christ. When you and I walk through open doors, we are using the unique abilities, personalities, and opportunities that God has given to each of us to draw others to the Savior.

Have you ever noticed why God called the people that He called to be involved in something significant? He chose them because they knew the people God sent them to. God called them to reach their peers in their everyday world. And that's whom God calls today, each of us to reach those around us. Here's how God works:

- When God wanted to reach out to Pharaoh, He chose from the royal family Moses.
- When God wanted to reach governors and kings, He chose the educated and religious Saul (later Paul).
- When God wanted to touch the lives of the common people, He chose the fishermen Peter, James, and John.
- When God wanted to affect the leading politicians and tax collectors, He chose Matthew and Zacchaeus.
- When God wanted to reach the business community, He chose Barnabas and Lydia.

• When Jesus wanted to talk to the religious leaders, He went to the temple. When Jesus wanted to touch the lives of those who were hurting, He went to where they were. The woman at the well was a person whom most would have shunned, yet Jesus met her need, and she became the vehicle for reaching a city.

Notice that Jesus rarely moved someone out of his or her natural sphere of influence. Jesus would touch a life and then let that person be significant for Him right where Jesus had found him. Legion, the demoniac, is another example. Luke recorded what happened upon the demoniac's deliverance: "The man from whom the demons had gone out begged to go with him, but Jesus sent him away, saying, 'Return home and tell how much God has done for you.' So the man went away and told all over town how much Jesus had done for him" (Luke 8:38–39). We too must find contentment in the situation where God has sovereignly placed us.

ALL ARE CALLED

In 1989, Lausanne II, the second International Congress on World Evangelism, convened in Manila, Philippines, drawing four thousand Christian leaders from across the world. Seminary professors and staff, pastors from various denominations, evangelical leaders, and missionaries attended. One hundred laypeople were also invited to give the perspective of the laity to these meetings. A friend of mine, William Garrison, who is an attorney in Fort Worth, Texas, wrote a twenty-seven-page document on the theology of the laity from Scripture and from history. Since there were thirty minutes in which to present it, and since everyone knows that an attorney cannot give a twenty-seven-page paper in thirty minutes, and since this was a multiracial, multidenominational environment, it was decided that a stockbroker from Hong Kong, Mr. Lee Yih, would summarize and present the paper. I had the privilege of being invited to present a seminar, so I was present in the audience to hear the following fantastic illustration—an illustration that says much about our call to proclaim Him.

Have you ever noticed how differently frogs and lizards acquire their food? The frog sits and waits for the food to come to him, and when an unlucky insect happens to come by, he simply sticks out his tongue and reels it in. If the lizard sat around like the frog, however, he'd starve to death. And so he goes into his world and he hunts. Now the frog in this analogy is the vocational Christian worker. He goes off to seminary, he gets a degree, and he goes on staff somewhere. And before you know it ministry opportunities are coming to him, and he has his hands full. In fact, when big frogs come to town they hide out in hotel rooms or they'll be swamped. But the lizard, on the other hand, is the layperson. Ministry does not come seeking him out. Instead he must move around his environment and assess his sphere of influence, establish friendships, serve people, and once he has earned the right to be heard, be ready to give an account for the hope that is in him.

I think the main problem today in world evangelization is the under-utilization of lizards. And a big part of the problem lies with the frog. Let's face it; he has a tendency to steal the show. What's more, the layperson looks at the vocational worker and says to himself, "I can never be as great as that," and he's probably right—as long as he defines the ministry in frog terms. The lizard needs to know how God can use him as the lizard that he is! And when he catches that vision, when he learns that evangelism is not an event, but a process, and when he tastes the joy of seeing a friend find the Savior, he'll never want to give the ministry back to the frog again.[2]

This analogy captured the conferees' attention, and for the next seven days these religious leaders, preachers, evangelists, and seminarians could talk about nothing but frogs and lizards. God used that simple illustration to show us that we are all called to the cause of evangelism, and it has continued to influence countless frogs and lizards. After I gave this story at a Leighton Ford Evangelism Leadership Seminar at a well-known seminary recently, a pastor from Ohio came up and handed me a card with the following written statement, "I am a frog who desperately wants to get more out of my lizards." Another wrote, "I want to be a frog, better at equipping lizards."

Paul instructed the Corinthians, "And he has committed to us the message of reconciliation. We are therefore Christ's ambassadors" (2 Corinthians 5:19–20). Yes, we are called. Undeniably.

A REAL-LIFE LIZARD

Some of you reading this must be content to be the frogs that God wants you to be. However, most of us have the flexibility of the lizard. One of our best friends is a real-life lizard. Hollis Howard was a high school art teacher in Oklahoma City and attended a local evangelical church with his wife, Kaye, in the early 1970s. There they sat under a Sunday school teacher who encouraged Hollis and Kaye in their relationship with Christ. They participated in small groups, had fellowship with other like-hearted lizards, and began applying God's Word to their daily lives. While feeling like he did not have the platform gifts of the frogs and larger lizards, Hollis used his art ability to assist speakers with chalk talks and to work with the church's growing children's worship ministry. During this time Hollis and Kaye wondered how a couple from a small town with limited public ministry opportunities could ever be used by God to affect other lives. These were years of intense learning, being discipled by other couples, struggling financially as a family, and being prepared by God for their next phase of life.

By the late 1970s, Hollis had moved his family back to their small hometown while taking a teaching position at a university nearby. Over the next few years, Hollis and Kaye began to share with their local church the things they had been learning. The "gifted" public speakers were not available, so in their own struggling way, the Howards began to teach Sunday school, start a children's program, and take leadership positions at church. God not only gave them opportunity but the power and ability to try new things, persist, overcome failures, and see changed lives. During this time, they stopped trying to copy the style and methods of others, and started to feel comfortable in the abilities, personalities, and the ideas for ministry that God had uniquely given them.

During this stage of ministry, Hollis had tremendous success professionally and became established as a professor. Kaye found her niche as a wife, mother, piano teacher, and women's Bible study teacher. They watched their children grow up, go to college, and get married.

Yes, you and I are lizards. In the early stages of our Christian life and ministry, we lizards typically focus on frogs, larger lizards, family issues, developing close friendships, and trying to find our place. We must be careful; some lizards never leave this stage.

Hollis and Kaye represented countless others as they gradually became fully developed lizards who saw ministry not just as a platform, not just as a program of a local church, but as all of life. Hollis invited friends and neighbors to use his well-stocked workshop, which became a once-a-week meeting place for men to work and talk. More often than not, conversation came around to their real problems and God's solutions. Kaye would have a friend over for a cup of tea to discuss a crisis situation. One afternoon each week, after classes, Hollis studied the Bible and answered questions posed by curious and interested students. On Sunday mornings, they invited members of the community who did not feel comfortable coming to church, to the "Lions' Den." This group gathered at the local Lions' Club building to study the Bible.

Do Hollis and Kaye still participate and lead in the activities of their church? Yes they do, but with a different perspective. They want to share Christ not just within the four walls, or even through the programs there, but in all of life. They work to share Christ and teach others in every area where God has placed them, where they live, work, and play. As lizards, they can go where frogs and official church programs cannot go. They proclaim Christ not with religious tools or activities, but by listening, giving encouragement, serving, observing, caring, and being sensitive.

Like Hollis and Kaye, let's become fully developed lizards—listening, caring, encouraging, and serving. Hollis and Kaye would tell you they are still experimenting, learning, and maturing in their own walk with Christ. They will never "arrive" spiritually, but will always persist in seeking to know Christ and making Him known to others. For every lizard—including you, including me—that is a lifetime effort.

> *When you think about walking through open doors . . .*
> ## Remember Joseph

Joseph is someone with whom we can perhaps identify. Others were jealous of him, and he was tempted, falsely accused, forgotten by friends, and neglected by family. Yet he was a faithful employee, a capable administrator, and one who always held out hope that things would get better.

While he was going through God's training program of pits, palaces, and prisons, he never stopped believing. He understood that God was in control of his circumstances. He realized that God had a special plan for his life, and when he was finally given the opportunity, he was prepared for a most difficult task. At one point he explained to his brothers, "You intended to harm me, but God intended it for good to accomplish what is now being done, the saving of many lives" (Genesis 50:20).

Joseph moved from being a shepherd to being the primary administrator for Pharaoh, from being a servant to representing a king. You are just as special in God's eyes. For years God has prepared you for this time, for this place, and for those people around you. Just as Joseph was, you have been chosen to preserve the lives of many in eternity. Do you sense God's preparation and special call on your life?

When we focus on loving God,
we can be available for Him
to love other people through us.

Chapter Two

LOVING GOD AND LOVING PEOPLE

"'Love the Lord your God with all your heart and with all your soul and with all your mind and with all your strength.' The second is this: 'Love your neighbor as yourself.' There is no commandment greater than these."

MARK 12:30–31

Jesus cited the above two commandments as the greatest of Scripture. Does this mandate sound simple? Simple it is, easy it is not. In fact, without Jesus doing it in and through us, it is impossible. For to truly love God with our whole being means that we yield to Christ's control in every area of our life. It means we make God the Father's desires preeminent to us; we trust God's plan for our life so completely that the events and people that touch us are seen as parts of a larger divine scheme that we may not fully see or understand. We know His plan is for good for us and others, all of whom He loves.

Because of this trust, we experience daily peace, contentment, and joy. Jeremiah 29:11 says, "For I know the plans I have for you, says the Lord. They are plans for good and not for evil, to give you a future and a hope" (TLB).

LOVING GOD:
OUR PRIORITY RELATIONSHIP

"Wait," we say, "this explanation sounds good, the way life is supposed to be in Christ, but it is not my experience. How does one learn to trust God like that? How does one ever get to the place where God guides and uses him each day?"

When a little child takes a walk with his dad, his small hand willingly slips into the larger hand being offered. The little boy's hand is soft and tiny, perfectly formed, and holds the promise of a robust and skilled man. But for now it is swallowed up in the strength and grip of his father. The holding of hands is an automatic exchange of love and an unconscious display of the child's trust in his daddy's ability to guide and protect. The young one walks with great expectation, skipping happily along. The destination matters little; it is the walking that is the important thing. Does he worry about the obstacles to overcome along the way? No; in fact due to his short stature, the child is not even aware of the upcoming curb or the busy roadway beyond.

But Dad, seeing all from his higher viewpoint, grips his son's hand tighter and merely lifts him over the curb. The boy giggles, imagining the lift to be a game rather than an escape from a fall. He is secure and happy, progressing safely along the way because of his willingness to hold his daddy's hand. He trusts because he intimately knows his father. It all began when the boy was an infant. A newborn first loves his father, then comes to know him well, and that leads to trusting him.

The Christian life is like this child's example. Psalm 46:10 says, "Be still and know that I am God." Coming to know and trust God happens the same way that we come to know another person deeply. As we walk hand in hand—trusting the other—we draw closer. Intimacy occurs when we spend extended time quietly conversing with another. As we sit and talk, we become comfortable and begin to describe what is really in our heart: our feelings, our desires, and the way we view things. And as we come closer together, we can almost predict what the other person is thinking before he says it. Similarly, when we love God wholly, making our heart's focus Him alone, we become more and more willing to submit to Him for anything He plans. That willingness frees Him to bring people into our lives that He wants to love through us.

God intensely wants this kind of relationship with each of us. The Scripture says, "For the eyes of the Lord range throughout the earth to strengthen those whose hearts are fully committed to him" (2 Chronicles 16:9); and King David wrote, "God looks down from heaven on the sons of men to see if there are any who understand, any who seek God" (Psalm 53:2). God promises that "You will seek me and find me when you seek me with all your heart" (Jeremiah 29:13). This call to and promise of relationship was repeated by Jesus Christ: "I am the good shepherd; I know my sheep and my sheep know me" (John 10:14). In *Experiencing God,* Henry Blackaby explained the process this way, "Don't just do something, stand there."[1]

"Stand there," Blackaby wrote. "Be still, and know that I am God," the Scripture says. It is this quiet getting to know God, by prayer and His Word, that develops our relationship with Him, our trust of Him, and our usefulness for Him. Even God's Son, Jesus, knew that He needed such time—time alone with the Father, to know and love God. "Very early in the morning, while it was still dark, Jesus got up, left the house and went off to a solitary place, where he prayed" (Mark 1:35).

It has been said that God will not use you in public until He has tutored you in private. One morning Ann told a friend of mine how this "tutoring" took place. "I started out this morning by reading my Bible and giving the day to God. I didn't know what the Lord and I were going to do today, but I knew we'd find something." That is the attitude of someone who has spent much time alone with God. The Lord's presence is as real to her as if He were a visible friend, sharing her day.

LOVING PEOPLE:
THE RESULTING RELATIONSHIP

As we spend daily time with God, we become available for God to lead and to use us in others' lives. God delights in loving us and in loving other people through us. As we learn to love God, His Spirit gives us the desire to share His love with others, and we want to act in loving ways. We want to be available, and He empowers us to have love for those in need.

Many times God will use us in others' lives and we do not know it. He will use us because we are available and loving. Ann, for instance, sensed God had brought Sally into her life to help her. Ann and her husband had two daughters, one adopted and one biologically theirs. Sally also had two girls of the same ages, and Sally herself was an adopted child. *How very gracious of God to bring into my life this woman,* Ann thought. *Because Sally has been adopted, she can offer advice about how an adopted daughter might feel in certain situations. Thank You, Lord.* Sally's easy manner made Ann comfortable to ask questions. They developed a warm relationship.

Many years later, after both Ann and Sally had moved and their daughters had grown into young ladies, Sally unexpectedly visited Ann. The women were reminiscing about their children's earlier escapades over steaming cups of raspberry tea and soft ginger cookies. Ann had just thanked Sally for having been there for her during all those years when Sally made a revelation that left her numb with shock.

"Ann, it is time for you to know my secret and the reason for this visit. The fact that I was adopted and therefore interested in your daughter's feelings was always secondary to a fact of more importance to me. Before I was married, I became pregnant and gave my first baby up for adoption. It broke my heart and has been the unspoken focus of my mind for all these years. I closely scrutinized how you and your husband raised and loved your child, and I listened between the lines of your words to understand your attitude about her and towards her. The security and warmth of your home, centered on God's love, touched my heart. That is the reason that I began a search to draw closer to God. I needed to know God's love for me like that, and I have been praying that God's love would be shown to my baby, wherever he was."

Sally had been watching Ann all those years, anxious to know Ann's attitudes about her adopted child and to see how her daughter was raised and loved. Ann was unaware of this, of course, and only now recognized that God had allowed her family to be a guide for Sally. She learned Sally had become a Christian and had grown to know God's love for her, too.

Ann's shock at the revelation soon turned to inward gratitude toward God for using her. She listened intently as Sally continued. "I've never quit hurting and desiring to know my baby. I left a letter with the adoption agency in case he should ever look for me, and I fervently prayed for that day. Well, the day has arrived and I need your advice."

So Sally had visited to seek Ann's advice: "How should I act so as not to hurt the adoptive mother?"

It is amazing what God is doing when we are least looking for His activity. When we love Him and are available, He is at work bringing opportunities our way. God is usually doing more than one thing at a time, only part of which we see. David Stewart, a hard-driving executive with a major oil company, was getting ready to retire to Eufaula, a quiet town of 3,000 in rural Oklahoma. His wife, Jerilyn, was originally from the area, and for years the Stewarts had spent much vacation and holiday time there. They had already moved into their retirement house, and David was commuting a long distance to work, sometimes even staying overnight in the city. He had met neighbors and made friends, and had come to appreciate the slower pace and quieter lifestyle that awaited. His heart's desire was that God would give Jerilyn and him a new direction and purpose for his retirement years. He wanted to have a way to influence people for Christ and to use his time for purposeful activities—not to exclude fishing, of course.

One of David's fishing buddies in this rural community was Sam, a good neighbor but not a Christian. Already God had provided several opportunities for David to witness to both Sam and his family, but each time David was met with coolness. Three young children and a lovely wife were in Sam's care, but none of them would commit themselves to God's care. As neighbors, David tried to find ways to improve relationships, but it seemed that the efforts of him and his wife toward Sam and his family were unfruitful. Praying and daily Christlike living before them were all they could do.

One summer evening, as Sam and David sat on the riverbank fishing, a neighbor drove up in a hurry. The driver began to scream, "Race home! Immediately! Sam's house is on fire!"

Sam and David jumped into David's pickup and sped away, not knowing whether Sam's wife and children, who had been home that evening, were trapped in the house or safe. It took about five minutes to make an eight-mile trip over dirt roads and section lines to Sam's house. During that trip, the talk was rapid. Sam's three children were small, and his wife would have had all she could do to get them out of a burning house. In addition, in the rural setting, there was a large propane tank near the house. *Would it blow up?* the men wondered.

"Leaving rapidly, we drove the eight miles in record time to find Sam's family safe," David recalls. "But the house was completely destroyed. My wife and I prayed that God would somehow use this incident to touch Sam's heart, but instead he seemed to grow bitter."

The next morning David and Jerilyn took Sam's family to town to outfit them with clothes and other necessities. As they walked into the store, they noticed the clerk behind the counter had a Bible. While Jerilyn and Sam's family shopped, David struck up a conversation with the young man. He discovered that the store was owned and operated by a Christian boys' ranch, a place where troubled or needy boys found shelter, protection, and love. After paying for all the purchases and taking Sam's family to temporary living quarters, Jerilyn and he went to locate Calvary Boys Ranch.

David described their visit to the ranch as "overwhelming," part of an answer to prayer. "I was planning to retire soon, and we had been praying that God would direct us to a fundamental, Bible-believing church and provide an opportunity for service as we left our city environs and traded them for the rural setting of our retirement home. Through our visit with the director of the boys' ranch [where we learned about a church associated with the ranch] God not only provided a church but many opportunities in teaching, construction, and other projects. Today we see God's hand at work in the lives of young men that come to 'The Ranch' from all over North America."

God opens doors in many ways. As David tried to love his neighbors, God opened doors for his family far beyond their expectations. They still love and pray for Sam and his family. None of us ever knows when God will open doors unexpectedly, but we can be sure that He will.

ETERNAL INVESTMENTS

If we choose to live our lives in this exciting day-by-day relationship with God, it demands not only that we know Him personally and allow Him to be the focus in our lives, but that we invest our lives in view of eternity. The only things that will last forever are God, His Word, and the souls of men and women. Therefore, if we are exchanging our lives for anything other than the Word of God and the souls of men, we are trading them for too little.

Daniel Webster, the great nineteenth-century congressman and statesman, wrote about the enduring impact of changing the lives of lost souls in a poem we once read in a calendar. (The title is unknown.)

> If we work upon marble, it will perish;
> If we work upon brass, time will efface it;
> If we rear temples, they will crumble into dust;
> But, if we work upon immortal souls,
> If we imbue them with principles,
> With the just fear of God
> And the love of fellow man,
> We engrave on those tablets
> Something which will brighten all eternity.

The apostle Paul had this same loving attitude in mind when he wrote to the Philippian believers, "My prayer for you is that you will overflow more and more with love for others, and at the same time keep on growing in spiritual knowledge and insight" (Philippians 1:9 TLB). Similarly, the apostle John exhorted, "Dear friends, let us love one another, for love comes from God. . . . Since

God so loved us, we also ought to love one another" (1 John 4:7, 11). Remember, though, that we cannot generate this love; it must flow from God through our spirit to others.

When we visualize God's plan for our lives, it is amazing to realize that God, in His sovereignty, His mercy, His unbelievable love toward us, chose us to be His tools to reach this world. God has chosen you. He wants to empower you and use you. He wants to use you, not just your money. He wants to use you, not just your influence. He prepares you by developing an intimacy with Him. But that intimacy with Him is not merely to make you feel loved but to want to give that love to others. He wants to use you to invest yourself in the lives of others.

BEING AVAILABLE *BETWEEN* SUNDAYS

Richard Halverson, former chaplain of the United States Senate, said,

> Christ's strategy is to scatter His people throughout the world between Sundays, penetrating society's structure from within. They are the true ministers of Jesus Christ in the world. Rightly understood, every believer is in full-time service for Jesus Christ. That movement is a lay movement, and the church's impact is the aggregate of all the laity's impact as they carry out their common tasks between Sundays.[2]

Yes, our impact occurs between Sundays. We combine what we do at church on Sundays—the worship, teaching, and fellowship—with what we do with God between Sundays. This creates the whole. The Christian life is the total of all seven days. Bill Hybels, pastor of Willow Creek Community Church in suburban Chicago, has made the point that church is "more than simply a refuge from the workplace." It is where Christians go to become refreshed and prepared to share Christ's love in the workplace. "Jesus cherished the time He spent in prayer and fellowship with His followers. But He also demonstrated a passion for ministering in the world."

We must recognize that our workplace is more than our place of employment: It is our place of *divine* appointment where we can be used by God. The same is true of our homes, neighborhoods, PTA, our children's teams, the jogging trail, the family reunion, and anywhere else where we meet the people that God has chosen us to touch.

The great Christian speaker and author Oswald Chambers has written these truths about the available Christian: "Don't try to be useful; be yourself and God will use you to further His ends"[3] and "Whenever we think we are of use to God, we hinder Him. We have to form the habit of letting God carry on His work through us."[4]

At times we will feel inadequate and sometimes outright fearful at the situations we find ourselves in when God is using us. But we can continue, knowing God is with us and will supply our needs. Ann admitted that fears came on occasion, but she realized the way to answer those fears. "Recently the phone rang, and on the other end was a sweet girl who had huge family problems," she told her friend. "All I know to do in these times, the only way I know to minister on the run, is to be in the Word myself. You have to be in the Word because you never know which part God might want to use. And you have to be willing to be used. With those two things, God's Word and your willingness, you just go. It's great, a little scary, but exciting because you never know what's going to happen. Each day is a whole new ballgame."

She has pinpointed the idea perfectly. That is really all that is needed, time in God's Word and our willingness to be used by God.

Henry Blackaby has suggested that "God takes the initiative to involve people in His work. When you see the Father at work around you, that is your invitation to adjust your life to Him and join Him in that work."[5] We do not have to go into our world and try to create situations. We just need to learn to be sensitive to what God is doing among the people in our world and join Him where He is already working. As Oswald Chambers wrote in his classic devotional book *My Utmost for His Highest*, "God engineers everything. He is sovereign. Remember wherever you are, you were put there by God, and by the reaction of your life on the circumstances around you, you will fulfill God's purpose."[6]

BEING AVAILABLE ON OUR JOBS

Several years ago I was asked to come to Chicago by one of our major suppliers. The supplier paid for my flight from Oklahoma City to Chicago and accommodated me in a nice downtown hotel. I went out that night to a fancy restaurant with the executive vice president of the firm and another fellow. The next morning, I got up and toured their plant and office facility, and at lunchtime they brought in a gorgeous buffet. At one o'clock they had twelve members of their management team come into the boardroom, and the rest of the afternoon was spent in a meeting.

They took me back to O'Hare International Airport, I got on the plane, and at thirty thousand feet in the air it dawned on me. I had not paid for that trip; my company had not paid for that trip. My church had not paid; it was not a planned "mission" trip. And yet, the night before, I had been able to share Christ personally with the executive vice president of that company. The next morning I had been able to meet with all of the children who were slated to take over the firm. Over the next few years I was able to share Christ with each of them personally. I realized that in God's strategy, the secular business community is paying the cost to send ambassadors for Christ to other cities, states, and countries around the world. What an effective mission movement God has provided. That, of course, means we must be available, willing to declare His love when doors of opportunity swing open.

Twenty years ago a major supplier gave our company $500 to use in a unique way. We decided to do something special for our employees with it. That summer we sent a few employees' children to an interdenominational camp in Colorado. The result was astounding, so every year since 1979 we have offered to send our employees' children, ages eleven to fourteen, all expenses paid, for one or two weeks to a camp where a relationship with Jesus Christ is taught. Do you think our employees like that? They sure do. A father came up to me at our recent sales meeting and said, "Kent, I want you to know that our two boys have gone to camp for the past two years, and they came back changed. Thank you."

We have found that there is nothing you can do that pleases parents more, and opens more doors of opportunity with them, than to help their children. What better way is there to help than to teach Jesus Christ to them? We have even seen God use the change in the children's lives to reach their parents. They ask questions like, "What is different about my children since they went to camp?" The answer: They met Jesus. Along the same line of helping the children, we give away children's Bible-based storybooks and Bibles whenever we offer books at our sales meetings or during special holidays. It is heartwarming to see parents grabbing those books. Even though some of these parents or grandparents do not know Jesus yet, they will be reading Bible stories to their children and grandchildren each day because they received a new book.

You may say, "But, wait. I don't have the authority in my business to designate money to send children to camp, or to buy books for everyone." Indeed, if you're a nonmanagement employee, you will have very little authority. The idea here is that God will open doors for you that are within your capabilities. After all, He placed you where you are and He knows all of your limitations. But He also knows why He put you in that place. People are there whom no one else can or will reach.

You are the available one, and God will use you. This may require your time spent listening during a lunch or your sensitivity to share a smile, a hug, or a book.

BEING AVAILABLE IN OUR NEIGHBORHOODS

This ability to be a missionary extends from the work front to the home front—your neighbors. All you must do is love people. Laurie and Chris are a couple who have made themselves available to be used by God. They have a heart for their neighbors and their children, but they have limited financial resources. Instead, God gave them great creativity. With two children of their own, Laurie and Chris often have neighbor kids stopping by, asking if Laurie's children can play with them. Laurie projects a "come on in, I'm so glad you came" attitude and keeps snacks available to give away. Other children feel welcome in their home. In addition, whenever neighbor children are playing in the street outside, Laurie and Chris go out onto their porch, chatting with the kids whenever convenient and offering a cool drink when possible. The kids invariably gather around and end up talking, including Laurie and Chris in their discussions. Laurie and Chris even bought a croquet set which they put up in their front yard for the kids, and sometimes for their parents.

Over time, family camaraderie has developed in the neighborhood. Last Christmas, Laurie organized a Christmas pageant for the children. All of the neighborhood kids were the actors and their parents became the audience. Laurie and another lady from the neighborhood had three or four rehearsals with the kids, which became a timely opportunity to share with a captive audience. The Christmas story and its meaning were shared before each rehearsal. "Who was Jesus? Why did wise men come to see Him? Why were shepherds worshiping Him?" piped little voices. The ladies got an opportunity to share the gospel and to establish deeper relationships with the children. The actual pageant became a party. The parents watched and were thus exposed to the story. Laurie wrote an article, complete with pictures, to send to the community paper, another opportunity for the gospel to go forth.

The success of the Christmas party gave way to an Easter celebration. Laurie organized and directed a big egg hunt in a backyard. Most of the eggs had candy in them, but twelve of them had small objects inside which represented an aspect of the Easter story. After the hunt was over, the kids sat around to open the special eggs and hear the story of Christ, His death, and His resurrection. Then more games were played and refreshments eaten. Laurie claims that all had fun, with the added bonus that several moms, a dad, and even a grandma came to sit around and hear the gospel. "It seems that whenever you have a holiday, people are a little more open and comfortable with you sharing Christ with them and their kids in such a direct way," Laurie and Chris say. The second annual pageant resulted in an article and pictures in the local newspaper, featuring the egg hunt and exposing readers to the real meaning of Easter.

As you can see, God uses both planned and totally unplanned

situations to bring people to Himself. We just have to be sensitive to what God is doing and to what part He wants us to play in His plans. Ministry is simply Christ revealing Himself through us to others. It is not what we do that is significant, rather it is God who makes what we do significant. Jesus Himself told us, "I am the vine; you are the branches. If a man remains in me and I in him, he will bear much fruit; apart from me you can do nothing" (John 15:5).

COUNTING THE COST

Jesus also gave a caution: "Anyone who does not carry his cross and follow me cannot be my disciple. Suppose one of you wants to build a tower. Will he not first sit down and estimate the cost to see if he has enough money to complete it?" (Luke 14:27–28). We must also remember that such planning and activities cost us something. There are costs to anything that is worthwhile. We know that and accept it in arenas such as sports, developing a skill, or education. It is true in any area in which you deal with people. What are the costs to being Christ's disciple—a disciple who cares for people in such a way that they are drawn to Christ?

One of the obvious costs is time. We live in a frenzied world, scurrying from place to place until the day is done. We fall into troubled sleep, only to awaken to do it again. Jesus, however, loved and cared for people in an unhurried way. He did not rush from meeting to meeting. He was not managed by appointment. "But we live in a different world than He did," we complain. That is true, but Jesus is still our primary example, our model. What can we do to make our lives more like His in this area?

It may be a painful thought, a costly one even, but we must ruthlessly decide to omit some good things from our lives so that we have time to partake of the best things. If we remain too busy, we will not even see the people or opportunities that God places in front of us until they are past and it is too late. We fail to recognize people's needs or God's still small voice in our race to get to the next thing on our schedule.

Time is critical to our spouses, children, and other people God wishes for us to influence and encourage. We must create leisure, or forfeit God's best. What a cost, but well worth it. Unless we have time, other people can be viewed only as interruptions and inconveniences, not as opportunities for love and care. For example, Laurie and Chris had to make sure that evenings and weekends had enough time built in to sit on their front porch. It would not happen automatically; it had to be their decision and action. They paid the cost.

Max Lucado, one of the premier storytellers of our time, referred to another cost in his book *On the Anvil*. In it he told the story of the tools in the master blacksmith's shop. Lucado described several piles of such tools in various places around the shop. One pile, over in the corner, was cluttered with tools that were currently unusable due to cracks, rust, or other damage. The blacksmith would have to work on them to make them useful again. Another pile caught one's eye as light streaming in from the door glinted off of their shiny surfaces. They were new and bright, sharp and ready for use. Any master craftsman would be proud to wield one of these. The last group was piled near the anvil. One at a time, these were picked up by the master and laid on the anvil. It hurt. They were put into fire until red-hot. Heavy hammers were then used to pound out bumps and bends in their metal. The blacksmith used skill and might to hammer them into perfection. He knew exactly when to stop the hammering so as not to damage the tool, but to leave it perfectly ready for its work. Then, as if that were not enough, they were plunged into cold water to seal their shape and strength. Next came the polishing until the master could see his reflection in the sheen of their metal.[7]

Do you see the point? Some of us are unwilling to be used at all. We are in the dark corner, taking comfort in each other, but not doing any good for the carpenter's work. Some are ready and willing, but most of us are in the third category, willing, but needing some work on our metal. Maybe impatience needs to be hammered away. Perhaps sensitivity or humility needs to be polished into us. Are we willing to have the master do whatever He needs to do to make us totally useful? That is the cost.

Be reminded also that Jesus assured us that "My yoke is easy and my burden is light" (Matthew 11:30). He works in us with the love of the Father, and the gentleness of the Good Shepherd. If we do not allow Jesus to work first in us, we will do work for Him in our own strength and wisdom, and it will be wrong. We will have had good intentions, but we will end up frustrated, having produced what the apostle Paul called works of "wood, hay or straw" (1 Corinthians 3:12). There are many Christians who are living just this way and wonder why they are missing the peace and joy that they expected.

Perry Bowers is a vocational Christian worker in the area of evangelism. Eight years ago he took a job on a church staff as director of evangelism. His dad was a non-Christian, who nonetheless wanted his boy to be a success in his new job. So he called and gave three suggestions as to how Perry should relate to people.

1. Treat us like people, not projects.
2. Take time to teach us clearly. We don't understand your big religious words like *sin, grace,* and *repentance.* We can't put our faith in Christ without the facts.
3. Do not be rude. Talk lovingly. Let us control the conversation. You can control the context.

What sage advice for us all.

So we each answer the question: Am I willing? Am I willing to spend time with God? Am I willing to be available to Him; to allow Him to make me useful? That is the recipe for a truly exciting, peaceful, and joyful life. The result of such a life is that other people are loved, cared for, and brought to Christ. That is Glory!

> *When you think about loving God and people . . .*
> ## Remember Esther

Esther was a great example of the principles of loving God and loving people. In her love and respect for God, she developed into an exceptional young woman. The king chose her to be his queen, proving that she was unique among all the young women of the realm. Her sacrificial love for God and for her people, the Jews, led her to risk her life to save them from the extermination plans of the evil Haman.

In Esther 4:16 she declared, "Go, gather together all the Jews who are in Susa, and fast for me. Do not eat or drink for three days, night or day. I and my maids will fast as you do. When this is done, I will go to the king, even though it is against the law. And if I perish, I perish." Esther was willing to die for her people if that was God's plan and will.

Are we willing to take risks so that others might have eternal life?

> *God wants to use us*
> *where we are, with what we have,*
> *right now.*

STARTING THE JOURNEY

"You did not choose me, but I chose you and appointed you to go and bear fruit."

JOHN 15:16

Consider Jesus' words above, spoken to His disciples and all who would follow Him: "I chose you and appointed you to go and bear fruit." What a thought: *You* are chosen, appointed by God Almighty! The angels are not chosen, nor only the mighty, but we are—ordinary, simple people. How awesome is the knowledge of it. Why would our amazing God choose to share His great love and plan through fallible men and women rather than by means He could more surely depend on, such as His own wonders and signs?

Again, think of it! God wants to use you. He chose you and wants to use you to declare His love.

POWER THROUGH CHRIST ALONE

"But," you say, "I can't face such a daunting task. I need more training, equipment, and experience. This challenge is too hard."

And it is—by yourself. The apostle Paul recognized this truth when he explained to the Philippians, "I can do all things through Christ who strengthens me" (Philippians 4:13 NKJV). Herein lies the secret, not that we work for God, but that Christ works through us. Without a relationship embedded in Him, nothing happens of eternal value. The only result is our frustration and sense of inadequacy. But when Christ is using us as His vehicle through which to love others, the results include our peace and joy as well as eternal miracles in others' lives.

Jesus walked and lived among men, and true kingdom building is just living a life and letting Him spill out, like light shining down from a hill. It is a life that shows as well as tells the gospel. Faith knows with confidence that the things that come our way are in His design. Such faith is not a separate activity, but a folding and blending with our everyday life. This takes incredible pressure off us. God does not need for us to be trained, experienced, or have the latest equipment (although those things are not bad). He needs rather for us to be available to Him, to be used by Him. His on-the-job training is far superior to any other method of learning.

"But," we counter, "I am so small, less than small. I see other people who can speak well, think fast in critical situations, know more about the Bible."

THE POWER OF MANY WATERS

Such an argument makes me think about Niagara Falls. We had not seen this beautiful sight until a few years ago, during a visit to Canada. While there, we took a day off and traveled to see the magnificent Niagara Falls. It is one of the most powerful waterfalls in the entire world, creating its power as its waters plummet down, ending in spectacular rainbows as the spray leaps back to the heights above. Millions of visitors have come to the falls and stood breathless at the sight of such splendor and might. God's own power and might are vividly displayed here as in few other places in the world.

But were you aware that the great Niagara starts far upstream where mere trickles of snowmelt combine to form rivulets of water? Thousands of such tiny streams merge into larger streams to form rivers. These rivers flow for hundreds of miles before finally merging into the quickening Niagara River, which soon churns to the precipice unstoppable, where it drops hundreds of feet in the cascading majesty of Niagara Falls.

THE POWER OF MANY BELIEVERS

God created Niagara, and He uses that same power as He deals with each individual. God does not need us, but He has blessed and privileged us by allowing the Holy Spirit to work through each of us. We may be like that trickle of water that is the start of the very small stream. As we join with other Christians who are submitting to God, we become a larger stream, and then a river. As God uses many believers in different ways to impact a person, the end result is like Niagara, God's power falling over that person to change him or her forever.

God uses the same method in our own lives. Consider this scenario as an example: Someone gives a young child initial information about God. Small children are very sensitive, and so the Holy Spirit uses that event in his or her life to plant a seed of truth. Then God helps to cultivate that seed through a number of different believers over a number of years. Taken by themselves, these encounters would be but a trickle of water here and there. But as circumstance after circumstance and person after person are added together by God, the seed of truth is watered. All of the people God brings into his or her life contribute to that area of growth, until ultimately the combination results in a soul being brought into a relationship with Christ. The power of God is awesomely displayed in my life because of the combination of waters from many sources.

This is not to say that salvation is a combination of encounters and circumstances. We know from Scripture that salvation is given to us by the grace of God, and received by us through faith (Ephesians 2:8–9). What we are saying here is that God has chosen to use us to cultivate an understanding and readiness in other people's hearts to accept Jesus Christ as their personal Savior.

Even with God's work being done through our lives, most of us do not see multitudes coming to Christ, or a miraculous display of God's power. Those things do happen sometimes, but normally God has chosen to work through a number of people, each adding something to a person's life, like a trickle and a stream joined together. Then, as that one meets Christ personally and begins to grow in his Christian life with the help of the mentoring of his fellow believers, change becomes evident in that life. The rock solid heart that could not be changed by a small stream could be totally cut away by the magnitude of God's power working through the combined effect of those streams.

You may interact with someone at the beginning of his spiritual experience, when he does not even recognize his need for God, but your life leaves him with an observation or reaction that stays with him and affects him later. Or you may meet someone who is in crisis—maybe that person's loved one is gone or sick, a financial disaster looms, children are causing heartbreak, or a marriage is in danger. During opportunities like these, God often combines the results of this person's previous encounters with Christians and your timely action and words to bring that one to Himself. When that happens, you have the wonderful experience of leading a person to a saving relationship with Jesus Christ.

Perhaps the person you are dealing with is a young believer and has questions or needs guidance. God puts you in the individual's path to possibly be a mentor or to simply show this new Christian how to take the next spiritual step. When new believers are in such a place, typically they are open to another who offers a position of stability and hope. Here is a door of opportunity. It may not stay open long, but for now it is there, and God will use an available Christian to bring that hope.

So we see that some sow the seed of God's love, others water and fertilize the ground, others reap the harvest of salvation, and still others tend the new Christian as he matures. So although you are one person, you are important in God's plan. His awesome power in you is enough; He can use you and me, no matter who we are.

SENT TO THE HARVEST

God *can* use you. He not only can use you, but He desires that you be available, as those who are sent to the harvest. Remember Christ's words as He looked at the crowds of spiritually lost around Him: "When he saw the crowds, he had compassion on them, because they were harassed and helpless, like sheep without a shepherd. Then he said to his disciples, 'The harvest is plentiful, but the workers are few. Ask the Lord of the harvest, therefore, to send out workers into his harvest field' " (Matthew 9:36–38).

In several instances, Jesus used the image of planting seeds and harvesting to describe the various ways that Christians interact with the people in their world to bring Jesus' message and love to them. Significantly, the harvest is of both believers and nonbelievers. When we "sow seeds," expressing Jesus' love and message through words and deeds, to nonbelievers, the result may be that they are brought closer to salvation. When we "sow seeds" to other Christians, the result may be that they take a step closer to spiritual maturity, return to a vibrant growing relationship with Him (if their hearts have been away for a time), or are comforted and encouraged by Him.

Any farmer will tell you that there are principles of harvest that have not changed through the centuries. Let's look at three of those principles.

The good news is the Lord can use each of us as harvesters in the workplace as well as the neighborhood. The first principle is *each of us can work during the harvest*. We do not need to be evangelists to be effective. During the early 1980s, an attorney met with my brother Kirk and me on a business matter. We had never met before, and the attorney was not a Christian. We met at a restaurant, and as is his custom, Kirk asked if he could pray before eating lunch. Kirk gave a prayer of thanks for our food, thought nothing about it, and went on to discuss business. The attorney, however, was flabbergasted because he had never experienced this before, and he did not forget it.

By the late 1980s, the attorney's life was falling apart. He remembered that businessman whose life was so attuned to God that he thought nothing of talking to Him in public. By this time the attorney's wife had been attending church, so he went with her, and there he met Christ.

I saw this man again recently at a leadership meeting for his church, and I did not even remember him. However, he remembered my brother Kirk and me, and he told me about how Christ changed his life and how Kirk's short prayer had impacted him so greatly. You never know how God is going to use your everyday walk with Him to touch someone.

Another principle we can take from the metaphor of the harvest is that *many seeds grow slowly and the results may not be seen for several years.* Those seeds in the workplace indeed may grow slowly. One employee, a new member of our clerical staff we'll call Jenny, once explained during a secretarial staff meeting how she learned about our company, Jacks Merchandising and Distribution. In 1979 she had been in the Oklahoma City Airport with her eighteen-month-old baby. Having just been bumped from a flight going to Dallas, she met some other folks who had also been bumped from the same flight. These people were employees of Jacks, and they were discussing their dilemma. They decided to drive a car to Dallas, and offered to take her and her child along. She could not believe her fortune to be with such nice folks, and during the ride she asked questions about our firm. She learned about the culture of the company and its values, which are based on biblical principles. She concluded her story by telling the employees, "You exhibited that culture by your kindness in allowing me to ride with you to Dallas."

Later Jenny told me, "The confidence that they had in the company and its values convinced me that I wanted to work for a company like that someday." Nineteen years later, having recently returned to Oklahoma City, Jenny acted upon that desire. The impact of those employees' lives had not only introduced her to Christian principles in action, but had paved the way for a new job with Christians who are modeling their values in the workplace. God is very patient. Have you learned to sow seeds without looking for immediate growth?

A third principle of the harvest is that *there are times when the soil is fertile and eagerly accepts the tender seeds.* Jesus echoed this principle in the parable of the soils in Matthew 13:1–9. Significantly, He talked about good soil when He said, "Still other seed fell on good soil, where it produced a crop—a hundred, sixty or thirty times what was sown" (Matthew 13:8).

One occasion when the seeds of showing Christ's love are easily planted is at a point of grief. Carl, one of our company's best managers, had lost his dad six months before our annual sales meeting. Carl's elderly mother was grieving her loss, as was her son. I had been sending cards and pamphlets to Carl regularly ever since his dad's death; it seemed like a small thing to do.

"I've read all the things you sent me," he told me during the sales meeting, "and I've passed them on to my mom and to several other family members. They have been a real encouragement to my mom.

"When we lose a loved one, we grieve for weeks, and there are friends around, and there is food, and cards, and gifts, and all that type of thing for a month or so, but pretty soon it is very quiet," Carl explained. "Six or eight months later, we are still really dealing with the issues of grief. You understand that. You haven't forgotten us, and you continue to send things to us. We really appreciate all you've done."

That confirmed to me the importance of taking such a crisis as an opportunity to minister to people and to love them. It is also important to do it over many months when they face a severe problem. You may not have the resources to buy many booklets or books, but cards, notes, and Bible verses of hope can be a tremendous help.

OPPORTUNITIES BIG AND SMALL

Sowing the gospel seed can take place in many settings, some obvious, others not. All represent opportunities to prepare hearts for His truth.

Nancy probably does not realize that she has a ministry, yet my friend Michelle tells me she appreciates Nancy's regular letters.

The two women met when Michelle lived in a large city. When Michelle later moved back to her rural hometown, she was a growing believer who found herself without other Christian friends and very lonely for the spiritual feeding she had been getting in the city. But Nancy started writing letters to her, and twenty years later she is still writing those letters.

Nancy will never know all the times that Michelle needed an encouraging word and a letter appeared in her mailbox that very day. Nancy had unknowingly become her spiritual mentor. She would write about a lesson God was teaching her, or would talk about a verse that was meaning a lot to her, and invariably it was something that Michelle needed to hear from God. Chances are that Nancy rarely if ever has learned how much God has used her letters in the lives of other people.

Michelle once described God's training plan for her. "When I needed to be taught a lesson, or to know something new, or to be encouraged, I'd look in the mailbox and there would be a letter. In Nancy's sweet way she would write, 'Well, I listened to this tape and it just meant so much to me.' And goodness, it might be just what I needed. It would convict me. I knew it wasn't Nancy's doing; it was the Holy Spirit."

IN GOD'S TIME ... HARVEST

Some people, like Nancy, write letters; others make phone calls in much the same way. God uses all efforts. He has promised, "My word that goes out from my mouth ... will not return to me empty, but will accomplish what I desire and will achieve the purpose for which I sent it" (Isaiah 55:11). When God's Word goes out, whether in a letter, a conversation, or a phone call, it will prosper and will accomplish whatever God intends it to accomplish, whether we see the results or not. Our responsibility is to plant, fertilize, and continue to cultivate. God brings the harvest in His time.

The opportunity to show God's love to another may seem insignificant to us, but it is not to God. Linda befriended a neighbor, Stephanie, a young girl without a car. It seemed natural to give

Stephanie rides, and Linda regularly took her shopping and spent time with her. Over a period of time they became friends, and eventually Linda was able to share the gospel with her and give her a Bible. The girl moved shortly after that, and Linda hopes to learn someday if those seeds of Christian love took root. That is how faith works; we keep taking opportunities to show love to people, believing that God's Word will always do His work and that God will keep working in their lives.

Linda's husband, John, has had similar opportunities to minister to people and to love them with Christ's love. For example, twenty-two years ago, John was teaching a boys' Sunday school class in his church when a young boy, Jason, lost his dad in a tragic accident. John did what he could to comfort the devastated boy; in fact, he tried to stay in close contact with him throughout the next few years. Jason grew up, graduated from high school, and moved away. He returned to John's town at a later time, with no money, no job, and no place to stay. John and Linda made an apartment of sorts for him in their garage, giving up John's workspace in order to provide a place with an outside door. There Jason could find privacy and yet be with the family.

John showed that his way to give Christ's love to Jason involved giving up not only his time, a great sacrifice for most of us, but also his privacy and convenience. Linda was, of course, involved as well, cleaning, cooking, and including Jason in family life while he got on his feet. Such love that never abandoned Jason, from elementary school to adulthood, had a huge effect on the young man.

John has been a Christian second dad to many young men, privileged to see God perform miracles through such bonds. Linda has been involved with young ladies in the same way; and as a family, John, Linda, and their children have quietly loved others for God with their own home, hospitality, and lives. It is interesting to note that John has a passion for such a tough ministry because he saw it modeled in his parents' home while growing up. Now John's father is enjoying seeing the seeds of ministry, planted by him in his early years of rearing his children, mature in his son and grandchildren.

Kirk, Nancy, Linda, and John have each learned the principle that God has chosen to use them, whether in the business world, across town, or next door. Are you being used by God and modeling this principle to others?

"WHERE YOU ARE"

"God wants to use you, where you are, with what you have, right now." Let's think about that second phrase in this principle: "where you are." Many times we Christians are not content with where we are. We may dislike where we live, where we work, where we are in the financial scheme of life, where we are in social order. If we had a choice, we would move ourselves to a different place. The apostle Paul would have been justified in desiring to be in a different place when he was in prison; in fact, if it had been my place, I would probably have questioned God's plan completely. Paul, however, didn't. His reaction was, "I am not saying this because I am in need, for I have learned to be content whatever the circumstances. I know what it is to be in need, and I know what it is to have plenty. I have learned the secret of being content in any and every situation, whether well fed or hungry, whether living in plenty or in want. I can do everything through him who gives me strength" (Philippians 4:11–13).

Similarly, Daniel could have really questioned what God was doing when he was taken into captivity by the Babylonians during his teenage years, but he trusted God and believed Him to be sovereign in all things. He remained steadfast in his love and worship of God, and God used him to impact the course of history during the reigns of three different Babylonian kings.

The important thing for us to learn from these two biblical examples is that *God has sovereignly placed us where we are.* We must realize that our everyday sphere of influence is the place where He will use us the most. And the location of our neighborhood, or the type of job we have matters little, for indeed God will use us where we are.

At times, Bible people seem bigger than life, and knowing the ends of their stories makes their paths seem logical and easy to understand. We must realize that their stories were put into Scripture as God's lessons to us. To see what God has done in the past and then to question His plan for us is to be saying, "God, you made a mistake with me. You made a mistake with my background; you made a mistake by giving me this personality; you made a mistake with my job, my income, my place in society." It is easy to be arrogant in our desire to have what we think is best for us, rather than to trust God's perfect plan and be content with the things He has given us. In God's master plan, He has chosen not only to use us where we are, but also with the qualities that make us who we are. He created in us our personalities and our abilities, and we are uniquely special to Him. We need to give up our expectations of how life should be and become grateful to God for where we are and what we have.

MOSES: LEAVING BEHIND OUR EXPECTATIONS

The Bible gives us a sterling example of a person willing to leave his own expectations to embrace what God planned for his life. Moses had been reared in Pharaoh's court as the son of privilege, yet after forty years he fled in terror for his life, and soon found himself in the wilderness, tending sheep for Jethro the nomad (Exodus 2:15–22). What a change in fortune! Jethro had befriended the frightened man, had taken him into his family, and had taught him the ways of the desert. For another forty years Moses would learn his lessons about God and about living in the wilderness.

Then God approached him. He revealed His plan that Moses would be the instrument through which God would save His people from Egyptian slavery and lead them to a new land. Moses actually argued with God in much the same way that we do when we do not understand what God is doing or why He is doing it (see Exodus 3:1–14).

Moses stood there before God, holding his shepherd's staff, a tool that could fend off predators with its blunt end and gently cradle a young lamb with its crooked end, and safely pull the lamb to the shepherd. It was the obvious mark of his profession and identity in the desert, as well as his security and added strength. God commanded Moses to "throw it on the ground" (Exodus 4:3), and Moses obeyed, only to recoil from it in fear when it became a serpent. God gave the order, "Reach out your hand and take it by the tail" (v. 4), and once again Moses obeyed. That obedience would have required faith in God and belief that God had a purpose for him because most snakes in the desert were poisonous, and to pick one up by the tail would enable the snake to strike. As Moses touched the reptile, it changed into a staff, and was ever after in Scripture referred to as the "staff of God" (v. 20).

The lesson is clear. What do we clutch in our hands? To what do we tightly hold as if our happiness depends on it? Does our security lie in our background, our talent, or our job? Whatever we depend on more than we depend on God, whatever is more important than God in our lives, needs to be cast down before Him. Wherever we may be, if we just open our hands and lay what we have before God, He will anoint us and use us. "God wants to use you, where you are, with what you have, right now."

We will find that it does not matter whether we are in the desert or in a city, riding on an airplane with a stranger in the next seat or buying groceries while conversing with the checkout clerk, sitting in the bleachers at a child's soccer game or sitting in an office—God is creating opportunities to love and serve people everywhere.

WHAT WE CAN OFFER

Sometimes we are concerned that we have little to offer. Note the next phrase of the principle: "God wants to use you, where you are, *with what you have,* right now." We do not need special funds or equipment. God has provided all we need, a relationship with Him and minds to react to the Holy Spirit's prompting. It is He whose still small voice prompts our hearts with thoughts such as, *I think I should send her a card,* or, *I should take a plate of cookies to our new neighbors and get to know them,* or, *I wonder why Bill Jones just popped into my mind? I haven't talked to him in ages. Maybe I should call him.* Thoughts like those, sometimes even illogical thoughts, are often God's leading for us to do something. A thought that we frequently ignore is that we need to pray for someone. That is the most important one to pursue, but it takes spiritual work and a willingness to act immediately so the opportunity does not pass empty into eternity.

As we go about our daily activities, regardless of how limited we think are our talents and abilities, we need to learn to obey God's prompting, even when we do not understand what He is doing. Cheryl and her husband Troy had been invited to share an extended holiday with another couple. Troy was able to take two weeks off from his job, and Cheryl was busy making all the other arrangements. Cheryl reminded Troy of a bee, fluttering from task to task, humming her way to her dream vacation. She had secured someone to stay with their youngest child, and their eldest daughter, Lorie, was attending a university some distance away.

Finally all seemed to be in readiness for departure on the following Sunday, except for a nagging feeling within Cheryl. During the previous weekend, Lorie had sustained a leg injury, which her doctor assured them required physical therapy rather than surgery. Even so, it was painful and Lorie had to climb stairs to her apartment and to many of her classes. Cheryl worried that Lorie's roommates, although good friends, would prove to be little help due to their own class schedules. Lorie was very independent and insisted that she was fine, but that assurance did not alleviate Cheryl's feeling that she should take an unscheduled trip to the university.

Cheryl did not understand this sense of urgency, but she reasoned that she could cook and freeze some meals, do some laundry and shopping for Lorie, and be sure all was well. It was not a logical thing to do. This was Tuesday and her big trip was only five days away. So she prayed that God would guide her through her husband, who loved the Lord as much as she did and seemed to have the ability to be fully objective at times like this. Then Cheryl told Troy of her feeling that she should go to her daughter, fully expecting that he would voice the opinion that this feeling was unwarranted and such a trip unnecessary. Instead he said just the opposite; he urged her to go.

So Cheryl flew the next day to the university town in Norman, Oklahoma, with plans to fly back on Thursday. While traveling she kept questioning herself, *Why am I doing this?* But she also remembered times when her own mother had gone off on a seeming tangent, and there had often been a reason for it, a purpose God had in it. *Maybe I'm supposed to be there for some reason,* she concluded to herself. She arrived at Lorie's apartment and spent Wednesday doing "mother" kinds of things, making soup, shopping, straightening Lorie's room, etc. The two shared a nice dinner together and settled down for a quiet evening. But such was not to be.

At 9:30 that night the phone rang, and one of Cheryl's friends—the only person besides Troy who knew where she would be that night—called to say a neighbor had asked if she knew anyone in Norman. "Do you know a chaplain there?" the crying woman had asked. She sounded hysterical. "I must have someone go to my daughter, quickly! My son has been in a terrible accident and is not expected to live."

"I said to Mrs. Jackson, 'I know someone who is visiting there, and if this happened to my daughter, she is just the one I would want to be with her.'"

As Cheryl's friend explained the situation, Cheryl's mind raced. Before answering her friend, the thoughts were tumbling on top of each other: *Should I be the one to go, or should I call a chaplain? What would I tell her?* Cheryl knew Mrs. Jackson and her daughter, but only casually, as Lorie and the girl had attended the same high school. *I am totally unprepared, totally incapable in my own strength. God, help me.*

Over the phone, however, Cheryl heard herself say, "Of course, I'll go."

Mrs. Jackson's instructions were to find the daughter, get her to her dorm room, and wait for her mother to call. She did not want Cheryl to give her daughter the news; she would talk to her. The daughter, of course, began asking all kinds of questions once Cheryl located her. All Cheryl could say was, "Your parents need to talk to you. Something has happened, and they wanted me to be here." Lorie had come as well, and her presence was a help, a peer who was calm.

Mercifully, the call came quickly and she was told the awful news of the tragic accident. Cheryl and Lorie stayed with her, helping her pack and comforting her until a family member could arrive to escort her back to her hometown.

For Cheryl, the experience was one of meeting God and letting Him guide her every action and word. In Cheryl's words, "God had His hand on my shoulder, and on my husband's, too, because he could have thought that my impulse was just a whim, a compulsion. As it turns out, it was God's direction." Two days later, the boy died. When Cheryl went to visit the house, the mother said, "Thank you. You did something for my daughter that I could not do. I have always been able to take care of my children, but God sent you to do it."

Since that time, Cheryl and Mrs. Jackson have spent time together and become very good friends. Likewise, Lorie and the daughter have forged a deep friendship. In both cases many opportunities have resulted to share God's love, verbally and with action. We are to be God's hands, His feet, and His love while we are on this earth. We must be willing and yielded to Him to begin right now.

OFFERING OURSELVES RIGHT NOW

Finally, remember that "God wants to use you . . . *right now.*" Start right now. Jim was relaxing in his backyard, enjoying the beautiful evening, watching a spectacular pink and orange Oklahoma sunset, thinking about gardening plans for the spring. His yard had a shallow strip of bedding along the back fence, and in his mind's eye he could see fruit trees, laden with sweet produce, his children picking and eating to their hearts' content. The whole vision made him happy, and he went the next day to the garden nursery.

"If I plant fruit trees this spring, how long would it take for them to produce fruit?" he asked.

"Oh, about five years, depending on the type," the nursery expert said.

Five years? That seemed like a long time, and Jim left without any tree seedlings, feeling sad and discouraged.

Five years later, Jim was again sitting in his backyard, relaxing and enjoying the sunset. The bedding strip along the back fence was still empty and bare, and a thought came to him. *If I hadn't been impatient to see results quickly, if I hadn't become discouraged, I would be eating fresh fruit right now!* Indeed, if he had just planted little seedlings and cared for them the best he could five years ago, those seedlings would be mature trees now. The same is true in our lives. Envision what you want to see five years from now. Get started with what you have, little seedlings of availability and love, and watch them grow.

As writer and preacher John Wesley once penned:

> Do all the good you can,
> By all the means you can,
> In all the ways you can,
> In all the places you can,
> At all the times you can,
> To all the people you can,
> As long as ever you can.

> *When you think about God using you . . .*
> # Remember Moses

Moses felt unprepared to be used of God. God had informed Moses that His plan was for him to return to Egypt, confront Pharaoh, and lead the people of Israel out of Egypt and into Canaan. Although we cannot imagine anyone arguing face-to-face with God Almighty, Moses did. (Actually, we might, too.) "But Moses said to God, 'Who am I, that I should go to Pharaoh and bring the Israelites out of Egypt?'" (Exodus 3:11).

God assured him, "I will be with you. And this will be the sign to you that it is I who have sent you: When you have brought the people out of Egypt, you will worship God on this mountain" (3:12). God even gave Moses a sign that would convey God's authority in Moses' message to Pharaoh; Moses could say, "I Am has sent me" (Exodus 3:14b). This was the most powerful statement of God's presence that could be uttered.

As we now know from biblical history, it was just as God had said. After God used Moses to show His unbelievable power, Pharaoh freed God's people and sent them out of Egypt under Moses' leadership to journey toward Canaan.

The great "I Am" wants to enable and send each of us to free people and lead them to Jesus. Do you have your vision from God? Have you spent enough time with God to understand this vision for your own life?

> *The secular becomes spiritual*
> *if done for the eternal.*

Chapter Four

WALKING DOWN ONE ROAD: THE INTEGRATED LIFE

"These commandments that I give you today are to be
upon your hearts. Impress them on your children. Talk
about them when you sit at home and when you walk
along the road, when you lie down and when you get up."

DEUTERONOMY 6:6–7

W ow, look at that!" the little girl exclaimed.

"What colors do you see, Deanie?" her mother countered.

"I see orange, and yellow, and red, and . . . oh, look, the orange is turning to gold! Look, Mommy, see it? And there is pretty blue all around the edges, and, ooo, it's shimmery! See, Mommy, see?"

The child's voice was at a high giggly pitch and escalating, and her body wiggled with pleasure. Mom held the child to keep her from falling.

"God must really love us to paint such a beautiful picture for us to enjoy. He wants us to be happy."

In the early 1950s—those "olden days" when seat belts and car seats for children were unheard of and the bench seat in the front could easily hold two adults and two small children—the small, curly-headed girl stood on the car's bench seat between her parents, exclaiming about the remarkable sunset as Dad drove. The scene remains vivid in my mind, because I was that little girl. I was just a toddler, but I was already overwhelmed by how much I was loved by God. Such conversations were an everyday occurrence in my life, and because of that, God and His Son Jesus were as real to me as relatives that lived far away whom I did not see. It is no wonder that I gave my life to Jesus at a very young age, as soon as I could understand the concept of sin and that it could keep me away from Him. When I came to learn that He died for me to pay the penalty for that sin, I was ready to ask Him to forgive me and to live in my heart. I have never doubted for a moment that He did exactly that. I grew up knowing that He loves me and that I love Him. What an unspeakably wondrous heritage I was given because my parents understood what it meant to live in touch with God in every area of their lives, and to share that with me.

My parents were one of the best examples I have ever seen of walking down only one road in life, one where the spiritual and the secular are so integrated that there is virtually no difference. In my childhood home there was as much talk of God and His Son Jesus on Monday or Tuesday as there was on Sunday. Jesus was as much a part of my everyday life as were my brothers and sister.

THE INTEGRATED
VERSUS THE SEGREGATED LIFE

Now that is integration. Although I experienced it early, most of us were not reared with that reality. A majority of us have lives more characterized by segregation, or a dividing of life into categories which do not necessarily overlap. We must all walk down that straight, solitary road where the spiritual and secular are so connected that there is no difference in our actions.

Unlike Davidene's integrated life, I (Kent) lived the segregated life. The following illustration shows how I felt for so many years. Notice that in the diagram, all the aspects of life are separate from each other. Ministry is just one of many activities. I felt pulled in many directions, all good endeavors, but their sum total was about to break me. I was exhausted, restless, and irritable as I tried to

The Segregated Life

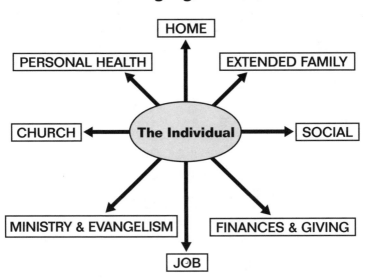

keep the areas of my life together. And I knew from talking to my friends, family, peers, and colleagues that they felt the same. We were all looking for the answer, thinking we would find it by studying about priorities or time management. But none of us was successfully managing our time or anything else. Yes, we were experiencing some isolated victories, but we were losing the war.

Walter Henrichsen, a contemporary Bible scholar and theologian, explained this phenomenon: "The secular things that we do become spiritual if done for the eternal and the spiritual things we do become secular if done for the temporal." What he meant was this: The things that we do Monday through Saturday become spiritual if we are giving our lives for the things that are eternal. Only three things last for eternity: God Himself, the souls of people, and the Word of God. But the spiritual or religious things that we do are nothing but secular, or worldly, if done for temporal purposes. Such temporal purposes could be working to please other people, or to make ourselves feel good, or anything that is not God centered.

As I thought about what Walt had said, I had to admit that I had spent most of my life trying to do religious things to please people, rather than considering my secular job to be a spiritual one when done with eternity in mind. God does want to use me where I am.

My personal crisis came one Wednesday as I was hurrying to get away from the office to get to church and fulfill my commitment to go out for visitation. While at the office I had been conversing with an employee, but I had to rush to conclude that conversation in order to leave on time. While driving to church, I had a rock in the pit of my stomach. The fellow at work had been trying to tell me about the heartbreak he was experiencing with his teenage son, and I had been in such a hurry that I had hardly listened to him. My heart convicted me to the point of tears. It was as if God was saying, "Wake up, Kent, evangelism and ministering to people are not activities; they are your life. Start listening to and talking to people every day." Now do not get me wrong. I am not against visitation or church programs. We cannot survive without the fellowship of our church family and the edification of our pastors and teachers to prepare us for living the Christian life outside of the church walls. But that night God seemed to say to me, "Do not go talk to someone you do not know when you have not even talked to the person at the next desk who is crying for help."

God wants us to start where we are, and we have not done a very good job of that. I came to realize that the segments of my life should all focus into one, my relationship with God. The result looks like the diagram on the next page, "The Integrated Life."

Notice how different our lives become when we focus on our walk with God rather than on activities. When our focus is thus reoriented, and we go about in our various spheres of influence, God sets the priorities and order in our lives. Ministry now encompasses and puts order in my life; it is not merely an activity in life. It works. It is peaceful, free of the guilt of slighting one area for another, free of the pressure of saying yes to too many things out of desire to please people. My desire is only to please God, and He is fully capable of directing my life and its activities when I allow Him to work.

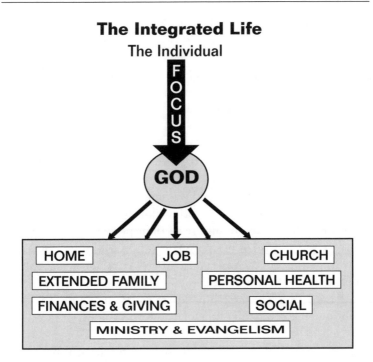

The Integrated Life

The Individual

FOCUS

GOD

HOME	JOB	CHURCH
EXTENDED FAMILY		PERSONAL HEALTH
FINANCES & GIVING		SOCIAL
MINISTRY & EVANGELISM		

INTEGRATING OUR LIVES

I quickly discovered that others had found the same to be true. Jim Petersen, vice president of the Navigators and a leader in world evangelism, has said,

> Historically, the trade routes served as highways for the gospel and traders served as the message bearers. Today's trade routes are the places businessmen and women travel to accomplish their business. National and international flights are filled with them, and some of them are Christians. The question is, can that Christian be as natural in sharing their faith as they are in sharing business? Can they be as artful in sharing the gospel as they should be? Can they learn to be?[1]

Petersen believes Christians face several hurdles in becoming natural as they share their faith, starting with the unnecessary segregation of the spiritual. "How do we deal with the meaningless divisions of the lives of many Christians into spiritual and material? This division leads us to believe that the material world is mundane and irrelevant and that only the spiritual is important."

That belief system is a lie, straight from the father of lies. All of your life—the spiritual as well as the material—is relevant and important to God.

Many people are running as fast as they can just to maintain their jobs, their marriages, and their positions in their church. They want to know if it is possible to order their lives so as to integrate serving Christ in their jobs with serving Him in their families and communities. Many leaders, positioned in large corporations, want to follow Christ, but are unsure of their proper approach in the marketplace. Christian businessman Al Lunsford says, "We know how to perform in the marketplace, but we are not as successful at integrating our lives and our businesses into the kingdom of God."[2]

Paul Stanley, a leadership expert, once said, "Life is so busy with so many competing time demands that ministry can be simply one of them. This seems to be a common thread running through every culture. But if one sees his ministry as part of his daily life, and not something that he does separately, then there is integration and great holiness."[3]

In the article "Kenya Takes Missions to Heart," Stanley described a frustrated physician from nearby Nigeria. "How can I find time for evangelism? I am a busy physician." A friend suggested that the doctor start by praying for those he cared for each day, and that thought revolutionized his concept of evangelism.

An evangelist, according to the Oxford Dictionary, is a "preacher of the gospel." And so we see that evangelism involves words, including prayer. It also encompasses action, or living your life in a way that maintains and preaches the gospel. St. Francis of Assisi reportedly said, "Preach Jesus, and only if necessary, use words."

ACTING AS AMBASSADORS

Our calling is to represent Jesus in every way that we can. We are His ambassadors, His spokesmen. An ambassador represents the one who sent him in everything he does or says. When the United States sends an ambassador to another country, he or she represents the United States every minute, whether talking about our government at that moment or not. The same is true of us as ambassadors of heaven. And just as our government takes great care to train their ambassadors before sending them out, God has planned for our training as well. "It was he who gave some to be apostles, some to be prophets, some to be evangelists, and some to be pastors and teachers, to prepare God's people for works of service" (Ephesians 4:11–12). God has chosen certain people, like our pastors and staff, to prepare us, God's people, for works of service in our everyday lives.

MINISTRY THROUGH
OUR ACTIONS AND WORDS

In order to learn how to recognize and take advantage of opportunities God gives us to minister to others, we must never forget our two obvious tools, actions and words. We show and then tell.

Concerning the actions of our lives, our goal is that in living close to Jesus we show others a different way, a pleasing way, so that they demand an explanation. For instance, Larry is a Christian businessman who owns and runs a resort. He hires Christians for staff positions and wants his resort to be a basis for ministry, but he does not want to run off his non-Christian clients by being too aggressive with the gospel. Therefore, Larry tells his staff during their training that their lives should be such that the guests are compelled by curiosity to ask what makes them different. That is a perfect opportunity to present their faith. He has learned that it is not just good service and a friendly demeanor that turn the key, although those characteristics are essential.

The things that catch the attention of non-Christians are unexpected actions, such as consistent and genuine smiles even when staff are exhausted or have faced difficulties that day. When a staff member has responded to a rude or disagreeable guest with a sweet and helpful disposition, not only that guest but others notice. When a crisis results in a peaceful response rather than panic, everyone around is amazed, and some want to know why. That is when speaking about Jesus is appropriate. And that is the show-and-tell evangelism in action.

The same is true in any work environment. People are watching us. It has been said that your life is the only Bible some people will ever read. That is true. When our lives are consistent in their joy, peace, and positive attitude, people know we have something different and better than they have. That is not to say that our lives are always happy and that nothing goes wrong—quite the contrary. But Jesus gives us hope and a way to cope that non-Christians do not have, but want. They just simply do not know what it is that we have unless we tell them. And they don't want to know unless our lives, by their difference, have earned their trust. When your words are backed up by your life, they will listen. This is the first one of our tools.

Our second tool is words, both verbal and written. We should take every opportunity to use one or both. Later we will devote a chapter to sharing God's love and message verbally. Here we want to remember the power of written words. One of our favorite ways to actually give the Word is to give away books. We love to find good gift books for individuals in both our work and social circles. One of our latest treasures is a beautifully artistic book about golf entitled *In His Grip* (Word, 1997). It contains pictures of the most gorgeous golf courses in the world, as well as statements by great golfers. It is a "lessons about life through the game of golf" format, but uses Scripture freely throughout. The text is largely about golf, with spiritual principles included. It is not preachy and focuses mostly on golf, but it is a marvelous tool to send to people who like the game. We send it to suppliers, customers, employees, associates, competitors, and friends in other social contexts. It is a great way to give a friendly gesture and exposure to the Word of God at the same time.

BOOKS AS GIFTS

We also give books away at work; in fact, almost any excuse is good enough for us. We have normally given books during special holidays, during our annual meetings, or when we have presented seminars. Christmas is an obvious opportunity to give gifts, but several of our employees decline to receive gifts due to religious persuasion. So we cover a table in the break room with unwrapped books of various types, and tell everyone that these books are free, and if they would like to choose one or two (depending on how many we bought), they are welcome to have them. Everyone grabs with enthusiasm. We always choose books which are biblical in perspective in a wide range of themes. Books on marriage and communication are sought after, but by far the first and fastest to go are Bibles and children's books, including Bibles for toddlers and young readers. We include paraphrased Bibles as well, since non-Christians find them easier to understand.

Many interesting situations have arisen due to these book giveaways. Dorothy, a long-term employee, came to me one Friday. She has worked for us for ten years, and is not yet a believer. My wife had an opportunity to share Christ with her this past year, and gave her a paraphrased Bible. She came to me and said, "Kent, my mother has been here all week, and she can't get her hands off my Bible, *The Message*. She has been reading it every day. She told me, 'I've never been able to figure out the Bible. It was religious to me, but I couldn't interpret it. I've been reading this book, and it's alive and I can finally understand it.'" I told her to give that Bible to her Mom and I would get her another one. These people are not even Christians yet, and they are begging for Bibles.

Last Christmas we again gave books, and this time we included twelve Spanish Bibles because we had many new Hispanic employees. The twelve Bibles were gone in three minutes, with many disappointed people still standing around looking for more. We told them that if they would let us know how many to get, we would supply more Bibles in Spanish. We ordered them, and thirty-six more Spanish Bibles found homes. Among books offered at that time were children's storybooks and coloring books.

One of the new employees, with tears in her eyes, told us that she had been so worried but now each of her children would have one gift for Christmas because of those books. Wow, our hearts broke. It humbled us to think that so many children would have Bible stories read to them by their parents, simply because they were free. In many cases, the parents as well as the children will be reading the gospel for the first time. It sure gives the Holy Spirit room to move, doesn't it?

Of course, giving away written words extends beyond the workplace. You can give small books (those that will fit into a mailbox) and CD's for any holiday or for no reason except that you think the recipient would enjoy it. It is such a small thing that they feel no obligation or pressure to give a gift in return.

There are inspirational books that have been beautifully produced with artwork relating to themes such as fishing, golf, gardening, and others. You could give written books and articles containing clear testimonies by well-known sports figures. You could also clip articles which contain a Christian perspective on such subjects as stress or men's/women's issues, and show them to a friend or coworker over lunch a few days after the subject has been raised. Friends, relatives, newcomers at church, neighbors, casual business contacts, and brief acquaintances are all likely candidates to receive such a word.

CREATIVE WAYS TO GIVE THE WORD

A favorite written/verbal project of ours is to read biblical and character books into a tape recorder for our young grandchildren. We make the tape together, Grandma and Grandpa, laughing and commenting on the stories as we go. We then give the tape and the books to the child, who listens and "reads" at bedtime or during the day. We began making these because two of our grandchildren lived several states away and we wanted audible input into their lives. We quickly found out that the grandchildren who live nearby loved them just as much.

There are so many ways to give a word, including clipped articles, bookmarks, magnets, cards (both bought and made), and Post-It notes. Be creative. Ask God for ideas and He will supply them.

Remember that our mission is to love God and love people. Our focus is to be on God alone. Then we will see people from

God's point of view, and they will become opportunities, not interruptions. For ten or fifteen years in business, I viewed people as interruptions. I am a hard-driving type of person and easily get focused on a goal and fail to see the person right in front of me. The Lord has had to teach me to be more sensitive and available to people, the way that He is to me. Now I have an open-door policy at work, and employees know that they can bring problems to me, personal or otherwise, anytime. When the person who has a personal problem and needs help is a woman, I know I can call my wife. She does not see people as interruptions and is quick to spend time with them.

SHOW AND TELL: A CONSISTENT LIFE

Show and tell means your life matches your talk. In order to have an influence for God, there must be consistency between what you do and say. A life that is evidence of the character of God gets attention, because it is different. And the difference is in the little things you do. For example, some folks see nothing wrong with taking office supplies, such as paper clips, home from work. Christians focused on God will not act that way; they show themselves as being different. Some folks make personal long distance calls on company phones; Christians focused on God do not. Some folks take breaks that last just a little too long, or leave a little too early, or simply quit working as hard as the day wears on.

Christlike employees will work like Christ would, for the entire time for which they are being paid. They take seriously doing the right things, even in small matters. Talking about God during company time is not done, because it is company time, not their own time. Such conversation is saved for breaks, lunch, or time scheduled before or after work. Their conversation does not include gossip or complaining. Other employees will watch these actions, take note of the difference, and eventually ask them why.

"But if I acted like that all the time, my friends would think I am a self-righteous snob."

They might, but it is unlikely, because people realize inherently if a person is just acting, or if he really loves them. They may test to see if such love is genuine and unconditional, but they do so hoping that it is real. If it proves consistent, they want it, too.

John gave me such a test after our company had put our values statement into writing. Our values were stated in business language, but they were based on the Ten Commandments. On the day that John approached me, I had just finished presenting the values statement at our annual sales meeting. The fourth value stated that the family is more important than the profitability of the business. Fifteen minutes later I was given the chance to live my words when John told me that he was traveling too much. It was hurting his family and his marriage.

John and I talked about his situation and we prayed about it, since John is also a Christian. Within minutes I had told John that we would move him to another city within a few weeks. We would pay for the move and take care of his house. I said, "If I am going to stand by the values I quoted a few minutes ago, this is the right thing to do." And we did. God has a great sense of humor, doesn't He? He called me to task within minutes.

I admit to having had a twinge of worry about the business, however, because we did not have enough business in the new city to sustain John's salary. Twelve months later, I received a letter from John's wife. She said, "Kent, thank you for allowing us to move. You'll never know the impact it had on our marriage." It wasn't until several years later that it dawned on me that during the year following John's move our business had grown dramatically, and most of the growth had been in John's new city. Did I mention that God has a sense of humor?

Having your actions back up what you say you believe is an important part of ministering to people. If we say we are caring, then we had better act caring. If we say that we are Christ's servants, then the acts of a servant should permeate our day. Bruce Wilkinson, President of Walk Thru the Bible Ministries, gave this challenge, "We need servant leaders, and we need to give up our parking place." He was giving an example of something that a CEO could do that would show a servant attitude in a real way to employees.

Wait a minute, I thought. *I am a CEO, and I like my parking place. I deserve it. I've been at this business longer than anyone, and I like parking next to the front door.* But the thought would not leave me alone. For eleven months I wrestled with it. Finally, I gave up my parking space, and people did not know what to think. I announced to my people that we would have a "servant-of-the-month," a person voted on by his peers, who embodied having a servant attitude and did things to show it. This person would park in my old spot. In a small way, we would elevate the servant, as Jesus says every servant shall be (see Mark 10:43–44). Now to get the full picture, you must understand that there are few places to park in the front of our building. Most parking is at the back of our large warehouse, so there is a fair amount of walking involved in getting to the front door. On the first day that I parked at the back, I got out of my car, slipped on the ice covering the asphalt, fell on the pavement, and scratched my elbow. It seemed like God was saying, "See what everyone else has to put up with?"

ACTING AS SERVANTS

You may be an employee with few benefits; in fact, you may feel forgotten. Remember, Christ called us to serve others. Realize that you have natural opportunities to demonstrate the role of a servant. Do so, and watch how God, over time, will elevate you.

It is not in our nature or desire to act like a servant. We do not have the power to consistently carry it off. Fortunately, God does not intend for you or I to do so; He intends to provide the power for us. Remember, Jesus said, "But you will receive power when the Holy Spirit comes on you; and you will be my witnesses in Jerusalem, and in all Judea and Samaria, and to the ends of the earth" (Acts 1:8).

Jesus and His disciples were standing outside of Jerusalem when Jesus made this statement. Judea was the area in which Jerusalem was centered. Samaria was further still, and of course, the end of the earth was as far as a person could go. This picture of an ever-enlarging sphere of influence can guide us as we think about our own worlds. My Jerusalem is my family, our employees, and our close friends. They are the people closest to me in my daily experience. My Judea is my customers, suppliers, and business associates. I do not interact with them everyday, but they are regularly in my life. I can have influence with them. My Samaria could be my Jewish competitors. I only see these folks a couple of times a year, but I care very much about them. I asked someone from "Jews for Jesus" how I could show God's love to my Jewish competitors. She said, "Have you thought about sending them a card at their holidays?" I never had. Why is it so difficult for me to look at life from someone else's point of view? I began to send cards to my Jewish friends on their special days. These simple acts have produced responses by note, phone call, and personal comment at our next meeting. One of them said to me, "For twenty years, the only person to send me a card was a family member. Thank you for remembering me." I add an Old Testament Scripture and a note from me. One Jewish family has become such dear friends that when our grandson Caleb was born, they planted a tree in Israel in his name, a real honor.

Where are your Jerusalem, Judea, and Samaria? For one woman, her Jerusalem is her family, friends, and the ladies she exercises with. Her Judea is her children's teammates, their parents, and coaches. Her Samaria is the PTA. Think about how your extended world looks and what you can do within it.

OPPORTUNITIES ARE EVERYWHERE

Opportunities to show and tell about Jesus can take place at any place, at any time. At times they come when we would least expect it. I remember a major company meeting when God gave an opportunity. Earlier in this chapter I described my hurried departure from work one afternoon, ignoring the man whose teenager was breaking his heart. Years later, I told that story at an annual company meeting to help illustrate why I do some of the things that I do as CEO. I had prepared to talk on a business theme, but God's Spirit seemed to encourage me to boldly share my calling as a CEO, to love and serve our employees.

I did not realize it at the time, but a rather new employee, "Wanda," was dealing with a teenager who was on drugs, so she related strongly to my statements. She began to cry and left the room.

When I finished my talk, one of the female employees came to me and told me that a woman was wailing in the ladies' room, and I had to help her. We found an empty conference room, and Wanda poured out her story through anguished tears. I volunteered to try to get help for her son, but I told her I was just as concerned that she and her husband be able to cope with this situation as individuals. If they were not stable, they could not help their son. So we went on to talk about her spiritual condition. When I got to the question, "How do you know you would go to heaven?" Wanda answered by saying, "Because I try to really help people like you do." That brought me up short and reminded me that we must serve people not just to help them—which is nothing more than humanistic philosophy—but in order to point them to Christ. We have to be sure that people understand that Jesus is the reason that we do the things we do, and He gives us the strength to do them. It is at this point that our actions need to be followed by words.

And so I told Wanda, "It is good that we can help people, but that is not what gets us into heaven. Jesus said, 'I am the way, the truth, and the life. No man comes to the Father, except by Me.'" I shared with her that sin's penalty is death, and that God showed His love to us through Christ. Christ bridged the gap with His death, and we can have a relationship with Him. I asked her, "Have you ever invited Jesus into your life? Would you like to give your heart to Him right now?"

She smiled and said, "Yes, I really would." So Wanda prayed to receive Jesus Christ into her life, and we both prayed for her son.

I promised to get additional help for her and her son, especially through the company chaplain. What a marvelous story of God confirming again that He is in the business of changing lives.

Let's recall once more the principle: "The secular becomes spiritual if done for the eternal." Simply put, God intends that we represent Him to those in our natural sphere of influence, in our daily secular activities. Whether we are at home or out in the world, at work or at play, with our closest friends or those with whom we least identify, we are to share God's love, serve in His power, and testify of His Son. We are to be as seed scattered throughout our world, as salt penetrating an evil environment, and as light shining in a dark place. No longer are we to be frustrated by rushing from one activity to another, living carefully divided lives. We are to slow down and realize that any person in our lives may provide an opportunity for ministry. The key is that we focus on God and see people from His point of view.

Is your spiritual life just one compartment, or does it permeate all of your being? Are those you encounter a distracting interruption in your day, or are they a spiritual opportunity? Could it be that you are seeking to serve God, but doing it in your own strength? Does Jesus Christ live in your heart? Have you lived a busy religious life without a spiritual relationship with God? Why not stop right now and talk to Jesus about it.

When you think about walking an integrated life . . .
Remember David

We cannot divide the spiritual from the secular in our lives. David's life was never separated into the spiritual and the secular. There is a saying, "What you see is what you get." That remark could have been made about David. The people loved him because he was transparent.

David began as a servant, a shepherd boy. His early life was devoted to protecting and caring for his father's sheep. During the process he grew to appreciate nature and the quiet wisdom of music. He grew close to God and learned about Him firsthand as God gave the shepherd the strength to fight and overcome the sheep's predators. Later David could claim with confidence to King Saul that the mighty Goliath would be no match for the strength that God could give him. After all, killing a hungry lion or a ferocious bear was in the daily line of duty for him as a shepherd. David had learned early to rely on God as a way of life.

David continued to have a servant heart when he became king. He declared to God,

> Who am I, O Sovereign Lord, . . . that you have brought me this far? And as if this were not enough in your sight, O Sovereign LORD, you have also spoken about the future of the house of your servant. . . . How great you are, O Sovereign Lord! There is no one like you, and there is no God but you, as we have heard with our own ears. (2 Samuel 7:18–19, 22)

David's life was an open book to his God and to his people. Whether in battle or on his throne, David called out to God for direction and help. He never forgot the lessons learned as a shepherd boy. We also need not go out in our own meager strength, but with our great God. Have you learned the secret of an integrated life?

*Whether acting intentionally
or spontaneously,
our focus must stay on God.*

Chapter Five

AN INTENTIONAL AND SPONTANEOUS LIFE

Whoever claims to live in him must walk as Jesus did.

1 JOHN 2:6

Are you still awake? It's hard to sleep here, isn't it?"

The frightened six-year-old boy nodded his head slightly. Timmy was lying in bed, staring with eyes open wide at the big man standing beside him. This bedroom was not like his cozy place at home; this room was all white and cold and smelled funny. His mommy had told him that he was going to get his tonsils out and that he would feel better soon, but now she wasn't here, and his throat hurt, and he couldn't even eat his favorite ice cream. And the big man who had been so nice before, but obviously had something to do with this awful situation, was talking to him.

Timmy did not know what to think, and he certainly had no intention of going to sleep.

"Come with me, Big Guy. We'll go find a nice warm place." Before Timmy could decide whether to agree or protest, the doctor had scooped him up, blankets and all, and was carrying him away. The child immediately began to snuggle down and feel secure. They headed to the baby nursery, a brightly colored place. Timmy heard a pleasant humming, coming mostly from the doctor who was carrying him. Yes, he definitely liked this. The two, doctor and his young patient, settled in a rocker, and as Timmy listened to the doctor hum softly, the child's eyes began to close. Lulled by the rocking, the music, and the absence of fear, soon he was asleep.

Timmy did not realize it, but his doctor was a Christian, lovingly called "Dr. Dave" by his staff and patients. This physician chose to make multiple hospital calls, especially when he had operated on children whose parents could not stay in the room with them. The nursery staff paid no attention to this unusual happening anymore; they were used to it. Another of Dr. Dave's daily habits was to arrive at the hospital early, with newspapers for every patient he knew, whether they were his or not. This gentle physician dispensed as much hope and comfort as he did medicine, and people responded. In fact, other doctors, and patients' relatives, would often ask Dr. Dave to stop by to see their patients. They knew the calming effect of his presence; he was a true reflection of the Great Physician.

Dr. Dave himself did not see his actions as being extraordinary; he just genuinely loved his Lord and loved people. He was simply using his sphere of daily life as a vehicle through which God could show His love to others through him.

Dr. Dave is a good example of intentionally planning to touch people. And like Dr. Dave, we all have areas due to our backgrounds and skills which make us uniquely suited to reach certain people, in almost any setting, whether a hospital room, a health club, or a hamburger stand. Howard Hendricks once said, "You can impress people at a distance, but you can impact them only up close." Mother Teresa of Calcutta believed the same thing, once noting, "I never look at the masses as my responsibility. I look at the individual. I can only love one person at a time. I can feed only one person at a time. Just one, one, one."[1]

Mother Teresa started by herself, lifting one person off the street. We often feel all alone like that. You may think you are the only Christian in your office, in your neighborhood, at the gym, or in the PTA. Mother Teresa went out by herself and did what she could, one act at a time, as God presented opportunity. She did that for fifty years. We can too, starting today.

ACTIONS THAT PLEASE GOD

Wherever we are, we can act intentionally or spontaneously—as Dr. Dave and Mother Theresa did—and be useful to God. Significantly, our focus must be on God. Even when we do not see the outcome of helping a downcast child or standing alone for Him, we can be sure God is pleased.

Consider Mary's loving action when she anointed Jesus' head. Jesus was in Bethany, dining with friends. Jesus' dear friend, Mary, entered—intent on an action that she had planned without care for what other people might think. She took an alabaster jar, in itself costly, and broke it, pouring its extravagant contents on Jesus. Perfumed spikenard filled the air, and I imagine that a group gasp did as well. For this jar and its contents were extremely costly, likely meant to be used for her burial, but instead indulged on her Lord.

The Bible tells us that some spectators criticized her sharply and whispered among themselves. It was a foolish waste, in their viewpoint.

"Leave her alone," said Jesus. "Why are you bothering her? She has done a beautiful thing to me. The poor you will always have with you, and you can help them any time you want. But you will not always have me. She did what she could. She poured perfume on my body beforehand to prepare for my burial. I tell you the truth, wherever the gospel is preached throughout the world, what she has done will also be told, in memory of her." (Mark 14:6–9)

What a wonderful statement, "She has done what she could." We need to remember that. We do not have to do it all. We do not need all the answers. Even if the timing does not seem perfect in our eyes, and others may not understand what we are doing or why we are doing it, we should proceed.

Do what you can, as Mary did. Jesus will be pleased. So do not worry when it looks as if other people are smarter, or have more time to do a bigger ministry, or more money to use, or a more perfect opportunity than you have. Just do what you can; it is all that Jesus wants you to do. And remember the tribute that Jesus gave to Mary. "What this woman has done will be a memorial to her." Jesus thought her small misunderstood act was wonderful, even if those around did not. So act to please the One for whom our actions really count.

BEING SPONTANEOUS

Small actions are significant, whether intentional, as shown in the above examples, or spontaneous. As we look for opportunities to respond to needs by showing love and care to others, at times we must be spontaneous. For those of us who grew up having been taught that there should be no exception in the area of commitment, this can be a challenge—to give ourselves permission to be spontaneous. For example, once I was hurrying to leave work for a meeting at church. An employee came to me distraught about his family; he needed to talk right then. The decision whether to skip the meeting was a difficult one. Missing the meeting would produce guilt in me, because I believed that commitment and dependability are Christian virtues that one should not alter. To spontaneously change my set schedule was not within my realm of experience; I typically did not allow myself that option. Many people feel the same way. So how do we know what to do, and when? Sometimes making a date or appointment with the needy person for a different time is possible and appropriate, but at times it is not. How do we know the difference?

God speaks to our hearts using a "still small voice," according to 1 Kings 19:12 (NKJV). When we live each day in concert with Him, starting it in His presence and praying to Him often throughout the day, He can easily guide us and our decisions from within. He tried to do that as I drove away from the office leaving the distraught employee, making me uneasy to the point of tears about leaving my fellow worker. The thing is, we must recognize and be willing to respond to His voice. As we grow in our faith, recognizing it becomes easier and easier. I must admit that on this particular day I drove on to the church meeting, but the experience changed my thinking and my perspective. I am now more apt to miss the meeting and be sensitive to my hurting friend.

ASKING "WHAT WOULD JESUS DO?"

While we are learning to respond to God's inner urges, a few thoughts can help us with our split-second decisions. One question that many people have asked recently is "What would Jesus do?" We see the initials WWJD on wristbands, car license plates, pencils, decals, shirts, and other paraphernalia. Used as help, this question can give us appropriate counsel. Jesus is, after all, our model and example. He was very committed to His Father and His Father's people, who gathered in the synagogues to worship. He attended faithfully, preaching and teaching as He went (Luke 4:16).

But Jesus never missed opportunities to minister to people's needs, even if such ministry differed from what was expected of Him by society or the church. He did not mind changing His course in the face of tradition, although He never deviated in doctrine. For example, when His followers were faint with hunger while on a journey, He allowed them to pick corn to eat, even though picking was considered work to the Jews and was forbidden on the Sabbath. Jesus' response when confronted was, "The Sabbath was made for man, not man for the Sabbath" (Mark 2:27). He realized that the need of the people was more important than the tradition, which brings me to the next helpful thought.

When confronted with a choice about what to do in a given situation, remember that people are more important than things. Remembering that truth will bring a certain perspective to the priorities involved. When I intended to rush to a church meeting when a coworker was in crisis, obviously the person was less important at that moment than a meeting. A meeting can be repeated or missed without eternal consequences; dealing with a person at the point of crisis cannot be repeated or postponed.

PLANNED APPROACHES

Let us share with you some of the planned approaches that Christians we know have used to present the gospel and to minister within their own worlds. One man we'll call Jeff is an avid fisherman. Now fishing, we are told, is a relaxing sport, one conducive to leisurely talking with a friend during a hazy early morning or on a lazy afternoon. This fellow lets it be known that he loves company, and he invites neighbors, relatives, and business acquaintances to join him. He invites one at a time, unless he can invite a man and his son. Jeff volunteers to teach youngsters to fish and even supplies extra equipment, which he buys for that purpose. He often fishes alone, too, but prefers using his talent and love of fishing to lure guys to spend time in his company. As friendships develop and deeper conversations result, the subject of Jesus and what He means to this fisherman inevitably becomes central.

Conversely, we do not fish, but we do own property which leads to a dock from which there is good fishing. We found out about this when we bought our place, and new neighbors hinted that the dock had sure been a good fishing spot with Jim (the previous owner). We picked up on their unspoken desire and encouraged them to keep using the dock. In fact, we told them to bring friends. We have had a wonderful time since then making friends and talking to folks whom we would never had met if it were not for the fishing dock. We fully expect God to give us opportunities to converse about Him during these visits.

Kaye, a seamstress, recently bought a fancy embroidery machine, and she has had great fun making gifts and decorating all sorts of fabric items. Many people who are new owners are very possessive of their equipment, but Kaye has used her purchase as a means to get other seamstresses to come over to try it for themselves. As with the fisherman, leisure enjoyment lends itself to talking, which leads to deeper friendship, which ends with revealing conversations. Even the fact that Kaye is so unselfish gives honor to God through her character, and other ladies do not miss it. Kaye is the one they are anxious to talk to when life gets difficult, and she leads them to God.

Another friend, Don, is an excellent football and basketball official and has been for almost twenty years. He is active in Fellowship of Christian Athletes, and uses his position as a ref to sport an FCA patch on the sleeve of his uniform. This in itself is not a huge step toward witnessing, because the athletes see it during the game, when they are all busy doing their jobs. But it does give testimony to what Don thinks is important, and that small act has led to some fantastic opportunities to point young men and women to Jesus. He recalled a high school varsity football game in October 1997 between Oklahoma high school rivals Hinton and Wayne. Hinton had possession of the ball, and Don, as referee, was standing behind the quarterback. The ball was snapped, and seconds later Don heard another snap—a noise like a loud crack of a tree limb, the unmistakable sound of a large bone breaking. He spotted the fullback on the ground, writhing in pain. Don immediately killed the play and motioned for the ambulance to come onto the field.

The football players who had also heard the sound had various reactions. Some stood still in shock, others paced and ended up in a large dual-team huddle, apprehensive and unsure of what to do or say. Several threw their arms across a buddy's shoulders in a small gesture of comfort, while one boy kept walking up to his moaning teammate and back again. This particular player finally approached Don, asking in an anguished voice, "What can we do for him?" Don, who was busy making way for the coaches and trainers to get to the fullback, simply pointed at his FCA patch.

The boy immediately left and within seconds the huddle had become a circle of players from both teams, on their knees praying. Don's reputation as a Christian had given unspoken permission to these boys to act out their faith.

Henry Ward Beecher once said, "If a man cannot be a Christian in the place where he is, he cannot be a Christian anywhere." Don is definitely a Christian in the place where he is.

Janet ranks among the world's better cooks, especially when it comes to pastry filled or covered with chocolate. Janet prefers to stay in the background of any event. She does not consider herself to be a leader, although the women willing to follow her might disagree. Yet Janet has recognized the talent that God has given her, and she has developed it. Often her goodies and her quiet presence are the answer and the comfort that a situation needs. She always seems to know when to appear, and at times her perception is nothing short of uncanny. Late one night a few years ago, Janet heard the tragic news that the father of a close friend had been shot and later died. The community was in shock, and friends back in Oklahoma City did not know what to do. But Janet knew. She got up before dawn, baked rolls and other sweets, drove for two hours, and arrived with homemade breakfast before anyone there had even thought about food.

Her actions required extra effort: Janet had a job, and she had to return home in time for work. Davidene later asked Janet about the decision. Janet made it clear she did not see this as any big thing; she was following what her heart told her to do. What effect do you think this action had on any unsaved family members who were there?

In chapter 1 you met Hollis Howard, the artist who has helped Sunday school classes and children's ministries with his gifts. He also teaches art at the University of Science and Art of Oklahoma (USAO). In addition, this versatile man also is a carpenter and has a workshop appropriately called the Carpenter Shop. Since both he and his father are fine craftsmen, his shop contains tools of all kinds. It must be the envy of every handyman in the county. Hollis has an "open shop" policy, and men come regularly not only to use Hollis's tools, but to get advice about carpentry and life. The number of men who enjoy spending time there became so demanding that now Hollis has a group every Tuesday evening.

Davidene's friend Susie is a dog-lover. She regards dogs as true friends, and will expound on their attributes every chance she gets. Susie has taken her belief that dogs can help people a step further than most. She actually trains her dogs so that they can become catalysts for ministry. Susie takes her golden retriever, Abbie, into places where the presence of a trained dog can lower stress, such as a nursing home, a hospital ward, or a disaster area. This gives Susie access to talking to people who are in crisis or who need someone to listen to them. What a great opportunity for God to use comfort to reach someone. It takes someone like Susie to think about using a dog, but I guess that is not much different than using fish (or anything else that works).

SHOWING INTENTIONAL LOVE
THROUGH CORRESPONDENCE

I (Kent) am a businessman, an arena full of opportunity. One of my favorite planned ways to plant a spiritual seed in my coworkers is to use e-mail. I send a note every day over everyone's e-mail, using quotes, humorous stories, Proverbs, and uplifting insights to give them a "thought for the day." These are not always biblical, but they are all biblically based. Last Christmas season I sent a story every day, to keep minds on the holiday's true meaning. I keep files all year and I draw from these files when I need them. As I see quotes and stories in the newspaper, in books and magazines, and coming in from friends on my own e-mail, I keep them and catalogue them. Later, when the occasion arises to need one, I have it. It does not take much time, just stick a piece of paper in a file, but the dividends are terrific. One employee wrote to me about the daily notes, "It is great that we never doubt where the owners stand in morals day to day, they talk the talk, walk the walk." Another told me, "Kent, your daily passages on e-mail have inspired me a number of times. Many have seemed tailored to my very situation that day. Keep on sending them."

The use of e-mails, cards, and letters is something anyone can do. If you cannot send a message to everyone in your office, you can certainly send an encouraging note to people one at a time as need and occasion arises. I have found that e-mails, along with birthday cards that I send to every employee and newsletters that I write and insert in paychecks, make others feel included and cared for. The monthly letters, called "From My Heart to Yours," deal with everyday issues facing each of us. They are not business oriented, but life oriented. We have found that the spouses often get them first and look forward to them.

Since our people are so receptive and appreciative of any effort to help their families, we have also instigated a very popular habit of offering books, tapes, and pamphlets on various topics.

The topics cover a wide range including marriage, communication, children, teens, finances, social problems, and others. We give away Bibles often, especially at the first of the new year, when folks seem more willing to think about making new habits like reading daily.

SHOWING SPONTANEOUS LOVE

The previous examples are all planned strategies for gaining opportunities to show God's love to people. But opportunities also come in very spontaneous ways as well, and we must be spiritually ready to respond to them. Janet, the baker, is now a stay-at-home mom, and her daughter, Tracy, has observed Mom's spontaneity. Tracy recalled one example and wrote the following story about her mother.

"When I was a sophomore in high school, two of our family's closest friends were Virgil and Linda Coffee. At this time, Virgil's dad was in the hospital, so Mom and I went to visit him. When we walked into the room you could tell Mr. Coffee was very sick and very miserable. My mom saw a bottle of lotion on the counter, and without hesitating she took off this dying man's socks and began giving him a foot massage.

"Feet are one of my least favorite parts of a person's body, and being a selfish teenager, I thought she had lost her mind. I said, 'What are you doing?' and she replied, 'I know how good it feels when someone rubs my feet. I just thought it might make him feel a little better.'

"And I remember how Mr. Coffee commented about how wonderful it felt and how much he appreciated it. I believe he died only a few days after this incident.

"I will never forget that day [my mom helped Virgil's dad]. It was a clear picture of what Jesus had done for His disciples, and was a clear picture of what we as Christians are supposed to do for each other; meet needs. People's needs are not always glamorous or pretty. Needs are not always easy to meet, and often come with a sacrifice. My mom is so good at empathizing with other people in their time of hurt and in their times of need. She does not do the normal things that a lot of people do when they are in a hurry.

Mom adds a personal touch like a hot meal, a handmade quilt or gift, a box of sweets, et cetera.

"I suppose what I've learned most from her is the necessity of availability. She does not pack her schedule so tightly that she doesn't have time to minister. She always makes herself available for His kingdom."

What an example to us all. Tracy is correct when she talks about tooling one's schedule so that there is available time. It is difficult to choose between good things, but most of us desperately need to omit some good things from our schedules so that we do not miss the best that God has to offer.

Hollis Howard also shows his love for God in spontaneous ways. As professor of art at USAO, he once taught a young married woman we'll call Diane, who was happily pregnant. Her husband was the school superintendent for the professor's hometown, so the professor and the superintendent were acquaintances. The superintendent was tragically killed when Diane was four and a half months pregnant, and her world spun apart. She was devastated. She had the baby, a daughter, and grieved that the baby's father had never seen her.

When summer arrived, Hollis and his wife, Kaye, invited Diane and her baby on vacation with them. They stayed in a house in Colorado, looking at gorgeous scenery, laughing and crying and starting to heal. They talked until hurts had worked their way out of her heart like splinters, and the wounds left behind had started to heal rather than fester.

To other people watching, it was an unselfish and possibly foolish thing to do, taking a depressed woman with them on their family vacation. After all, they had two daughters of their own, and just how much fun could such a week be for them? Actually, it was wonderful fun, and the sacrifice for them became the door of opportunity through which God could start to claim this young woman's heart and life. When your heart goes out to someone and you think, *What could I possibly do for them?* ask God to give you an idea, then get ready because He will.

Your company can be a fertile ground for such opportunities of giving and helping, whether you are a manager or an employee earning an hourly wage. Look for opportunities to help.

When Florida was a new territory for our company, Lance Humphreys, our son, was living there to open up the routes, hire, and train salespeople. Lance had hired Ed, a wonderful Christian man whom Lance came to know as a friend as well as a coworker. Within a year, Ed was diagnosed with cancer, and Lance spent much time with Ed and his family as the cancer quickly spread. Lance helped run Ed's route as he became more ill, and eventually visited him often in the hospital.

As Ed's illness worsened, Ed asked Lance to consider his friend Larry to be his replacement. He wanted the same employment opportunity for Larry that he had enjoyed, and together Lance and Ed planned how to tell Larry. Later, after Ed died and Lance hired Larry, Larry's wife wrote the following letter to us.

"Before my husband, Larry, became an employee of Jacks, we saw how the company's top management cares for their employees. Larry's friend, Ed, was dying. Near the end, Lance Humphreys was by Ed's bedside comforting Ed's wife and children. There were also many in the Oklahoma City office who were showing this family how much they cared for them. Once we knew that Ed was in the hospital, we went to visit him. What we did not know was that Ed had proposed a plan to Lance. When we arrived, Ed introduced Larry to Lance. They wanted to hire Larry to take over Ed's position. Larry was surprised and saddened. Ed assured him that this was what he wanted. During Ed's funeral we were pleased to see how many of Jacks management came, and they surprised us even more by financially assisting Ed's family after he was gone. Few, if any, companies would have done this for the family."

Larry's wife was impressed with the "many differences between Jacks and past companies." In her letter she noted how Lance told Larry to think about the job, pray about it, and talk to his wife. "He also took both of us out to dinner to get to know me. I was shocked. Larry had been with another company for fifteen years and never had that company wanted to meet me or to know my feelings. I'm not sure they knew my name. When a company makes an employee feel valued, it snowballs. It makes him happier at home and influences his family."

THE DANGER OF COMPARISON

At this point we raise a word of caution. You may be thinking, *They have thought of things to do that I would never have thought of. I wish I could be like that. How did those people get so wise and creative?* They didn't; they aren't. The group in the examples above is comprised of homemakers, a retired businessman who loves to fish, a physician, a sports referee, a college teacher, and a few active businessmen thrown in for good measure. Regular folks like you and me. Then how did they start ministries that are so varied? God did that.

These people do have one thing in common. At some point in their lives, each of them made a decision. The process started with their love of Jesus and their desire to spend time with Him daily, reading the Bible and praying. Over a span of time, their love for Him turned into passion, so much so that they decided to give their lives to be lived with a focus on Him and a love for what He loves, people. They are motivated every day and hour by their focus and love.

When you are entirely focused on someone, totally in love, how do you act? Totally focused on pleasing and being with that person, you find yourself constantly looking for more ways to show your love. Our relationship to Christ can and should be like that. As we spend more time with Him, as we fall more in love, our passion becomes being and doing everything we can to please Him. He uses His wisdom and creativity through us to love others.

HOW TO HAVE A PASSION
FOR OTHERS: KNOW CHRIST

If your life lacks passion, look at your passion for Christ. That point came in our lives at about the same time, as teenagers, but under wholly different circumstances. Let us tell our stories. I (Kent) had given my life to Jesus when I was nine years old, and I dived fully into learning to know Him better. I centered my social life on church and was there many times a week. Within a few years, I was the leader of the youth group. Since our church went through a period of time about then in which we had no youth minister, I jumped into leading Bible studies and other activities. Adding schoolwork to the mix, I seemed to be carting a load of books with me everywhere. I was exhausted. One Sunday evening, I arrived home from church, threw my Bibles and other assorted texts on my bed, and declared in an aggravated voice, "That's it! I have had it. If this is all there is to the Christian life, Lord, I don't want it. I'm tired, and this is fruitless."

What was wrong with the whole picture? I had only been doing what I thought God wanted, and it left me with no joy or peace. I was frustrated and bewildered. My parents and church teachers talked about ministry, and I was trying harder than anyone I knew, but it was not leading anywhere that I could see.

That night I started afresh with the Lord. I told Him that if I was valuable to Him, He would have to show me. I wanted to get to know Him, not just activities that centered on Him. I began getting up an hour earlier to read the Bible and pray. I kept up this habit for the rest of high school, actually for the rest of my life. For thirty-five years I have started my day this way, and I cannot imagine life any other way. Thus began a passion for people. There is nothing wrong with the church activities, and I remain active in my church today. But I had not had a foundation on which to build through those activities. Now God was building the foundation.

By the time I was a senior in high school, all I could think about was that my friends and I would soon be separating, going our ways to work and college. I had to talk to them about Jesus. I began praying for each one individually, and as God prepared the way with conversations and events, the time became right to tell them the gospel. One at a time, I took them out for a soft drink after school, then drove to a certain tree by the lake, and told them about God and His Son. One by one, they accepted Christ as their Savior, and I was hooked. I never want to live a life that does not see people changing because of what God does. And I want Him to use me to do it every chance He gets.

I'm ready, looking for opportunities. God gives the ideas and ways. I just have to be willing and available. That's what all of these people have in common.

DAVIDENE'S STORY

I came to this point about the same age as Kent did but in a very different set of circumstances. I was reared in a family with Christian parents who loved the Lord and loved their four children. I gave my heart to Christ early, and grew up in the church. I was a happy teenager; life was easy and fun. Then it came apart. When I was seventeen, my mother experienced a clinical depression. In those years depression was not well understood, and an illness which is helped rather easily today was a secret scourge then. People did not discuss it, and Dad lost his church positions because of it. Because it was not talked about openly, I was left to wonder how it happened, and what would happen next.

As days became weeks and months, and as Mom went through hospitalizations and treatments, my fears and confusion escalated. I was convinced that the same fate would befall me, because everything I believed, the bases of my life, had come from Mom and Dad. I had never questioned my parents' commands or teachings, and I had patterned my behavior after theirs. And so I reasoned it was inevitable; I would fall prey to the same outcome. I did not know how to begin to tell what it was that she had done or believed wrongly. What had led to this?

In the fall of that year I began college. During the nights I found it hard to sleep, so I buried my tired mind in studies and questions. I did not tell a soul, but I was ready to undertake a step that I thought was possibly blasphemous. I told God that although I loved Him, I could not risk my life on the same things that my mother had. I wrote down all the things that I had spiritually embraced from my parents' and church's teachings, things I had not questioned because I had trusted my teachers. I filled pages and pages with ideas, principles, and theologies.

I held up the pages to God, and said something like: "God, I cannot believe these things any longer, unless You choose to show me that they are truth. I will only embrace what You prove to me."

Thus began a year and a half of study. Every night I read the Bible, proceeding from Genesis to Revelation, reading over and over again. As I found an idea that the Bible seemed to confirm, I wrote the reference beside the idea. I was convinced, however, that I would not accept it as true unless it was found repeatedly throughout Scriptures.

After a year and a half, I had made a remarkable discovery. All of the things my parents had taught me were truth. A spiritual misunderstanding had not been the basis for Mom's illness after all, and I had a tremendous freedom in knowing that God had revealed Himself to me in a very special way. I am unshakable to this day about the things that the Bible teaches, and I love to show those things to others. That experience formed my Bible study method, my passion for daily time with God, and my desire to invest in the lives of others. By the way, Mom's faith and her unshakable trust in memorized Scripture led to her recovery. She is still faithfully serving God at this book's writing.

YOUR QUEST TO KNOW HIM

We all have such times in our lives in which a critical juncture forces such action. The decisions that come from these crossroads form life's motivations ever after. Have you arrived at such a place? Is your focus and passion on God and people? When it is, He will direct your daily life and its ministry.

Remember that God uniquely and individually gifts you. He does not want you or me to wish that we were like someone else, or copy his or her actions in order to please Him. In fact, we are told in 2 Corinthians 10:12, "We do not dare to classify or compare ourselves with some who commend themselves. When they measure themselves by themselves and compare themselves with themselves, they are not wise." God has a plan for each of us that is different from each other. God does the ministry. He gives both the ideas and the means to make them come to fruition.

Remember God's promise in Proverbs 3:5–6, for He will give direction when our focus and hope is in Him: "Trust in the Lord with all your heart, and lean not on your own understanding; in all your ways acknowledge him, and he will make your paths straight."

> *When you think about intentionally sharing Christ . . .*
> ## Remember Paul

Paul understood that we are to "proclaim [Christ]" intentionally (Colossians 1:28). He was the most driven of all our biblical examples as he testified about himself "I press on toward the goal to win the prize for which God has called me heavenward in Christ Jesus" (Philippians 3:14).

Paul also took advantage of every opportunity to respond to others, whether in the halls of government, in prison, or in churches. He challenges us to be ready as well. "Let your conversation be always full of grace, seasoned with salt, so that you may know how to answer everyone" (Colossians 4:6).

Paul took his responsibility seriously and gave his life completely to the purpose of always being ready to minister to people. Are you preparing yourself to share Christ?

When the door of opportunity
opens, walk through it!

Chapter Six

WATCHING FOR DOORS OF OPPORTUNITY

Each of you should look not only to your own interests,
but also to the interests of others.

PHILIPPIANS 2:4

Jesus showed love and compassion everywhere He went, every day. The writer Matthew wrote that Jesus went through all the towns and villages, "teaching in their synagogues, preaching the good news of the kingdom, and healing every disease and sickness" (Matthew 4:23). The apostle John told how Jesus met the needs of the woman of Samaria, then His disciples, and finally a grieving father (John 4). He met each at their point of need and met those needs, whether they were for healing or for teaching.

Each person had a different set of circumstances, but over and over through the Gospels we see common ground. Jesus dealt with people's illnesses, death, mental anguish, and skepticism, and He attended special events, such as weddings and holidays ("feasts"), and all these factors seemed to create stress and crises that He was able to defuse.

THE STRESS OF OUR LIVES

A big event in people's lives triggered needs, and the same is true today. Often a felt need is the open door that prepares a person to acknowledge his deeper, real need and Christ's solution to it.

When we become sensitive to what these are, we can more accurately observe people's felt needs and pray that God would use each need as an open door to share Christ. The results are God's responsibility; our responsibility is to be available and faithful.

One instrument, the Holmes-Rahe Stress Scale, has evaluated the big events in people's lives and developed a scale assigning stress level for each event. The scale is helpful in sensitizing us to the levels of stress that people feel relative to other events in their lives. The greatest upheaval would be 100 points, and descending stressful events have lesser numbers. The next page shows the top thirty events.[1]

These stress values were prepared by Insurance Underwriters' Institute to prepare actuarial tables on persons likely to be bad risks for medical and hospital insurance. If a person's total values for a twelve month period are 100–199, he has a mild crisis and has a 17 percent chance of a serious health problem within two years. If a person scores 200–299, he has a serious life crisis and has a 51 percent chance of a serious health problem within two years. If total values are more than 300, the person has a critical life crisis and has a 79 percent chance of a serious health problem within two years.

Stress is an indicator that there are needs in a person's life. These needs are "open doors," or opportunities to love and care for that person as Christ did. The greater the stress level, the greater the need.

We have found that there are at least seven types of circumstances that swing open the doors of opportunity to love and help people. They are:

- Physical needs, specifically illness or hospitalizations
- Grief caused by any great loss such as death or divorce

The Holmes-Rahe Stress Scale

LIFE EVENT	RANK	LIFE EVENT	RANK
Death of a Spouse	100	Death of a Close Friend	37
Divorce	73	Change to a Different Line of Work	36
Marital Separation	65	Arguments with Spouse	35
Jail Term	63	Foreclosure on Mortgage or Loan	30
Death of a Family Member	63		
Personal Injury or Illness	53	Change in Responsibilities at Work	29
Marriage	50	Son or Daughter Leaving Home	29
Fired from Job	47		
Marital Reconciliation	45	Trouble with In-Laws	29
Retirement	45	Wife Begins or Stops Work	26
Change in Health of Family Member	44	Begin or End School	26
		Change in Living Conditions	25
Pregnancy	40	Trouble with Boss	23
Sex Difficulties	39	Change in Work Hours or Conditions	20
Gain a New Family Member	39		
Business Readjustment	39	Change in Residence	20
Change in Financial State	38	Change in Schools	20

- Marital difficulties
- Birth of a child
- Financial difficulties
- Problems with children
- Holidays

Any change is an instigator of stress, whether that change is good or bad. But when the change is major, the door is open wider. The door may provide an opportunity for evangelism, but often when the person is experiencing the stress of change you will have opportunities to show compassion, give comfort, and offer encouragement. During a devastating crisis, your door of opportunity could be all of these. For Angela, we found opportunities to be the giver of renewing spiritual truth.

ANGELA'S STORY

Years ago Angela worked in our office. She was young and bright, just out of high school when she entered employment. During her first year with us, her dad died of cancer. He had been a wonderful man and she was extremely close to him. Four years later, her mother died of cancer. She had been through two major life-changing episodes in four years. I watched her closely and prayed that God would make me sensitive to her and her pain. But every time I asked her how she was, she answered in a positive way. Davidene and I had discussed her situation several times and had grieved with her. We did not know how to help her through her pain except to pray and encourage her. So we waited, observed, and prayed for her.

Several months later she appeared at the door to my office, broken and sobbing. I listened as she agonized over her feelings of isolation. She truly believed that God had left her. My own heart broke for her and soon tears were streaming down both of our faces. I shared with her that she was of great value to God; He loved her and had not abandoned her. We ended our conversation by praying aloud, a new experience for her.

When we finished, her countenance had changed. There was a look of peace rather than sorrow, and joy had replaced fear. Angela was a different person. Later, she wrote to explain how that time of expressing her anger and grief helped her understand God and her own feelings. She was convinced that such times of listening and praying with those who are hurting can help.

After losing her mother at age twenty-two, only four years after her father's death, Angela wrote, "I felt completely alone. Who could I turn to; whom could I trust? Now I was not only disappointed with God; I was angry. I had convinced myself that I was being punished for something I had done, or maybe something I had not done. . . . I struggled with this for some time and my faith was diminishing. I seldom prayed, and when I did there was not that 'connection' I had known before.

"Over a year later, I muscled up all my courage and went to see the one man I knew could give me the advice and wisdom I needed, our CEO. After sitting in his office for an hour, crying so hard I could barely be understood, I became convinced that it was not my fault, I was not being punished. I was only punishing myself for letting my relationship with God fail. Before leaving the office, Kent asked me to do something I felt very uncomfortable doing; he asked me to pray aloud with him. For the first time in months, I prayed for God to forgive me for turning away from Him when I needed Him most.

"Because of this, I am a better Christian today than ever before. I honestly believe in my heart that if this man had not been openly demonstrating his beliefs so strongly, I would never have gone to him."

THE PROVISION FOR OUR LIVES

I (Kent) must admit that even though I knew that Christ could meet Angela's needs, I was uncomfortable. I believe that if I had not been observing Angela and praying for sensitivity, I would not have been prepared when she appeared at the door. I had to trust fully in God because my only confidence was in Him.

Have you ever been nervous when put in a position like the one I just described? Is the thought that you might have to come up with the right words to say to a person in crisis frightening to you? The disciples felt the same way. Jesus' answer to them is His answer to us, "Whenever you are arrested and brought to trial, do not worry beforehand about what to say. Just say whatever is given you at the time, for it is not you speaking, but the Holy Spirit" (Mark 13:11).

We may not be literally arrested and sent to jail, but we do feel sometimes as if facing such situations is a trial. But it is not our responsibility to plan everything. The Holy Spirit will bring to our minds exactly what we need at that time. The key is to be available to the Holy Spirit, walking with Him daily so that our lines of communication are open. The more time we have spent with Jesus in His Word the Bible, the more prepared we are. With God's Word in our heart and minds, the Holy Spirit has a lot He can use. Jesus told His disciples, "But the Counselor, the Holy Spirit, whom the Father will send in my name, will teach you all things and will remind you of everything I have said to you" (John 14:26).

Preparation is not easy, but it can be done with a commitment to study God's Word and a passion to know Christ's character. Being aware of the needs of others, however, is sometimes more difficult. Such awareness may not come naturally, yet God can develop your sensitivity as you look for opportunities and ask Him to make you more sensitive. I realized early that sensitivity is not a natural strength of my personality type; in fact, normally it is nonexistent. Being a hard driver who tends naturally to run over people on the way to a goal, I work hard at developing this characteristic.

You may need to focus on developing that sensitivity. Sometimes we aren't as sensitive because we have focused on a project or find other duties distracting us. My assistant of eighteen years told me that I did not recognize her as a person for the first six years of her employment. I pray for sensitivity and I make a conscious effort to slow down so that I can observe others more carefully.

Here are several methods to help us increase our sensitivity to others.

INCREASING OUR SENSITIVITY
THROUGH PRAYER

First, *we can pray for people,* especially by name. Such prayer helps us to focus on others rather than on our own daily concerns. Beginning your day with prayer can be as simple as saying a short prayer while you are still in bed, or as time-consuming as you desire. Either way, the important thing is to begin each day focused on God and on other people. It sets the tone and motivation for everything said and done that day.

Prayer is hard work, and for years I had no method to help me pray regularly. Over time, a system developed that has revolutionized my prayer life. I would like to share it with you.

Often I would hear of a family in need, and I promised that I would pray for them. A week or two later, when I would see them again, I remembered that I had good intentions, but had not prayed. It has been said that the smallest good deed is better than the grandest intention. So, I began the practice (nearly fifteen years ago) of writing down needs on a 3x5 card, taking seriously my commitment to pray. When God began to answer these prayers, I started to get excited and wanted to do it even more. First there were friends at church, then coworkers, business associates, those involved in spiritual ministries, and even casual acquaintances.

Over the years as I wrote down specific requests and prayed for them, I became more interested in people's situations and wanted to do more. This was particularly true when someone was involved in a long-term illness or grieving over the loss of a loved one. Then Davidene began to bring other names and requests to me, and a mutual sharing of those needs evolved. It all starts with prayer.

INCREASING OUR SENSITIVITY
THROUGH ACTS OF ENCOURAGEMENT

Second, *give encouragement.* Look for ways, however small, to encourage others. For example, at work we tend to be constantly in a hurry, on a mission with a goal in mind. So it is encouraging when someone will stop by another's desk for a brief "good morning" and a smile. A person feels special when a friend inquires about his child, his progress on a project, or his spouse's ball game last night. A note of support, encouragement, or congratulations left on a coworker's desk or a teenager's table does wonders for the person's outlook.

When we show kindness during the good times, we will be more sensitive to a person's trauma during the hard times. We are developing a relationship, and conversations can follow.

INCREASING OUR SENSITIVITY THROUGH GIVING GIFTS

Third, *offer well-written tools.* Giving a card, magazine article, or book puts your focus on others, and finding the right one will make you more sensitive to their needs. When possible, choose greeting cards and other literature that are based on God's Word.

Surprisingly, we found that this simple encouragement was so rare that people were overwhelmed. God began to heal them physically and emotionally; many were able to receive specific promises from cards, the Scriptures, and booklets. We began to understand that we were just a conduit for God's love to those around us. These were people that we saw everyday where we lived, worked, and played.

It is amazing how this simple ministry has expanded. In one recent month, five different coworkers lost a family member. We were able to offer them prayer and other helps. We have learned that critical times in a person's life do not end quickly, so we tailor what we send and the length of time we send them to each person. A person in grief may receive items from us once every few weeks, then once a month for up to a year. Over a period of years of looking and reading, we have compiled a list of our favorite pamphlets, bookmarks, cards, and books. We update the list constantly as new material comes on the market. We have included our current list in Appendix 1, as well as an offer to help you obtain these for yourself if you are interested.

You may be thinking, "If I give that much stuff away, I will be the one in financial crisis." Let us assure you that such is not the case. These items can be as small as a thirty-nine-cent bookmark or a one-dollar pamphlet. We have, however, found that it helps to have an amount for "ministry" in our budget. We have personally budgeted for ministry since our earliest days of marriage. In our company, we set aside a specific amount to minister to our employees. Let me share just a couple of the reactions we have received as a result of this endeavor.

"Thank you for sending us the book on hope," wrote a father who lost his son to suicide. "Each day is a struggle as we deal with grief. Some days we don't leave our house or answer our phone. We are praying hard to God for strength to endure our terrific loss of our special child. We take each day one hour at a time, and hopefully one day we will start functioning normally again. Thank you for caring about us. Believe me, the book helped."

An international student attending one of our universities was going through an emotionally distressing period. We found out about her situation from a friend, and so we sent her some encouraging cards. She responded, "The Scriptures on the card you sent were water to my soul." She went on to give enough details about her life and her willingness to receive help that we were able to contact someone who could help her where she lived. It is often true that when you are in a situation when you cannot help the person, you can make arrangements with someone who can. God orchestrates that kind of cooperation among Christians a lot.

HABITS OF SENSITIVITY

As we look for ways to be sensitive to people, there are at least three habits to incorporate into our lives.

The first is *the habit of prayer.* Earlier we mentioned prayer as one way to develop sensitivity. Now we want to emphasize prayer as a habit of sensitivity. As we pray for people, we develop a spiritual focus in our interaction with them. We cannot overemphasize the value and necessity of prayer in the process of becoming sensitive to people. Prayer changes our focus and unleashes God's tremendous power. Recall two powerful promises of prayer in Scripture:

"If you believe, you will receive whatever you ask for in prayer."
(Matthew 21:22)

Do not be anxious about anything, but in everything, by prayer
and petition, with thanksgiving, present your requests to God.
(Philippians 4:6)

The second habit we need to develop is to *stop and talk to people at every chance.* That sounds obvious, but it is not easy because we are so often in a hurry. Instead of racing into the house when returning home from work, we can go over and talk to the neighbor who is standing outside for a minute. Instead of jogging to be the first one at the office copier, we can say hi to the person at the next desk as we pass. It is shocking how often we do not even see someone we could interact with because of our focus on our goal.

The third habit to add to our lifestyle is to *ask others for help,* especially in the neighborhood. We are a prideful people, and we resist asking for help. But people are usually glad to help, and it opens opportunities for conversation because the other person can talk about something he knows about. That, in turn, opens possibilities for relationships.

These three habits can be used often by God to open doors for ministry to people. As we watch for the door of opportunity to swing wide, as we are sensitive, as we care for others, we will have chances to show and tell of God's love. We close this chapter by presenting several ideas for opening doors, based largely on opportunities we've experienced. Most of these are from our world of business. They are not meant to dictate how God will use you in your world of work, school, neighborhood, etc. As you read them, ask God to give you ideas that will touch others as you work, play, raise your family, and interact with friends.

DOORS OF OPPORTUNITY
DURING MARRIAGE DIFFICULTIES

Difficulties in a marriage can become a crisis that opens doors of ministry. For example, consider asking a troubled couple to go with your spouse and you to a marriage or parenting conference.

You may want to help them financially if this is possible for you. You may tell them, "We want to help you go with us by providing baby-sitting for you. This is really selfish on our part because we want to spend this time with you."

Maybe you could give anonymously to your church and then say, "Our church has scholarships. Let's both go!" If you cannot help financially, plan far enough in advance that both couples can save for it.

We have offered to send couples to marriage conferences, and the results have been great. Some couples are willing to go by themselves, but we have been known to get a group together to go just so that we can invite a couple we are concerned about as our guests. As CEO of our company, I can also offer this benefit to my employees, and many have taken advantage of it. As one employee wrote recently, "I thank God that you have the marriage conferences, the parenting conferences, and the children's camp programs available to your employees." (See Appendix 2 for offerings from Family Life, a ministry of Campus Crusade for Christ, and from Eagle Lake Camps, a ministry of the Navigators.)

Another thing we do at work to help families as well as individuals is the chaplain program that we initiated through Marketplace Ministries (listed in Appendix 2). Many of our employees do not attend church regularly, so when they face a crisis they have no church of their own to call. Marketplace Ministries provides our company with a chaplain who visits once a week and gets to know the employees. He or she becomes a friend, being available and holding Bible studies before work hours. When employees face a problem, they can call on the chaplain at any time. Our chaplains have helped our people through some terrible times in their lives.

The company chaplain has been present for births and deaths, trouble with teenagers and spouses, and happy times such as weddings. Since the information of who sees the chaplain and what is said is confidential, employees have great trust and freedom getting the help they need. If you have the authority in your business to look into having this program, or to suggest it to someone else, I would strongly recommend it. The return on your investment in employee morale, productivity, and loyalty is tremendous. Best of all, lives are changed.

We want to be involved with our people when they are in the hospital, and we have spent many hours and days sitting with folks who are there. But with several hundred people that we care about, we cannot be there in person for everyone. Our chaplain really helps the employees and our company.

DOORS OF OPPORTUNITY
DURING HOSPITAL STAYS

Most of us, however, do not have a company chaplain. What can we do as individuals? Here's a second suggestion, a second door of opportunity. When a neighbor or coworker is in the hospital, we can go to visit them, rather than simply sending a card. We can offer to pray with them, and do so right then in their presence. As the conversation in the hospital room unfolds, there may be a natural opportunity to talk about stress, life's crises, family reactions, and other problems.

We can then make a request: "Do you mind if I share this with my pastor so that he and my church family can pray for you?" In some cases, we could even look for an opportunity to ask if we could bring our pastor with us for a visit. The important thing is to go with a prayer for sensitivity to that person's needs and an awareness of the chances God will give for us to minister.

Be bold. In asking a person if you can pray for him or her, you are not imposing on the person, but showing the depth of your care. We have never seen a case in which an offer to pray was not appreciated, and it often opens the way for more spiritual conversation.

DOORS OF OPPORTUNITY
DURING HOLIDAYS

Another open door God provides to care for people is during holidays. It is easy to imagine how Christmas lends itself to giving of ourselves to others, but don't forget the less emphasized holidays. Father's Day and Mother's Day are often neglected holidays except by a parent's children, but these are great days on which to surprise someone you care about with a small token. If they do not have children, tell them that the gift is because they have a mother or father!

We decided to emphasize the week before Mother's Day at work. We gave each woman a different small gift each day. The gifts included cards, candy, a flower, and a small book. The morale in the office was sky-high for a long time. On Father's Day, I inserted tracts about Father's Day in the paychecks. Another year we sent a letter, and a third year we sent a small book. I sent these not only to our employees, but also to our contacts in the business world. One letter I received back from a supplier said, "Thank you for your letter. What pleased me most was the information that was inside, the tracts on being a better dad. Raising a family is often difficult." We have found people to be highly appreciative of any effort to make them feel special, especially since daily life does not often produce that effect.

Good material on the family, children, or marriage is usually freely received. Later on, when we want to say or send something that is spiritual in nature, people are receptive.

The Fourth of July is another overlooked opportunity as a rule. One year we sent a letter, along with the book *Preserve Us a Nation,* by Charles Crismeier, to friends and business associates. This book relates many stories about the heroes of our nation's early years. It emphasizes our nation's biblical roots. The reaction to that book from our suppliers was eye-opening. One supplier wrote, "As we celebrate our nation's birthday, this book is indeed an appropriate reminder. Because I travel quite a bit, I am never far from a book. This book will be with me on my next trip." Another replied, "This book will remain among my treasured readings. Thanks for thinking of me."

Of course, the holiday that means the most personally is a person's birthday. How long has it been since you have received a birthday card from someone other than your family? Another holiday like that is a wedding anniversary; not even family members remember that one. It means a lot, therefore, when someone remembers your special day. We make it a practice to send birthday cards, and once in a while, we send a card or an encouraging note to someone, not realizing that it will arrive on their birthday.

On one such occasion, the lady involved wrote back, "Bless you for your kindness to me in sending the precious book, *A Mother's Journey.* I'll attempt to explain to you the significance of your obedience to the Lord's prompting. The book arrived on my birthday. Because of the nature of our schedule, it was the only acknowledgement of my birthday. Also, the Lord told me that He had something for me when I opened your package. I knew what it was; the Lord was kissing me through you. Thank you for your sensitivity. Every time you have given to us it has met an exact need."

I can't tell you how many times people have told me that a card or pamphlet has arrived at an exact moment of need. Of course, there is no way I could know that; it is God's work. He is faithful and true in His love. The awesome knowledge that He is willing to use me to touch others keeps me on my knees in gratitude to Him. What a privilege and a joy it is to be His child.

DOORS OF OPPORTUNITY
DURING CRISES

Crises are often severe and heartrending. Such things as watching a loved one waste away with a disease, or hearing about the tragic death of a child, tear us apart. It may even make the local newscast or the front page of the newspaper. We wonder what we can do that would really help, but there is always something we can do. At times, history creates its own special days, usually out of crisis.

We will never forget one such day in Oklahoma City, April 19, 1995. The terrorist bombing of the Federal Building downtown created a chaos and opportunity to minister to people unparalleled in our state's history. Within three days of the event, we sent out a letter to several hundred friends, missionaries, and business contacts to tell them about it and to thank them for praying. People responded from all over the world.

It was a time to share our grief with others, and out of it positive influence was built. Of course, no one in Oklahoma City was personally untouched by the tragedy. If a resident did not directly lose a loved one in the event, he knew someone who did. We all attended funerals for weeks, and we helped friends recover for a year. One such person, Richeal Thatcher, worked in our office. Her sister, who was seven months pregnant at the time, was killed in the building. To make things worse, her body was not recovered for days. The torture one goes through while wondering if her loved one is still alive and suffering is terrible.

We tried to uphold Richeal in every way we could, and two years later we were still sending cards. In the meantime her dad was diagnosed with cancer, and she was told that she would be a witness at the trial in Denver. She had been through a lot in a short time, and we wanted to minister to her. In December of 1997 she wrote us, "Thanks so much for all the lovely cards you sent, as well as the prayers. Thank you also for the books you continue to send. I share them with my mother. Max Lucado has become a favorite."

Last year, Richeal wrote to the employees of our firm this letter:

"In life, we are constantly reaching out to grasp whatever we can. We start as infants reaching out and up to latch onto whatever objects lay within our reach. We hold tight to our parents' hands as they teach us to walk. We hold on first to them, then to God as we go out into life. All that my parents have taught me and all that God continues to teach me have helped me savor life and realize that material objects are never permanent nor to be depended on. The foundation of my life has been my faith, trust in God, values, and morals. When I came to work for Jacks Service Co. in 1985, I noticed that the management clearly demonstrates that God comes first, family second, and your job third. I observed that they put the company on the line with a Mission Statement that they stand behind, values they are frequently called upon to uphold, and morals that are tested daily.

"The friendships I have made at Jacks are a constant support in my life. Friends have held my hand after surgery, celebrated with me on my wedding day, comforted me when my dad was diagnosed with cancer, quietly prayed with me (and for me) the morning of April 19th when my sister was missing, and later cried with me as we laid her and my unborn niece to rest. They were there with me in thought and prayer as I took my turn on the witness stand. . . . The cards and inspirational readings I have received (and still continue to receive) tell me that Jacks' foundation is indeed God and that they want to share this with all of their employees. My stay at Jacks has enriched my life. I'm glad I latched on!"

You may wonder what effect one Christian trying to love people can have in a company. But one Christian influences others to do the same, and after a period of time, a company culture is developed that can really minister to people and honor Christ. Did you notice that although we as management had influence, most of Richeal's help came from her many coworkers? Just ordinary people, showing God's love to others.

Ask God for creative ways to meet the needs of the people you are in contact with everyday. As your sensitivity toward others increases, you will find people coming to you for advice. They want to talk to someone who they feel cares about them. Then you can take them by the hand and bring them with you to Jesus.

The way you do this will be different for each person. For example, I have given many stories about sending cards and books. That is just one way, one well suited to me, to minister. How each of us ministers is influenced by our backgrounds, personalities, gifting, experiences, abilities, and talents. The point is that when a door of opportunity is open, walk through it.

The key is not how we do it, but that we do it. If someone is in grief, four different Christians may help that person in four different ways. One may give a book, another may cook a meal, another goes by to sit and listen, another may sit by the phone and organize relatives coming into town for the funeral. Do not limit God by thinking that a method that is natural for me is what you should do. God probably has plans for you that you will be much more comfortable with, based on what He has gifted you to do.

The creativity of our great God is unlimited. Each of us is unique, placed by the Father to be His personal representative to those who need Him. The Creator of the universe has chosen to work through us. How amazing! As we become more sensitive to those around us, we will experience the words of Jesus in John 14:12, "I tell you the truth, anyone who has faith in me will do what I have been doing. He will do even greater things than these, because I am going to the Father."

> *When you think about being sensitive . . .*
> ## Remember Mary

Mary, the sister of Martha, exemplified the practice of observing and being sensitive. Jesus said of her in Luke 10:42, "Only one thing is needed. Mary has chosen what is better, and it will not be taken away from her." The setting for this unusual statement came during dinnertime at Mary's house. Jesus and His disciples had come to visit at the house of Jesus' dear friends, Lazarus, Martha, and Mary. Martha was busy in the kitchen, overwhelmed by the work involved in feeding many people. Mary was overwhelmed by the presence of Jesus, and was sitting at His feet, soaking up every word He uttered.

Few had Mary's sensitivity to the moment. Others in Jesus' life were constantly asking Him to do things such as heal the sick or challenge the religious leaders. Mary asked only for the privilege of quietly observing and listening to the Master.

Are we rushing around like Martha, trying to make things happen? Or are we quietly observing people and asking Jesus to make us more sensitive, learning from the Master?

> *We must dedicate ourselves to developing the habits of availability and listening.*

Chapter Seven

WALKING THROUGH THE DOOR, AVAILABLE AND LISTENING

Just then his disciples returned and were surprised to find him talking with a woman. But no one asked, "What do you want?" or "Why are you talking with her?"

JOHN 4:27

The above verse appears as part of the story of Jesus' meeting the Samaritan woman during midday. The meeting was significant in many ways, but we will consider two.

First, the encounter took place only because Jesus was available to His Father. He was ready to obey His Father's prompting to travel through Samaria, a land avoided by Jews, who considered Samaritans to be unclean and unworthy of interaction. We know from the above verse that the disciples were surprised He was talking with a woman, but they probably also wondered what He was thinking to pick that route. They followed nevertheless, knowing from experience that being with Jesus was a daily and unpredictable adventure.

AVAILABILITY, A KEY ATTRIBUTE

Jesus displayed a key attribute of those who enter doors of opportunity. He was available to God and other people. When he had reached Sychar, Jesus told His disciples to go into town, an action that left Him alone when the woman arrived to draw water.

Now Jesus was available for whatever would happen. And the apostle John recorded what happened next:

> When a Samaritan woman came to draw water, Jesus said to her, "Will you give me a drink?" The Samaritan woman said to him, "You are a Jew and I am a Samaritan woman. How can you ask me for a drink?" . . . Jesus answered her, "If you knew the gift of God and who it is that asks you for a drink, you would have asked him and he would have given you living water." (John 4: 7–10)

Notice Jesus was available not only to God the Father, but also to the woman. He made a trip out of His way to talk to a woman He did not know about eternal life. In Jesus' day, men did not hold conversations in the village square with women; much less would Jews talk with Samaritans (see verse 8). Yet Jesus was available to meet her needs, even though she was unsure herself what they were. God knew that she was ready in her heart, that she was waiting expectantly for the answers that the Messiah to come would give, and His Son responded to the opportunity.

The results of Jesus' willingness to be available, to be inconvenienced by taking a longer route to Galilee, and to spend time with this woman were overwhelming. Not only did she become a believer, but many in the town did also after hearing her testimony and Jesus' words (see verses 39–41).

LISTENING, AN ACTIVE SKILL

A second attribute that Jesus displayed during the encounter with the Samaritan woman was a keen ability to listen and really hear the individual. Listening is an active skill, rather than a passive one. It gives the listener the discernment to know what a person means as well as hearing what the person says. Review the conversation between the Jewish teacher and the Samaritan commoner:

> The woman said to him, "Sir, give me this water so that I won't get thirsty and have to keep coming here to draw water." He told her, "Go, call your husband and come back." "I have no husband," she replied. Jesus said to her, "You are right when you say you have no husband. The fact is, you have had five husbands, and the man you now have is not your husband. What you have just said is quite true." "Sir," the woman said, "I can see that you are a prophet. Our fathers worshiped on this mountain, but you Jews claim that the place where we must worship is in Jerusalem." Jesus declared, "Believe me, woman, a time is coming when you will worship the Father neither on this mountain nor in Jerusalem." (John 4:15–21)

When Jesus understood the meaning behind her words, "I have no husband," she was so amazed that she rightly called Him a prophet, and then quickly changed the subject. Jesus again went straight to the heart of the matter, and when the give-and-take of conversation was over, she was an ecstatic new follower of her Lord.

UNIQUE SITUATIONS EVERY DAY

When opportunities came, Jesus regularly demonstrated those two important characteristics: availability and listening. Both are important for us to use in our interaction with people as well. "But," one might say, "things don't happen like that today. That situation was unique." Yes, that was a unique situation, as are all of the events throughout history in which God has dealt with men and women. Yet, even as God led His Son two thousand years ago to go out of His way to speak to a stranger, He continues to do so every day in the twenty-first century to those who are listening for God's direction and are available to Him and to people.

Vickie Jenkins, a vivacious, quick-witted, and loving mother of three, once wrote for me—and you—how God made a clear

opportunity for her. She entitled her story, "A Ride on a Carousel."
Here are excerpts from her story:

"It was a summer day; I stepped outside to greet the morning.
The wind was a gentle breeze as it blew against my face. There was
a soft whisper in the air, and I smiled as I thanked God for His
many blessings. God had been good to me. He had given me a
wonderful husband and three beautiful children. I had a great job
as a secretary. My life was like a ride on a carousel. I had my share
of ups and downs. Going round and round, I never knew where I
would end up next. Little did I know, I was about to venture to yet
another ride on the carousel of life.

"I had gone to work, and that afternoon I found myself
driving home by a different route. I did not know why. All of a
sudden, I saw the Children's Convalescent Center. I had lived in
Oklahoma City for many years, but had never noticed the center
before today. The next thing I knew, I was turning into the parking
lot of the center. What was going on? I stopped the car and turned
off the ignition. In my solitude, these words seemed to speak to my
heart, 'Go to the children.' I obeyed and went inside."

Vickie entered the reception area of the center and when the
receptionist asked her business, Vickie announced, with some hesi-
tation, "I would like to see the children."

She soon found herself in the office of the center's chairman.
After the woman greeted Vickie and had some brief words about
the center, she invited Vickie to tour some of the rooms. "Are you
ready?"

Ready for what? Vickie wondered. She resumes her story:

"I followed her through double doors and down a long narrow
hallway. I was surprised by what I saw. The rooms were lined with
cribs and adolescent beds, and there were six children in each room.
All of the children were critically handicapped. There were children
on life support, their bodies motionless. Other children were in
wheelchairs, and some had casts covering their arms and legs. I had
a weak feeling in my stomach as I watched the children struggle
with the slightest movement. I was speechless as I wondered why I
had stopped here. This was not the place for me. What was God
telling me? As I left, tears flowed down my face. I said a prayer.

"That night, I found myself tossing and turning as I tried to sleep. The children were on my mind. I asked God to reveal to me His plan. My heart was peaceful only after I had concluded that He wanted me to work at the Children's Convalescent Center. The next day, I went to work, knowing what I must do. I explained the situation to my boss as I told him that I must leave. I left the office and drove straight to the center. Now what? I had just quit my job!

"I walked into the office and asked if there were any jobs available. Any kind of office work would suffice to be close to the children. The only position that was available was for a Certified Nursing Assistant for the night shift. I was not a CNA, and I thought I could never work with handicapped children. Nor did I want to work at night. *When would I spend time with my family? When would I find time for myself?* It is amazing how God takes control of our lives and leads us down certain pathways. The obstacles that we think are impossible, are removed by the grace of God.

"After completing a course of training for certification at Canadian Valley Vo-Tech, I worked at the Children's Convalescent Center, as a Certified Nursing Assistant, caring for the critically handicapped children. My heart reached out to each one of them as I gave them my love and my care. In return, I received many blessings. God allowed me to see children in a special way; I saw each child as a promise from Him."

Today, as Vickie works at the center, she regards the children as "miracles full of love, hope, and dreams, rolled into rainbows of possibilities, challenges, and accomplishments. They held my hand tight and my spirits high. Each child was as extraordinary as a single twinkling star set in the velvet of the night sky. Today I thank God for the blessings and promises He has given to me."

Yes, God continues to call His children to serve today. We may not hear a voice or prompting as Vickie did; circumstances, Scriptures, the biblical counsel of friends, and the words of magazine articles or news stories are other ways our limitless and creative God can direct us. Importantly, like Vickie, we should follow God's direction.

Vickie's life changed because she made a spontaneous decision to obey God's urging in her heart when she drove home by a new route. She became permanently available to minister to the children when she took planned steps to accomplish a vocational change. Both types of availability, spontaneous and planned, are necessary in our Christian walk.

ABOUT PLANNED AVAILABILITY

I (Kent) have seen both kinds of availability work in the marketplace. I plan to be available to people by communicating to them that I have an "open-door policy." Anyone in the company has permission to come to me at any time. This includes warehouse employees as well as management, and many of them have taken advantage of the opportunity for personal and job-related help. I also watch the people whom I interact with daily to try to sense when they are under pressure. They may just need a smile or an encouraging word. Sometimes they need more.

I remember a day when one of the secretaries seemed down. Was Tina simply being overly thoughtful, or was she sad?

"Are you all right?" I asked her.

"Yeah," Tina replied in a most dejected voice.

Knowing now that something was wrong, I assured her that I would be available if she wanted to talk. Later that day, she came to my office and admitted that her heart was indeed heavy. One of her very best friends was having tremendous emotional problems, possibly to the point of contemplating suicide. She was convinced that something needed to be done for Teresa, and soon.

"Does Teresa want help?" I asked. Tina thought she did.

"Would she talk to me?" Tina thought about that for a second and then a faint smile broke across her face.

Tina phoned Teresa, who was relieved that someone would try to help her, and it was arranged that the three of us would meet for dinner at a quiet restaurant where Teresa could talk. I phoned my wife to tell her what had happened, and Davidene committed to pray during the dinner. I was nervous, but I said a prayer committing the time ahead to God, praying that He would direct our paths. He promised in Proverbs 3:5–6 that He will "make [our] paths straight" when we "trust in the Lord with all [our] heart and lean not on [our] own understanding; [and] in all [our] ways acknowledge him."

God did direct our paths. And he gave me freedom and a peace that truly "transcends all understanding" (Philippians 4:7). Even better, He did the same for Teresa. She was already His child, but she was severely depressed. She received hope from God's Word that evening, and a plan of action to seek more answers. My wife Davidene started the process with her, meeting every week for Bible study, support, and encouragement. Teresa has become a dear friend to all of us. God has changed her life and guided her direction in miraculous ways, and we rejoice.

The same open-door policy that I have instituted as a CEO can take place anywhere: in the lunchroom during a coffee break or meal, in the living room, even in the backyard. It is basically a desire to be there for other people. It can happen when a coworker seems down and wants to talk, and you take the lunch hour (in which you had planned to rest) to listen, or when a neighbor strikes up a conversation over the back fence and talks about a need you were unaware of.

PLANNED AVAILABILITY
THROUGH MENTORING

Mentoring another person is another method of planned availability. Mentoring is a relational experience in which one person with experience or knowledge in a certain area (the mentor) gives assistance to another person (the mentoree) in an intentional or planned manner. We will discuss three of the many possible ways to mentor: intensive, occasional, and passive. (In most cases, the mentoree asks the mentor for help or advice in a certain area, except in the case of passive mentoring, which we will discuss last.)

Intensive mentoring occurs over a prolonged period of time and involves both teaching and accountability. About fifteen years ago I spoke to the students at the Baptist Student Union at the University of Oklahoma. One young man stood out to me. Brian had lots of questions, questions filled with thought and a desire to be influenced to live with God no matter where his adult life might take him. I spoke again a year later, and Brian was still there, intensely seeking God's will for his life. He asked if we could have lunch together and I gladly agreed. We had a good time sharing about God together, focusing primarily on living for Him in the marketplace.

Years passed and I occasionally saw Brian, since he had gone into business in our area. Then one day I received a phone call from him, again asking for a lunch meeting. During that lunch, Brian gave me a book on mentoring. Then he asked a question.

"Would you consider doing this?" he asked. "I have underlined some things in this book, and if you would read it we can meet next week to talk about it."

I had never seen anyone so eager to pursue God and learn how to honor Him in business. I was not sure what I was getting into, but I decided to be available to meet with Brian weekly and any other time he wanted. We are now very close friends, and we have both had an impact on each other's lives. We have both owned and sold businesses, and been where God is working. We both took advantage of the opportunity God gave to influence and to be influenced by another person.

That's the joy of intentional mentoring. Friendships will develop and deepen; both the mentor and the mentoree will influence each other's life for the good. As we say in business, it's a win/win situation.

Occasional mentoring is another way to help and encourage a person. It occurs when a mentor has knowledge and understanding in an area in which a mentoree desires short-term advice and guidance. As a college freshman, I (Davidene) remember getting settled into my room in the girls' dorm when a tall, lanky, wide-eyed girl poked her head through the open door.

"Hi, my name is Evie," she ventured. Her eyes looked like those of a deer caught in a car's headlights. She stood half in and half out of the room, a curious combination of fear and excitement, of intensity and insecurity. I didn't know what to make of her.

"Hi, I'm Davidene. Come on in."

Thus began a lifelong friendship with the most sensitive and creative person I have ever known. Evie's room was on the floor below me, but we visited regularly. I soon learned that Evie had been reared as an orphan. Part of her first seventeen years had been spent in a children's home, during which time she was taken to church and fell in love with the Lord. Her relationship with God remained her focus throughout her life's experiences. When I met her, she had been living on her own, roaming between Kansas and Oklahoma, staying in local YWCAs. Due to her lifestyle, her spiritual growth had been limited to the Sunday school Bible stories of her childhood years. Although they had laid a wonderful foundation for her increasing love of God, she was looking for more. She had multitudes of questions and no one to answer them.

Weeks later Evie burst through the same door and found me on my knees beside my bed, praying. She did not care that she had interrupted me; she only saw a hope for her hungry heart.

"How do you do that? Can you teach me?" she blurted out.

I was so surprised by her outburst that I wasn't even sure what she was talking about. I soon realized that Evie wanted to be taught how to pray. She was like an eager child, thrilled at the opportunity to have intimate conversation with God. Throughout our college years, I was an occasional mentor for Evie. Her questions and our discussions were a highlight of that period in my life, and I believe that I grew spiritually more than she did because of the demand that her questions gave me to search God's Word.

When she asked a question that I could not answer, we both went back to my parents' home to be mentored by my mother. We began to make frequent weekend trips to my home, and Evie had her first glimpse into a marriage and family centered on God. Today Evie is married to a vibrant Christian man, has three children who have been reared to love God, and is a creative homemaker, writer, and artist.

I found through Evie that being an occasional mentor is not hard. It does not require a position of authority or even very much knowledge. We simply have to be one step ahead of the person following us on our spiritual journey and be willing to share what we do know and have experienced. When we do not have an answer, we have the options of learning together, or of going to another more knowledgeable person, as Evie and I did with my mom.

Finally, *passive mentoring* occurs when a person lives a model of the values he holds to the point that he or she inspires emulation. This occurs at various times as we model a life that wins respect; we become models for those who watch us. The mentoree need not be someone our age, either; those watching may be much younger. For example, a stay-at-home mom can make her home a place where neighborhood children are welcome, especially after school when their parents are both at work. A ready hug, snacks, and a smile can help a child feel secure and warm, even when that child is not yours. As the children come to know you well, questions and discussion ensue (especially during a snack time), prompted by their lives at home and at school. In your answers you gain the opportunity to impart your views about life and the God who loves them.

These children, by the way, may be six or sixteen. One of our son's friends came to our house for so many years that we bought extra cereal (his favorite snack) just for him. By the time he was a senior in high school, we were buying three extra boxes a week, and talking about serious life issues along the way.

The methods that we have discussed so far, by which we can use planned availability, have dealt with individual efforts. A married couple can also work together to influence one or more couples in their neighborhood. One program we heartily recommend is sponsored by Search Ministries (listed in Appendix 2). Its Search Open Forum creates a comfortable environment for a religious non-Christian or the unchurched alike. It begins when Christians invite their unbelieving friends and/or neighbors to a discussion about life and God issues. These often include some of the objections that folks have to Christianity, such as "Why do the innocent suffer?" "Isn't belief in God a crutch?" and "Why do some say that there is only one way to God?"

The beauty of the Search Open Forum is that people will come to it who would not come to church or attend a formal Bible study. It is low-key evangelism by design. There is a thirty-minute social time, including light refreshments, followed by an hour discussion, followed by more food, usually desserts. It lasts for four weeks, and is held in a home, emphasizing hospitality.

PLANNED *AND*
SPONTANEOUS AVAILABILITY

Often you can use both spontaneous and planned availability in your neighborhood. Be creative. Laurie demonstrates both kinds of availability as she shows and tells others about her love for God. If another mother is ill, Laurie may fix dinner and take it to the family. That is a spontaneous act and requires that Laurie change her plans for that day to create time to cook. On the other hand, Laurie also has "Project Nights" for her neighbors. This is a planned event one evening a month. Everyone brings a project they are working on, and then work together and chat.

Laurie has found that, with time, the relationships grow and conversations get deeper among the women. Since the evenings take place at Laurie's house and she plans them, Laurie becomes the one to whom other ladies come when help is needed. Laurie is purposely available.

Laurie has told us that both she and her husband, Chris, consider their home to be their basis for ministry. Therefore, practicing hospitality is a goal and a tool for them. They keep frozen desserts ready, they keep the house somewhat orderly (as much as possible with two young energetic children), and they invite people to dinner regularly. They include their children in the planning and in praying for friends and neighbors, so that it is a family affair to love others.

Laurie and Chris make plans to be available to people, and they are ready for those spur-of-the-moment encounters that are not planned in advance. That's planned *and* spontaneous availability, and any of us can do it. It often involves showing hospitality. Biblical hospitality is living lives that we can invite people into.

Interestingly, availability was part of Laurie and Chris's lifestyles before they met and married. They saw such ministry modeled in their parents' homes. They each grew up seeing God work through their parents' love of people and the flexibility in their schedules to meet needs. Chris practiced availability as a college student. During his four years at school, he lived in the dorm every year, requesting the room by the elevator (which no one else wanted because of the noise). He did this because all of the residents on the hall would have to pass by his room to get to their own. He kept his door open and a jar of candy ready to lure students in. He became a friend, confidant, and spiritual mentor to many. He used planned availability. Chris also organized a weekly dorm Bible study for Christians and non-Christians, and occasionally he ordered pizza to increase the attractiveness of the study. Laurie used tutoring as her way to get time with students. If a student needs tutoring, she is already frustrated and very likely over time will want to talk about her burdens. Laurie was available.

Those are good strategies we would recommend to college students. We're not saying you have to get your dorm room next to an elevator or always buy pizza, but plan ways to develop relationships and have your own open-door policy, where other students feel free to visit and know they'll find a listening ear.

GUIDELINES FOR BEING AVAILABLE

When Laurie and Chris married, they wanted to find a church home. As they looked, they met many new couples, their age and older. They began to notice that some of the couples seemed frazzled and hurried all the time. A representative couple had three children, the eldest nearing teen years. Both parents worked a job, held positions in the church, took their children to various team practices and skill rehearsals, and had no time for anything extra because they were busy and exhausted. That is when Chris and Laurie realized that being flexible and available would take concentrated effort to control their schedule so that their schedule would not control them. It is a dilemma that we all face.

That raises a key question when it comes to making ourselves available to others: How do I make decisions when the choice is between several good things? Here are a few suggestions we would offer for making wise ministry choices. They can help you know when to be involved.

- Does this activity emphasize people rather than programs? The Scriptures make it clear that people are important. The apostle Paul reminded young Timothy, "And the things you have heard me say in the presence of many witnesses entrust to reliable men who will also be qualified to teach others" (2 Timothy 2:2).
- Does this activity involve my circle of influence (family, business, social, etc.)?
- Does it have the possibility of having eternal results? "For no one can lay any foundation other than the one already laid, which is Jesus Christ. If any man builds on this foundation using gold, silver, costly stones, wood, hay or straw, his work will be shown for what it is, because the Day will bring it to light. It will be revealed with fire, and the fire will test the quality of each man's work" (1 Corinthians 3:11–13).
- Am I making an investment in a person? "We proclaim him, admonishing and teaching everyone with all wisdom, so that we may present everyone perfect in Christ" (Colossians 1:28).
- Am I looking for people with a heart for God? The Lord honors such people; He always has. "But the Lord said to Samuel, 'Do not consider his appearance or his height, for I have rejected him. The Lord does not look at the things man looks at. Man looks at the outward appearance, but the Lord looks at the heart'" (1 Samuel 16:7).
- Can someone else do it? Will someone else do it? We must do things that others cannot or will not do. Remember, only three things last for eternity, God Himself, God's Word, and the souls of men.

BECOMING GOOD LISTENERS

As we learn more about how to be available to people, we will understand the necessity of becoming good listeners. We must rely on the Holy Spirit to enable us to hear not only people's words, but their hearts' yearnings as well. We need to develop our listening skills so that we can discern the meaning behind words.

Every time communication takes place, there are many messages:

1. What person A means to say
2. What person A actually does say
3. What person B hears
4. What person B thinks it means
5. What person B means to say
6. What person B actually says
7. What person A hears

And so it goes. You can see how easily misunderstanding can occur in conversation. In order to be successful, communication involves thinking as we hear, then formulating thoughts, and finally sharing those thoughts. We tend to rush the process in our everyday lives, much like we tend to rush our schedule and other things.

Listening is a skill that did not come easily to me (Kent). I was reared as the eldest of five children, four of whom are boisterous leader types. Dinnertime at my house was a contest of who could jump into the conversation the fastest and talk the loudest. The ability to interrupt with authority was essential to having a part in the fun. We loved our raucous way of bantering, and still do to this day. But it did not lend itself to my learning the skill of listening. Davidene, on the other hand, was reared in a family that had quiet, slow conversations. If she wanted to talk to her dad about something and he was studying, he put down his book, pushed it away, and gave her his undivided attention. When Davidene and I married, we were in for some serious adjustment.

Shortly after we moved into our first little house, we had friends over. Davidene had spent the day preparing, excited about entertaining in our own home. The evening had been a success, and our friends were getting ready to leave. As we stepped out onto the front porch to bid our friends goodbye, Davidene was feeling happy and warm about everything, especially our house now becoming a home.

As they drove away, Davidene glanced up and saw through the beautiful branches of a pecan tree a large orange moon, partially covered by clouds that gave it the appearance of having wispy stripes. Then she said to me, in almost a whisper, "Honey, isn't the moon gorgeous?"

I'll let Davidene tell what happened next. "I meant, of course, 'I love this evening, I love our home, I love you, and I feel totally romantic.' Kent responded by saying something about the weather! I ran into the house feeling unloved and misunderstood."

I (Kent) heard only the word "moon," and looking up I saw it almost smothered with clouds, bad news for the weather tomorrow. So I said, "Yes, but we might be in for some rain." I meant, of course, nothing more than those words, but she raced into the house, sobbing. I remained on the porch dumbfounded and wondering what had gone wrong.

In those days, I did not listen much, and rarely heard meaning behind words. We have now been married for more than thirty years, and I am gradually making some progress in this area. Now our three children are grown and married, and I come home from work to my wife. She has dinner ready and we sit down to eat. I listen, really listen, while she pours out the thoughts and feelings about her day. I do not interrupt, but wait until she is finished before I jump in. I ask questions and try to understand what she is saying over and around her words. She loves it. It seems that I can do no wrong for the rest of the evening. What a marital secret, a true key to happiness! This kind of listening can help you in any kind of verbal interaction with anyone you encounter in life, from family and friends to store clerks and neighbors.

SUGGESTIONS FOR LISTENING

Here are some suggestions to help you listen more and so understand the needs of others better.

- Do not interrupt. When we interrupt, we in effect are saying, "What I want to say is more important than anything you are saying." It is only logical that if I am busy in my head thinking about what I want to say, I am not listening to the other person. Here's a tip for extended listening: If you are in a counseling situation, ask permission to take notes. This does several positive things. It helps you to remember the key points thirty minutes later when the person is finished telling his or her story, and it helps you remember what you want to say without needing to interrupt because you have written it down. Most important, it tells the person that you are taking this seriously and truly want to hear him.

- Stay focused. Minimize external distractions and pay close attention.
- Interpret both words and emotions. Body language helps to give away emotion as well as words. If the speaker clenches a hand, there could be underlying anger. Arms crossed over the chest are often a sign that the person is feeling defensive. Fidgeting could reveal nervousness. Eyes downcast could mean the person is depressed, feels guilty, or feels ashamed. Be aware of the pitch and tone of the person's voice, too.
- Resist filtering. Be open minded; avoid judging and jumping to conclusions due to your own values. Realize that difference in values gives their words a different meaning than if you were saying the same words.
- Summarize the message back to the speaker. "This is what I think I heard you say. Is this correct?" In that way, the other person can clarify if you have misunderstood.
- Take your time wording a reply. Silence is not fatal. You can preface your remarks by saying, "Wait just a second while I think about how to phrase this." The person will be grateful, not impatient.
- Let the other person do most of the talking.
- Encourage others to talk about themselves. Do this by asking questions about topics that interest them. They will leave thinking you are the best conversationalist they have ever met.

OUR MODEL

Jesus was the best example we will ever see of someone who perfected the skill of listening and the habit of being available. It is valuable to read the Gospels and make note of all the times that these two characteristics were evident. Notice how He used them, and what effect they had on the people He was ministering to. This is an extremely difficult thing for me to do, even after years of working at it.

If you struggle in this area as I do, then share your frustrations with a friend or a small group of people who will advise and pray for you. Ask God to help you develop your skills. Our Lord takes great pleasure in showing His power in our weaknesses. That gives us hope!

> *When you think about availability and listening . . .*
> ## Remember Abraham

Time after time, Abraham listened to God. That sounds like a simple activity, doesn't it? The things that God asked him to do were not simple or easy. God asked Abraham to leave his home city of Ur to travel to an undisclosed location. This was quite a request, because Abraham's family had lived there for generations, and Abraham was very wealthy. Besides, travel in those days was not exactly safe or convenient (Genesis 12:1, 4–5). Then God asked him to believe that he would father a son long after he was young enough to do so (Genesis 15:2–6). After fulfilling His promise of a son, God asked Abraham to sacrifice him (Genesis 22:1–12). But because Abraham consistently and faithfully remained available to God and instantly obeyed Him, God was able to use Abraham to build a mighty nation.

Yet the Bible praised Abraham more for his faith than his actions. Genesis 15:6 says, "Abram believed the Lord, and he credited it to him as righteousness."

As God opens doors in your life, will you trust Him enough to walk boldly through them? Will you be available to those God places in your path? Will you quietly allow the Spirit of God to recognize the real needs and problems of each person as you listen attentively to them?

> *We must have the heart*
> *of a servant and the spirit*
> *of an encourager.*

Chapter Eight

SERVING AND ENCOURAGING AS YOU WALK

"Not so with you. Instead, whoever wants to become great among you must be your servant, and whoever wants to be first must be your slave—just as the Son of Man did not come to be served, but to serve, and to give his life as a ransom for many."

MATTHEW 20:26–28

Jesus, the Master, spent much of His earthly life demonstrating to us how to be a servant. Nowhere in Scripture was that portrayed more poignantly than in His act of washing the disciples' feet. After He had washed their feet and dried them with a towel, He explained the significance of His actions.

> "Do you understand what I have done for you?" he asked them. "You call me 'Teacher' and 'Lord,' and rightly so, for that is what I am. Now that I, your Lord and Teacher, have washed your feet, you also should wash one another's feet. I have set you an example that you should do as I have done for you. I tell you the truth, no servant is greater than his master, nor is a messenger greater than the one who sent him. Now that you know these things, you will be blessed if you do them." (John 13:12–17).

The story of Jesus' washing the disciples' feet raises one question. Why was it important for Jesus to be a servant? After all, He had spent much of His ministry doing good and miraculous things for people. Kindness, caring, and compassion were His hallmarks, so why add servanthood?

OUR MOTIVE IN SERVING

Look in the dictionary and you will see that the words *servant* and *care* do not differ much. But Jesus' example set a new standard for spiritual servants that adds a dimension to our understanding. Serving people and meeting their needs can look the same. Often they involve menial tasks and work done behind the scenes. A spiritual servant has a particular motivation. The servant does what he does strictly out of obedience to his master. Jesus was obedient to His Father, and the spiritual servant is obedient to Jesus' command and the Holy Spirit's prompting.

Though we have emphasized being sensitive and available to meet needs, let's remember that our success is not important. Only obedience is. We serve others simply to honor the Father and follow the example of His Son. There is no thought for gain other than the satisfaction of doing the deed.

For example, let's say that Mary has a huge job to do at the office. She works all day, but does not get the task completed. She is frustrated and worried because the boss needs the project by tomorrow morning, but she cannot stay late to finish it because her daughter has an important appointment. Bob offers to stay and do Mary's work for her. He explains that he has no time constraints and would be happy to do this for her. Bob could have one of several motivations for his offer. He may want the boss to notice and realize what he did. If so, the action would still meet Mary's need, but it would not be a servant act unless he truly did not care for any reward other than to be able to perform this act of kindness.

Jesus' acts as a servant taught us that serving is a humble attitude, in which the person expects nothing in return; serving is simply an act of obedience to the Master that we love. This was as true of Jesus as it must be of us. Paul explained the concept to the Philippians in the second chapter of his letter to them.

If you have any encouragement from being united with Christ, . . . then make my joy complete by being like-minded, having the same love, being one in spirit and purpose. Do nothing out of selfish ambition or vain conceit, but in humility consider others better than yourselves. Each of you should look not only to your own interests, but also to the interests of others. Your attitude should be the same as that of Christ Jesus: Who, being in very nature God, did not consider equality with God something to be grasped, but made himself nothing, taking the very nature of a servant, being made in human likeness. And being found in appearance as a man, he humbled himself and became obedient to death—even death on a cross! (Philippians 2:1–8)

HOW TO ENCOURAGE AND IMPART VALUE

Servant deeds encourage both the servant and the recipient. The fostering of encouragement is very important, because it is easy to lose hope, a common malady in our society today. As we strive to give support through serving, there are some strategies for making the other person feel valued:

- Give honest, sincere appreciation
- Become genuinely interested in the person
- Smile
- Remember the person's name
- Do not criticize, condemn, or complain
- Be a good listener
- Talk about things of interest to the other person

STORIES OF SERVICE

The following two examples demonstrate how people show and tell God's love though acts of spiritual service and encouragement. Several years ago a couple at our church, Monty and Louise, both had hepatitis. The church sent food, yet the two could hardly eat and often felt weak. Their friend Gary performed the ministry they remembered the most. One day he arrived unannounced and mowed their lawn with no fanfare or great spiritual message—he just loved them and showed that love.

Years later, Monty's neighbors had a death in their family and were experiencing grief. Monty remembered Gary's gift of love and mowed his neighbors' lawn. He did not tell the family that he was the one who had done it, and he was not sure that they even noticed. He did it for the Lord, he said. Now he makes it a habit to help others unheralded as much as he can.

Earlier this year Monty wanted to watch basketball on a Saturday. That game would involve several hours, so he decided to drive to the homes of three female neighbors, a single mom, a widow, and a caregiver to an elderly parent, and collect their knives and scissors. Then, as he watched the TV back home, he sharpened the knives. Later, he returned them without a word; the ladies were happy and grateful for that small help.

Dean and Linda are parents of a grown son, Greg. When Greg was in high school, he befriended a new student who lived in a nearby neighborhood. Chris was a bit of a loner and appreciated having a friend. As the boys spent time together, Dean and Linda became aware that Chris's home life was quite different from theirs. Chris's parents were alcoholics who frequently locked him out of the house. He regularly broke into the garage to sleep on some old furniture that was stored there. After one altercation with his parents, he was arrested and sent to jail.

One day Linda answered the doorbell to find Chris standing on the porch, his probation officer at his side. He had been released from jail and had no place to go. His parents had moved out of town. The officer asked if Chris could stay with them until a place was found for him, so they agreed to keep him for two weeks, until he was moved to a group home.

As time passed, Greg received occasional phone calls from Chris as he moved from place to place. One December evening, after Greg had graduated from college, Chris called Linda to say that he had been evicted, had no money, no job, and no place to go. He wondered if he could stay with them again. Most people would have considered Chris to be a loser at life and a very poor risk to bring into a home. Dean, however, had faith in God's power and believed that if Chris could be parented onto the right track, he could possibly make it on his own later. At 11:30 P.M. on that cold Saturday night, Dean located Chris and brought him into their home. Greg was astonished and proud of his parents' decision to share their lives with his friend. Chris lived with them for seven months, until he and Greg got an apartment together. Eventually Chris secured his GED and wandered away again.

Chris's lifestyle and problems were not solved in that short time. But Linda and Dean now say, "We can only pray that we might have planted in him some seeds of Christian faith, which will eventually sprout. Chris is now thirty years old, and although we have lost track of him, God knows where he is and how he is doing."

Dean and Linda's willingness to sacrifice their own privacy, time, and money for the sake of a boy in whose life they saw little result was true servant love. Their experience reminds us of Paul's encouragement: "Let us not become weary in doing good, for at the proper time we will reap a harvest if we do not give up" (Galatians 6:9).

PRAYER ... TIME ... MATERIALS

There are other things that we can give that constitute being a servant and bring encouragement. The most important is prayer. Many years ago, I was speaking at a conference. I had taken time off work, I had left my family at home, and I would get one hour to invest in the lives of those in attendance. Was the cost worth it? I was impressed with the thought that I could invest more than that hour in these lives if I just knew how to pray for them. Prayer has the power to change hearts, and I would be willing to put my time and the work of prayer into these people. In fact, it would make my time more worthwhile.

That was the first time that I made the commitment to pray seriously for those people who would allow me. Now, every time I speak, I ask that each audience member give me a 3x5 card with their name and address on one side and a prayer request on the other. I ask that they be heartfelt requests, and that they be very specific. Several times a week while I walk or ride my stationary bicycle, I read one card at a time and pray for the person represented by that card. When these cards are added to those from family and friends, I have many to pray for each week. Davidene claims that it is my prayer life that is keeping me healthy, because the more I have to pray for, the longer I exercise.

After three months of praying for someone, I send him or her a letter of encouragement. I remind the person that I am praying and ask how things are going. Often they reply by letter with an update and another request. Prayer is time-consuming work, but how rewarding! God has done some miraculous things through the years, and I get excited just thinking about being a part of that. Some requests, especially for people to come to know Him, have taken many years to be answered. It is a victory every time I find out about such a new believer. Prayer is a powerful friend to a servant, and we commend prayer to you.

Of course, time is also a powerful friend. While investing a little time, you become a servant who encourages. During Christmas 1998, a man asked for me to have lunch with him and a friend who needed some advice. The Christmas season is busy, but I gladly spent the time with him. He sent me a note later which said, "Of all the gifts I received over the holiday season, the one hour that you gave me was perhaps the most valuable of all. I'm looking forward to receiving the materials you mentioned."

A third thing we can give is actual material goods. We know folks who do not have garage sales when their clothes or other assets are no longer of use to them. Instead, they give those items to a boys' ranch, a rescue mission, or other Christian organizations. That's a great way to serve the need of others and honor Christ. Some choose to give away old but serviceable cars or trucks to a needy organization, or they sell a van and give the money away. Some give computers, cars, or other assets anonymously, receiving no recognition, and then they find their joy increased.

A SERVANT'S CREATIVE WAYS

In the workplace, think of all those who serve you, from custodians and food service workers to security or the parking attendants. Think of creative ways to support those who serve so faithfully. Prayer, time, and materials are important, but there are other practical things to do. For instance, bring a soft drink or a snack to an assistant. Help someone by giving a recommendation for a new doctor or dentist. I have found that whatever you do well can be used as a gift to freely help others. Your heart, your experiences, your abilities, and your personality form who you are. These are your unique qualifications for service.

Do you serve your coworkers so that they are more successful? What have you done to support your spouse in maximizing his or her gifts, and in achieving your spouse's goals and dreams? Serving is simply meeting needs, which can be emotional, spiritual, physical, financial, or social.

Here are two good questions to ask to determine whether you have a servant's attitude: (1) Do I serve those who could never repay me? (2) Do I help those who cannot help themselves? If your motive is to show the love of Christ, and not to gain reward or glory, God will bless, and you will find yourself with many creative ideas.

A SERVANT'S ENCOURAGING WAYS

Have you ever thought about what words you would like as your epitaph? I have. Philemon 1:7 is my life verse: "Your love has given me great joy and encouragement, because you, brother, have refreshed the hearts of the saints." I can think of no better way to be remembered than as one who refreshed the hearts of those around me. We are surrounded with negative, critical, fearful, and angry people. There is always room for one who will encourage.

You can be the principal encourager in your office, in your home, at your church, and in your social group. Let's summarize some of the loving actions you can take in these settings (and add a few more). At work, you can (1) put a note on a coworker's desk, (2) leave an encouraging e-mail, (3) leave a "thank you" voice mail, (4) send a card, and (5) write a note at the top of a completed project. At home, you can (1) call your spouse and leave an answering machine message of hope, (2) leave a note at a family member's breakfast place when you leave early, (3) send or bring flowers for no occasion, (4) send your child a card stating how proud you are of him or her, and (5) congratulate your child on a recent accomplishment.

Beyond your coworkers and immediate family, you can encourage others you see only on occasion but appreciate nonetheless. Consider what you can do for friends:

- Use a card, booklet, or other item to celebrate their important times (weddings, birthdays, promotion, graduation, or new home).
- Stop by to talk about their loved one who passed away.
- Leave answering machine messages remembering shared good times. For example, Jack called a friend he knew was at work with the following message: "Remember that two years ago today we were hiking in Colorado? What a great trip that was! Thanks for your friendship."

Similarly, consider what you can do for others whom you appreciate and who need encouragement:

- Send an encouraging note or thank you card to your favorite positive radio personality, a government official who took a difficult stand, or the person who delivers your newspaper.
- Send a small gift to a missionary.
- Write an appreciation note to your church staff, or the one who helps your teenager, or a faithful teacher, or the one who keeps the babies at your church.
- Remember the one who cleans your office, fixes your car, works the cash register at your neighborhood grocery; remember such people with a smile, cheerful conversation, and verbal appreciation for their work on your behalf.

Yes, you can probably lead the parade of encouragers in your sphere of influence. The line is long of those who point out shortcomings, but if you seek only to affirm, uplift, and encourage, without any expectations, you will have multiple opportunities daily. Seize the opportunities; walk through those open doors.

Finally, a suggestion of a way that we as servants can encourage hearts is to be aware of those people in our lives who have had an impact on us, and let them know of their value. Spend some time thinking about the people who have most affected your walk with Christ and your desire to live for Him at work and at school. Put those names on a list. You may have a few names of people you have never met—authors whose writings have greatly influenced you. Then write letters to all of them.

I did this, writing letters to twelve men, telling them how their lives had changed my life, and thanking them. Although I did not do this to get a response, a few did write back, overwhelmed at my appreciation. I came to realize how much these men had needed encouragement and an affirmation of the usefulness of their lives. When you do this, you too may get some thanks. But remember, you're doing it not for thanks but because it's the right thing for servants to do as they serve and affirm others.

Sometimes in the daily challenges that life gives us, we miss what is really important. We may fail to say hello, please, or thank you, congratulate someone on something, give a compliment, or do something nice for no reason. Charles Plumb, a U.S. Naval Academy graduate, was a jet fighter pilot in Vietnam. After seventy-five combat missions, his plane was destroyed by a surface-to-air missile. Plumb ejected but parachuted into enemy hands. He was imprisoned for six years. Years after Plumb's release, his wife and he were surprised by a gentleman who approached them in a restaurant.

"You're Plumb! You flew jet fighters from the aircraft carrier Kitty Hawk. You were shot down!"

"How in the world did you know that?" asked Plumb.

"I packed your parachute," the man replied. Plumb gasped in surprise and gratitude. The man pumped his hand as he said, "I guess it worked!"

Plumb assured him, "It sure did. If that chute had not opened, I wouldn't be here today."

Later that night, Plumb lay sleepless and troubled. He had been a fighter pilot, top dog of the ship's social hierarchy, and had given little if any thought to the fact that his personal safety depended on the "lowly" sailors who worked long hard hours doing the tedious and thankless job of packing the parachutes. Plumb now says, "I kept pondering what he might have looked like in a Navy uniform. I wonder how many times I might have seen him and not even said 'Good morning' or 'How are you?'" Plumb's fate had been in the hands of this man who had been sitting beside a wooden table far below the deck, folding the silk that would save his life.

Plumb now speaks on lessons learned from his experiences in captivity. One question he likes to ask audiences concerns their "parachute" in life. "Who is packing your parachute? Everyone has someone who provides what he needs to make it through the day. We all need many kinds of parachutes, physical, mental, emotional, and spiritual. We need support in all of these areas. As you go through this week, this month, this year, recognize the people who pack your parachute."[1]

As servants, we need to acknowledge those people in our lives who have had an impact on us, letting them know of their value.

HOW TO SHOW AND TELL: A SUMMARY

As a way of review, we have talked in this and previous chapters about various aspects of loving God and loving people. They are actually not separate entities as much as a sequence of events that happens over time. When it comes to how we show and tell others about God's love, it works like this:

- We *observe* people around us. As we do this,
- We *see needs*. As we recognize the needs,
- We are *sensitive* to those needs.
- We *listen* to understand what people are going through.
- We are *available* to them.

- We *care* for them in every way that the Holy Spirit indicates.
- We *serve* them, and
- We *encourage* them. And as our relationship progresses,
- We *love* them as Jesus would. We look for and are ready to
- *Communicate* the gospel of Jesus Christ to them.

Jesus meets the needs of men's souls. He satisfies as nothing else can. We are simply the channels through which His love flows. A servant heart and an encouraging spirit are the vehicles that He uses to transport His love to a hurting world.

Ruth had both the heart of a servant and the spirit of an encourager. Life's circumstances warranted that she have neither. The story began with Naomi and her husband, Elimelech, who lived in Bethlehem. When famine reached their homeland, Elimelech moved his family to Moab, where food was plentiful. Naomi's two sons found wives from among the Moabite people; Mahlon chose Ruth. Within ten years, all three men had died, leaving three widows.

Naomi decided that she would return to Bethlehem to try to remake her life. She insisted that the two girls, her sons' widows, stay in Moab and find new husbands from among their own people, and one of them obeyed. But Ruth had great loyalty and love for Naomi, and she firmly refused to be left behind. Her statement, engraved in Scripture, has became famous. "Don't urge me to leave you or to turn back from you. Where you go I will go, and where you stay I will stay. Your people will be my people and your God my God" (Ruth 1:16).

What an encouragement that must have been to Naomi. Her daughter-in-law returned to a foreign country with her, determined to serve and care for her until death. Ruth obeyed Naomi's every instruction without reservation, resulting in Ruth's marriage to Boaz and God's blessing.

When Ruth bore her first child, a son, to Boaz, Naomi's women friends came to tell her the joyous news. "For your daughter-in-law, who loves you and who is better to you than seven sons, has given him birth" (Ruth 4:15). Have you made sure that those around you, especially in your family, know that you are with them? Are they confident that regardless of the circumstances you will be there, encouraging and supporting? If you encourage with Ruth's kind of commitment to people, you will be greatly used of God.

> *We should be ready to*
> *declare God's truth verbally.*

Chapter Nine

SHARING AS YOU GO

"Return home and tell how much God has done for you."
So the man went away and told all over town how much
Jesus had done for him.

LUKE 8:39–40

When we live to honor Christ (note Philippians 1:21), we can and must present the gospel. This will mean knowing and using Scripture and also telling others our own story—telling of God's love and deliverance of us. As we do so, we will see God in action. We may not always see the results; yet, as we are faithful, God will honor our efforts.

Remember God's promise regarding His Word, "My word that goes out from my mouth . . . will not return to me empty, but will accomplish what I desire, and achieve the purpose for which I sent it" (Isaiah 55:11). This is a strong motivation for us to memorize Scripture. Even if you know only one verse, God will use that verse mightily in your heart and in others' lives. The more verses we know, the more eternal power the Holy Spirit has to use through us.

In addition, our own story of redemption can be powerful. Jesus instructed us to tell our own story in Luke 8. Jesus had healed a man possessed of many demons. When this man became free due to Jesus' mercy and power, he wanted to follow Jesus, but Jesus told him, "Return home and tell how much God has done for you" (Luke 8:39).

THE POWER OF OUR TESTIMONY

This man was no Bible scholar, had no education that we know of, and was not even reputable. But he now had his own story of what great things God had done for him, and Jesus knew the power of that testimony. Each of us has just such a story to tell.

On another day, Jesus healed a blind man, who joyously told people about what Jesus had done. The Jewish leaders came to examine him, asking detailed questions, to which the formerly blind man did not have all the answers. Finally he told the leaders, "One thing I know: that though I was blind, now I see" (John 9:25 NKJV). That statement was as irrefutable as our own experiences with Jesus are.

We do not have to have all the answers; we just need to be willing to tell our own unique story. Our friend Kaye was telling us about the first time that she had the joy of leading someone to Christ. Kaye had noticed a new woman in church and invited Ruth to join her for coffee at home. The intent was to introduce Ruth to some of the ladies of the church. Kaye has a large room that she designed as a kitchen/living room combination so that even while cooking, she is never away from the action and conversation of her family and guests. After a relaxing morning coffee, the other women said goodbye, but Ruth kept sitting at the table. Soon Kaye felt uneasy. God's still voice in Kaye's heart seemed to be saying to her, "She wants to know how to be saved." Kaye's mind countered that thought with, "But I don't know how to do it!"

For a few seconds an inward battle raged, until Kaye finally blurted out to her new friend, "Would you like to know how to be a Christian?"

To her amazement, Ruth said, "Yes."

"Oh," Kaye answered. Kaye told us what happened next. "So I began to just say what I knew. And when I asked her if she would like for me to pray a prayer that she could follow, she said, 'Uh huh.'" The shock in Kaye's voice was surpassed by the joy in the other lady's voice.

Kaye had discovered the key: "I just said what I knew." When you combine your story with memorized Scripture, God has a powerful tool indeed.

What would have happened to this lady if Kaye had not explained God and salvation to her? The answer is that we do not know. You see, God is sovereign, and He has many Christians whom He could have chosen to influence her life if Kaye had not been willing or available. We do not want to suggest that if we miss or ignore an opportunity to share, that someone will miss salvation. But one thing is sure, Kaye would have missed the thrilling experience of having led her to Jesus Christ and eternal life with Him.

CORN FOR THE DUCKS

"Quack, quack, quack."

Kent and I stood at the top of the hill watching the humorous sight. It was as if the ducks were hollering, "Wait, wait, wait for us! We're coming as fast as we can. Don't leave!"

The spectacle had commenced as soon as the ducks heard the screen door slam shut. That sound initiated a flurry of action, as the birds paddled full speed across the cove toward us. They paddled with such force that their progress was marked with ever bigger wakes, creating "V" patterns behind them. Their yellow webbed feet were making a furious dance, churning the water for the creatures below. The sound of my shaking can of corn—a favorite food for these birds—motivated them to greater effort, and, as they reached the shore, they performed a lopsided jump to the dirt ledge and continued to run up the slope. They did not use their usual slow duck saunter, or the more efficient flying technique; in their excitement they literally ran.

Kent and I had to chuckle at the sight. The ducks quacked

loudly all the way to the top of the rise, and did not stop until corn was thrown to them. At this point they settled down to enjoy the feast. A few ventured forth to peck the kernels right off the palms of our hands, and we knew that soon they would slowly meander back to their watery home, satisfied.

As we glanced up, though, we saw other birds who had heard the commotion. The coots were inching their way up toward us, and the geese were nearby as well.

It had not always been this way. When we first bought our lake house, the waterfowl were wary and suspicious of us. When we ventured outside, they fled in a flurry of wings and squawks. Eventually they became used to us and tolerated our presence, but still they preferred being in the water when we were around. We began to bring corn with us, spreading it out for them, whether they came to eat it or not. Early in this process, they waited until we had returned inside to come and eat, as though they did not want us to know that they were accepting what we had to offer. As time went on, however, the ducks dropped all pretense and came to know us, trust us, and eat from our hands.

The coots, small, plump waterfowl with dark gray bodies, black heads, and bright yellow beaks, never came to eat out of our hands. They were still standoffish after a year, but will now accept the corn and join the ducks for a while. They will even mingle to partake of the treat, although the two groups separate again immediately thereafter. It seems as if this mingling must be unusual in their everyday lives.

The geese are a different story. They always stay by themselves, a group protected by their sentinels, ready to flee or fight. They have never hurried forward in anticipation, but they have over time learned to trust and now know that we are not there to hurt them. They no longer act as if they will attack at any second, but politely wait for their turn for corn. Even our two- and three-year-old grandchildren have no fear of repercussion, but gleefully approach them with food.

This winter we have had great concern for a young mallard with a broken leg. He struggled to move, and got around by flying to a landing place and then sitting down immediately. He had great difficulty diving for food due to the pressure such activity put on his broken limb, and we wondered if he would survive. When he saw us, he flew fairly close and plopped to the ground. We walked as close as we could without making him nervous, then threw piles of corn right in front of him. This way he could eat his fill easily, then fly back to the water. He did survive, which we consider a personal achievement, and now waddles with a limp and can almost keep up with the rest of his flock.

A PARABLE OF GOD AT WORK

Letting God work through you in others' lives has much in common with our experience of feeding the birds. It is not a quick process and you cannot expect immediate results. It takes time for people to trust you and me, and our actions must be consistent and predictable to earn that trust. Our interaction with others must always be to help, to meet needs, to comfort and to care. If we ever hurt them, we will lose all the ground we have gained so far. One mistake can cost dearly; people do not easily forget.

Here's an example from the birds. Once our energetic grandson, Caleb, was piling leaves into huge mounds on an autumn day, then jumping into the pile accompanied by shrieks of laughter. His leaps and yelps scattered leaves and adult nerves alike. He did not notice that the geese had come up from the lake behind him, and when he turned and ran toward them, high-pitched voice and all, they took to flight in stark fear. It took days for them to venture back onto our land. People are even worse in their reactions. Caution and care must be given to their fragile spirits.

THE PARABLE OF THE BIRDS

Yes, the people in our lives are like the various kinds of birds. Some are like the ducks. They are the easiest to convince that we are friends. They may at first act as though they are not taking in the seed, by not obviously listening or reacting. But they eventually come close, willingly taking from our hands the good news we offer. They come back repeatedly, wanting more, asking loudly for nourishment, answers, support, and guidance. They get so excited about the Lord that they run to us, wanting all we have to give as quickly as they can digest it. They are a joy, and from them we see results from our efforts.

The badly wounded ducks, like our mallard with the broken leg, give us cause for concern, keeping us on our knees in prayer. Their wounds can take various forms, from abuse in childhood, to a fractured relationship, a lost job, a major misunderstanding, or any of a host of other deep wounds. God is faithful to guide us in our desire to give specific help to these injured ones, and we rejoice when they recover. Sadly, some do not recover. They resist our efforts and God's love, and break His heart.

Other people are like the coots. They want the corn, but are much slower to approach it. It takes longer for them to trust us, and we are gratified when they finally start eating. Eventually they come as regularly as the ducks, even mingling with them to get the first and best kernels. Although they are more comfortable in their own group, they willingly if tenuously join us for such a treat. And the final result is that they are just as fat and well fed as the ducks.

Sometimes these people who are "the hesitant coots" come from different socioeconomic situations. At other times they are from cultures different from our own and find it difficult to relate to what we are trying to say and do. For example, in Kent's company, we have a large group of Hispanic employees. Many cannot speak English well, and some cannot speak it at all. At Christmastime, we wanted to give our employees a meaningful gift, which would include the true Christmas story without preaching to them. So we came up with the idea of giving a package we called "A Night at the Movies." In the package we put three movies on videotape, *It's a Wonderful Life, Jesus,* and an *Adventures in Odyssey* episode (from Focus on the Family), plus a package of popcorn. (In fact, we liked the idea so well that we sent out hundreds of packages to our customers.)

For our Hispanic friends, we had copies of the *Jesus* film (distributed by Campus Crusade) done in Spanish. We did this because, although most of them can understand English, they speak Spanish in their homes, and we thought that this story would be more personal to them in their own language. They were much more likely to react in a friendly way to us after this exchange had taken place, because they saw that we were willing to meet them in their world. They are like coots joining ducks at work, but we gave them the good news separately, and they appreciated it. They have started coming back for more; what a blessing.

Another flock of birds is the geese, beautiful, stately, and aloof. These commanders of the sky keep to themselves to find security. They never cease to be on the lookout, wary and skeptical. But even they can be won. They may never interact easily with the other birds or with us, but they can come to see us as friends, not foes, and accept our offerings. They will seek us out when they are in our cove, and they know where to come for food.

Do you know folks that fit this description? Indeed, they pervade our lives, all looking for something to sustain them and to satisfy their hunger. It is up to us to initiate interaction with them. If we do not, we will coexist in the same world and they will never know we had the food all along. If we do not show them and tell them—"throw the corn" so to speak—they will never know. Paul wrote to all believers, "How, then, can they call on the one they have not believed in? And how can they believe in the one of whom they have not heard? And how can they hear without someone preaching to them? Consequently, faith comes from hearing the message, and the message is heard through the word of Christ" (Romans 10:14, 17).

GETTING READY TO HARVEST

You have probably met all three kinds of birds. (If you haven't, don't worry; you will.) Although the analogy of the ducks means something to us because we spend time at the lake, it would not have meant much to Jesus' disciples. When Jesus wanted to show His disciples how urgent was the need for them to interact spiritually with other people, He used the metaphor of the harvest. "The harvest is plentiful but the workers are few. Ask the Lord of the harvest, therefore, to send out workers into his harvest field" (Matthew 9:37–38).

In agrarian Israel, His followers would have readily understood. The country was a large producer of dates, figs, grapes, nuts,
and grain. The people were well acquainted with the harvest cycles
and the land. Jesus' comparison of people to a harvest in need of
being planted, tended, and harvested would have had great meaning for His disciples.

PLANTING THE SEED

Let's look at the metaphor to understand the movement of the
gospel in the hearts of men and women. The first season of harvest
is planting. A farmer readies his soil by turning it up to loosen it.
He may add chemicals that the soil lacks but that the new crop
needs. He breaks up big clods of dirt so that the soil is prepared for
planting. Peoples' hearts are like that soil. They may be hardened
by life's tragic and damaging experiences, they may lack the ele-
ment of openness to understand God, and they may have too
much skepticism and need patience infused into them.

We may meet a person in this phase of his spiritual life, and the
Holy Spirit may nudge our heart to smile when his actions do not
warrant it, or to be friendly and tolerant to one not deserving of it.
God may want us to show long-term friendship when it would be
easier not to be a friend. At the time we do not know exactly what
God is doing; that's OK, for we need only to follow His prompting
in our heart. These small actions and words comprise the first steps
in harvest.

After the soil is ready, the farmer plants seed. In spiritual terms,
this planting of seed could be anything that the Holy Spirit could
use to initiate growth and acceptance within that person for God
and Jesus Christ. It can consist of words and/or action. Sometimes
your story of Christ within will cause curiosity to build and questions to come from the listener. Sometimes your reactions will
bring the questions. When God's Word and your story combine in
another person's heart, it grows. God usually uses the combined
plantings of many people and events to effect change in another.

We know a godly lady named Helen Crawford. She has a
unique way of planting in the hearts of others. Actually, her

method should not be unique; it should be used by many of us. She prays with nonbelievers. Years ago she read a life-changing article by Bernie May, a Wycliffe editor, about praying with non-Christians. When May would talk with an individual and see a point of need, he would ask if he could pray with the person about it. Always given a yes, he would simply ask God for their needed help.

With that approach fresh on her mind, Helen had a great opportunity to practice such prayer when attending a conference in northern California. The conference grounds admitting office and public restrooms were located just off a main street. As Helen was coming into the ladies' restroom, she noticed a woman's face in the mirror. "It was black and blue and taped up," Helen said, and she heard the woman's words of horror upon seeing herself in the mirror: "Oh, my God!"

"The Holy Spirit," Helen recalled, "prompted me to put my arm around her and say, 'But God spared your life; may I thank Him for you?' She nodded yes and I gave a short prayer of thanks as we both cried."

Another Christian, Tracy Rader, planted a seed in an unusual way. Her grandmother, Mrs. Little, was eighty-nine years old and had been a widow for seven years. After years of nurturing her children and grandchildren in this home, this sweet lady wondered whether she should now move to a place that would provide care for her. As she talked it over with her family, the treasure of memories that the old house held touched her granddaughter Tracy. Eventually Mrs. Little did decide to sell the house, and Tracy wrote the following letter to the new owners of her grandmother's house:

Dear Owner,

Hello! My name is Tracy, and I'm the granddaughter of Mrs. Little, the previous owner of your home. I know this is not normally done, but I wanted to write you a note about your new home. I wanted you to know what a precious home you have bought, not because you could turn around and sell it for twice its worth, and not because there is a winning lottery ticket in a cabinet.

You see, forty-three years ago, my grandfather and grandmother decided to move to this neighborhood and make this house their home. When they moved in, they filled the rooms with furniture, the basement with tools, the cabinets with dishes, the yard with flowers, and the entire home with love. Not the kind of love that you see today—where commitment is promised until things get tough, where kind words are spoken until stress gets too high, where faithfulness is vowed until something better comes along; no, they filled this home with God's love.

If these walls could speak, they would go on and on about the many special memories here. You see, Christ was not only invited here, but was welcomed. He has been here with every birthday party, every Christmas celebration, and every Thanksgiving dinner. He has witnessed and participated in each gathering for weddings, new babies, and even deaths. This home is saturated with Him. His mercy oozes from the walls; His kindness flows from the faucets; His forgiveness has seeped into the carpets.

My grandmother will move on to a new home, and God's love will follow her there. He will continue to make her home His. He will never leave her or forsake her. These are promises He made in His Word, the Bible. These are promises He makes to you, too! May God continue to live here and may this home continue to be filled with His love.

Sincerely,
Tracy Rader

Tracy planted the seed boldly. Can you imagine the reaction of the new owners of that house when they read her letter? Perhaps it made them want to know more about what made these people the way they were.

TENDING...CULTIVATING...WAITING

Planting is followed by tending. If weeds are not controlled and moisture not added when needed, the little sprouts could fail.

Tending needs to take place so that nothing will pluck the seeds out of the ground. As the young plants grow and their crop starts to develop, the farmer waits and time does its work. Eventually the crop is ready to harvest. You see, an immutable rule of harvest is that you reap later than you plant. In fact, harvest is in a different season altogether. It is true of spiritual harvest as well. If your inter-action with someone comes at a time when that person is ready to accept Christ as his personal Savior, then God has already used many other people and circumstances to get him ready. Converse-ly, if your dealing with someone seems small and fruitless to you, God is simply using you to help cultivate in a process that has not yet come to fruition.

The process is God's. He created it, He uses it, and He is re-sponsible for it. Our only responsibility is to love Him and to love people, constantly. God uses us as part of a larger group of sowers and gatherers. We are in this together. Jesus explained this to His disciples:

> "Do you not say, 'Four months more and then the harvest'? I tell you, open your eyes and look at the fields! They are ripe for harvest. Even now the reaper draws his wages, even now he harvests the crop for eternal life, so that the sower and the reaper may be glad togeth-er. Thus the saying, 'One sows and another reaps' is true. I sent you to reap what you have not worked for. Others have done the hard work, and you have reaped the benefits of their labor." (John 4:35–38)

That truth should encourage you as you plant and tend seed. As the apostle Paul reminded Christians, "Let us not become weary in doing good, for at the proper time we will reap a harvest if we do not give up" (Galatians 6:9).

Another rule of harvest is this: You always reap more than you plant. One corn seed produces a plant that contains many kernels; one apple tree yields thousands of apples. The same is true spiritu-ally. God emphasized this principle in Isaiah 60:22: "The least of you will become a thousand, the smallest a mighty nation. I am the Lord; in its time I will do this swiftly."

DEVELOPING RELATIONSHIPS

Alan Andrews, the U.S. director of the Navigators, has offered the following simple steps to having relationships with friends and neighbors that lead to verbal communication:

- *Know the value of prayer.* It is such a delight to get up each day and pray specifically for my friends who do not know Jesus. What a joy it is to pray God's blessing on their home and family.
- *Take time to relate to your friends.* I, like you, am very busy. I've had to learn that loving people into a relationship with the Lord Jesus takes an investment of my time. I've had to learn to count that use of time as a privilege rather than an intrusion.
- *Wait on the Holy Spirit to lead.* As we pray and take time with our friends, let the Holy Spirit be the leader. It takes patience on my part, as I've had to learn to listen as God works in my friends' lives. I've had to learn to move at His speed and direction; He knows when it is right to say a word and when it is better to wait. I've had to remind myself that I am involved in a process, not an event.
- *Allow my relationship with Jesus to naturally flow into my relationships.* I do not need to preach or be overly urgent in sharing Jesus, but I do need to make certain that others see my relationship to Jesus as central to who I am.
- *When the time is right, I must invite my friends to look at the Scriptures.* Ultimately, it is the power of God's Word that will melt the heart of an unbelieving friend.[1]

All of Andrews's points are equally important, but let me amplify on the fourth point. As we allow our "relationship with Jesus to naturally flow into [our] friendships," we should also let others know that our lives have difficulties and problems just like everyone else's does. You and I will not look real to others if our lives appear totally smooth. Also, non-Christians will not share their

problems with those who they think cannot relate. We can, however, let them know that it is our relationship to Jesus that affords
the answers to these situations and stresses of life.

BEING CREATIVE WHEN WITNESSING

God again shows His creativity and uniqueness in the ideas
He gives for sharing His Word with others. Chris and Laurie, who
love their neighbors to Jesus quite literally, have found a new way
to share. They have what they call "Gary Smalley Parties." Chris
and Laurie have lived in their neighborhood for quite some time
and have interacted socially with their neighbors a lot. Thus the
neighbors know them well and trust them and their motives; they
have earned the right to talk by the lives they live before them.
Chris and Laurie invite five or six couples to their home to watch
a Gary Smalley video about marriage. These couples are a mix of
Christians and non-Christians. Chris and Laurie chose Gary Smalley videos as their tool because Gary is funny and lighthearted. He
is a gifted counselor and author; as a speaker, he presents practical
marriage and relationship instruction with a touch of Scripture
and lots of humor. Neighbors watching the videos find themselves
laughing and having fun, even as Smalley is presenting truth.

The gathering takes a break in the middle of the video for refreshments and neighborly chatting, then resumes watching. One
of these parties became a springboard for a marriage Bible study
with five couples, some of whom were non-Christians.

Another time, Laurie held a women's neighborhood Bible
study in her home. The women studied the book of John, and they
called it "Ladies' Night Out." The dads kept the children on those
nights. The ladies had Bible study for about an hour and a half,
then went out for ice cream or some other treat. We asked Laurie
what the results were of trying such a study, and she related that it
was evident that the Holy Spirit was working in the lives of the
women, beginning to transform lives. It also opened up new doors
for spiritual conversations in the neighborhood.

These neighbors have been so open in studying the Word of
God together that now when they are standing outside watching

the children play, there is more freedom to discuss spiritual issues. One neighbor had a sister-in-law staying with her for the summer to help take care of a new baby, and the sister-in-law became involved in the study. During that time she grasped a vision for a vital and growing relationship with God and became very excited. When she returned home, she influenced her non-Christian brother and sister-in-law and began to communicate Christ to them.

Christmas, of course, presents special opportunities to share our faith. Christmas is Christ's birthday, and people who sing carols and see occasional nativity scenes may listen to the gospel more readily. Davidene and I have enjoyed using Christmas as a starting point for sharing Christ with our neighbors. Last Christmas we gave each neighbor one of two books. One of them, entitled *Mary, Did You Know?* included a CD of the thought-provoking Christmas song. The other was a beautiful gift book entitled *The Christmas Cross*, by Max Lucado. Our reasoning was that a beautiful "coffee table" book that could be left out as a decoration was more likely to be read by several people throughout the season.

There are many books that are suitable to give to non-Christians so that they will not feel cornered. *The Christmas Cross* was one of our favorites this past year. When families have children, we normally give a picture storybook. Parents always seem to appreciate a gift that includes their children.

ALWAYS BE READY TO SAY . . .

We could fill two more books with stories that show how God gives opportunities for His children to communicate with other people whom He loves. The types of communication and the circumstances vary, but there are a few things that we should always be ready to tell people.

First, tell them there is hope. Hope is that vital ingredient to a happy life that most people have lost to some degree. Always be ready to let your friend know that there is hope. Just a couple of verses tucked away into your memory will bring great hope to those who are questioning, confused, or in crisis.

For instance, you can recite the truth of Jeremiah 29:11: "'For

I know the plans I have for you,' declares the Lord, 'plans to prosper you and not to harm you, plans to give you hope and a future.'" Recite to them Jesus' words: "I have come that they may have life, and have it to the full" (John 10:10).

Second, tell them that the Bible has the answers. What a relief to know that we do not have to have the answers; rather, the Bible has the answers to every problem, to every question. So do not be afraid to admit that you don't have the answer to someone's question, but readily offer to find out what it is. Then study for yourself and come back to them to show what you found, or study the Word with them.

Remember the truth of Hebrews 4:12: "For the word of God is living and active. Sharper than any double-edged sword, it penetrates even to dividing soul and spirit, joints and marrow; it judges the thoughts and attitudes of the heart."

Third, tell them that Jesus is the way. People desperately need to know that there is a way through their floundering world and to heaven. To have someone say, "I know how you feel, and I know the way," is a gift from heaven to a wandering lonely soul.

"Jesus answered, 'I am the way, and the truth and the life. No one comes to the Father except through me'" (John 14:6). The gospel, or "good news," is simply the explanation of how to come to the Father through Jesus.

The basic questions and answers about the gift of salvation are as follows.

Question: What does it mean to be a Christian?

Answer: The term *Christian* means *Christ's One.* The term was coined in the first century and it refers to one who belongs to Christ.

Question: Why do I need to belong to Christ? Are my good deeds not enough to get me to heaven?

Answer: Mankind has a major problem, sin. Romans 3:23 tells us, "For all have sinned and fall short of the glory of God." Anything we do that falls short of God's glory is sin, and we have all sinned. The penalty for that sin is explained in Romans 6:23: "For the wages of sin is death, but the gift of God is eternal life in Christ Jesus our Lord." This death is not just physical, but spiritual and eternal. That is why Jesus' gift of life is eternal in nature as well.

Question: What did Jesus do?

Answer: Jesus paid the penalty of sin for us when He died. John 3:16 says, "For God so loved the world that he gave his one and only Son, that whoever believes in him shall not perish but have eternal life." Someone has to die to pay the penalty for sin; either we have to die and live in eternity away from God, or we have to accept Christ's death and live in eternity with God.

Question: How does one accept Christ's death? How does one receive this gift of eternal life?

Answer: The apostle John wrote, "Yet to all who received him, to those who believed in his name, he gave the right to become children of God" (John 1:12). When a gift is offered to you, it is not truly yours until you take it, receive it, and hold it. This receiving takes an act of your will before it is yours. And when you do receive Jesus, God grants adoption into His family; you are His child, and other Christians on earth are your brothers and sisters in God's family. What a remarkable position!

Question: And how do we receive this gift?

Answer: We receive by believing in His name. "Believe in the Lord Jesus, and you will be saved," Paul and Silas said (Acts 16:31). This believing in His name is significant, because His name is the Lord Jesus Christ. To believe that someone is Lord over you gives that person total authority over your life. It is absolute surrender to live under His authority, to obey Him as Lord, and to live to honor Him. You are a subject in His kingdom, now and eternally. Jesus is His human name, and that is wonderful. Because He took a human form on earth, He can completely understand us. He was tempted, abused, hated, loved, had friends and family, had enemies, and died a painful death. There is nothing we can experience that He does not fully understand and feel with us. And He is the Christ, Redeemer, Messiah, Savior, Provider, Protector, wise and loving God. He has all honor and is worthy of our all. He is all powerful and can safely promise us peace, joy, and comfort. He is all we will ever need, now or ever.

The kind of commitment we make to receive Him is total, and the kind of commitment He makes to us when we do so is complete and eternal. What joy!

The apostle Peter boldly communicated the gospel of Jesus Christ. In Acts 4 we learn he was controlled by the Holy Spirit (verse 8), used the Word of God as he declared the gospel (verse 12), and was therefore confident (verse 13). Although he was uneducated, it was obvious to all that Peter and John had been with Jesus (verse 13). Peter's explanation to observers was, "We cannot stop speaking what we have seen and heard" (Acts 4:20).

As we prepare to communicate the gospel, education and training are not necessarily required. The essentials for us are spending time with Jesus, being surrendered to the Holy Spirit, and using His Word. God chose fishermen, Peter, James, and John, and He chooses ministry nonprofessionals, like you and me.

In our weakness we are forced to rely on Him, and therein lies power and good success.

We respond to others with urgency while investing for eternity.

Chapter Ten

SHOW AND TELL IN A FRAGILE WORLD

So then, just as you received Christ Jesus as Lord, continue to live in him.

COLOSSIANS 2:6

The lake was calm, the water still and shimmering like glass. The fishermen were sitting quietly in their boats. The early evening sky was turning pink and orange, promising a brilliant sunset to come. The scene reminded me of a painting done in pastels. Six of our dearest friends were enjoying a skiing outing on our boat in this near perfect setting.

Nevertheless, I was uneasy. Kent, usually a terrific boat driver and ski instructor, wasn't himself. He seemed agitated, at times turning erratically, too quickly. Something wasn't right.

The evening had started with laughter as our group piled into our ski boat. The hot July day had begun to cool. Kent had felt a little weak the last day or so, but we had stayed indoors during the heat of the afternoon sun and had taken a refreshing swim before skiing. After about an hour in the boat, Kent suddenly felt light-headed and began to gasp for air. He staggered to the backseat, still struggling to breathe, and passed out briefly.

Our medical emergency had begun. During the next few minutes the men in the group laid Kent on the backseat; my sister, Janet, began to monitor his pulse and breathing; and my brother-in-law, Chris, drove the boat to the dock in record time. Upon arriving at the dock, one friend ran to call 911 and another quickly collected the things we would need at the hospital. But most important, our friends united in prayer. I'll let Kent pick up the story from there.

As I lay on the table in the emergency room, the tears rolled gently down my face. They seemed to spring from deep within my soul and came nearly uncontrollably as I looked into Davidene's face and tried to explain my emotions. They were not tears of pain or sorrow, but tears of inexpressible joy. I was overwhelmed and deeply touched by the responses of my family and friends. It grieved me that I had caused such turmoil in their lives in the last few hours, but the love that had been freely shared had brought peace to my spirit and tears to my eyes.

My thoughts wandered back to the previous hour, as I lay in the boat, with friends gathered around, waiting. Thinking that I had only a mild case of heat exhaustion, I resisted the thought of an ambulance. My sister-in-law, however, who had been monitoring my pulse, wanted me to be checked out in a hospital as soon as possible. I am thankful for her insistence; she won, and I took my first ambulance ride. Shortly after arriving at the small country hospital, I vomited a great amount of blood and the medical team realized that my problem was not heat, but internal bleeding. For the next four hours they sought to stabilize me, empty my stomach, and find a way to get me to a larger hospital without putting my life at even greater risk.

During all of this I sought to be upbeat, answer questions, listen to all the phone calls, and laugh. Then I heard the doctor explain the risk of a long transport ride to Davidene, and I realized that I was in serious condition and could die of uncontrolled bleeding. I really was not fearful; I believe that the Spirit of God gave me miraculous peace. Five years earlier, I was told that I have relapsing polychondritis, a rare disease that is potentially fatal. At that time I had made the choice to go on with life as I had been living it, taking medicine prescribed by my doctor. Over the next five years my general condition had improved, but the large amounts of steroids and other harsh drugs had caused ulcers, which were now pouring blood into my stomach.

The well-trained medical staff in the emergency room, aided by the medical flight team, prepared me for another ambulance ride and a forty-five minute flight in a specially prepared small plane. By two-thirty in the morning I was in a major hospital only minutes from my home. There I was able to get help from a medical staff that could nurse my ailing body back to health.

It is expected that with medicine and care, my condition will be handled. I'll probably always have to be careful now that I've pushed my stomach to the "wall" with harsh medication. Although necessary, the medicine did finally take a toll on my body. Should I have seen signs? Was God trying to tell me something? I'm sure there were many lessons there, some I am still learning, but a major one was a reminder: Life is fragile. Remember that as you walk through open doors, do so with urgency and confidence. Invest your energies in people wisely. Remember this quote, "Life is fragile; invest it wisely."

OUR FRAGILE LIVES

Life is fragile on two fronts. It is fleeting for the people we care about, and it is fleeting for us. No one knows how long he or she has to live on this earth. We want to influence people for Christ *now*, even though their response may come later. Urgency is necessary because our time on earth (and the time until Christ returns) is uncertain. Now is the time to show and tell of God's love to those around us.

Years ago we had a wonderful warehouse manager, a man who cared about his employees and was loyal to the company. Lynn Miller was strong, robust, and energetic. No one could outwork him, and none cared to try. He was there early and late when the need arose, without ever a complaint, and we thought the world of him. Lynn, his wife, Carol, and their two children were an extremely close-knit clan, but tragedy seemed to surround the family. Lynn's son, Mark, had leukemia. He had it as a child, fought it bravely, and had chased it into remission. Mark was good-looking, athletic, and a hard working student, and we all wanted a long, good life for him. As Mark grew into his teenage years, the family started to relax a little. Then, when he was seventeen, leukemia struck again, this time without mercy.

In despair we listened to Lynn's daily reports and watched as he left work early to deal with emergency after emergency. We felt acutely the urgency of Mark's life, and we tried to care for him and his family in every way we could. The day arrived that Mark went into eternity, surrounded by his loving family. We grieved with them, and prayed that their recovery after years of suffering would be as quick as possible.

Shortly thereafter, we were waiting for Lynn to arrive at work one morning. Instead, we received a frantic phone call from Lynn's wife. Lynn had been feeling very tired and had sat on the sofa for a few minutes before leaving. During those few moments, he quietly drifted into eternity without a moan or struggle.

What a shock to all of us who were so focused on Mark that we never dreamed of the urgency in Lynn's own life. We simply cannot wait for the perfect time to love people. We must do it now, because they may not have time, and we may not either.

"OBEDIENCE HAS A TIME FRAME"

Several years ago I was scheduled to speak at a Sunday morning breakfast meeting. A group of Christian laymen had planned an evangelistic breakfast and were expecting about one hundred twenty men. That same weekend, our son, Lance (then seventeen), was attending a prom in another city. We had loaned him our car for the weekend, thinking it to be a better highway car than his, and we had decided that he would attend the prom and an after-party, stay overnight with friends, and return to Oklahoma City the next day. Lance got to bed at 2:00 A.M., but could not sleep. After lying there until 4:00 A.M., he decided to get up and drive home since he could not sleep anyway. He reasoned that he would be home before the rest of the family got ready for church.

The car had a sunroof, which Lance had opened to keep himself awake. After two hours of driving, Lance closed the windows and sunroof. Five minutes later he awoke suddenly to find himself heading toward a guardrail.

In his dazed state, Lance made a left turn, sending the car across the median and into oncoming traffic. His next move was to over-correct by turning hard to the right; the car responded by careening back onto the original side of the road, tumbling and rolling until it came to rest at the bottom of a hill in a ravine.

The car was totally wrecked, and Lance should have been killed, but God spared him. He crawled out of the car dazed and sore, but not permanently hurt. One shoe was missing, but he walked and hitchhiked the short distance to the turnpike tollbooth, where he asked the surprised operator for a phone.

While Lance was on the phone talking to us, a Highway Patrol officer arrived at the tollbooth. "There has been an accident," the officer told the toll operator. "The car is totaled, and I don't know how anyone could have lived through it, but I can't find the body of the driver." The man responded, "The body is standing right here." Our son, after all that, had a sprained thumb.

The call every parent dreads had come: "Dad, I've rolled the car, but I'm all right." We were so relieved. Lance assured us that although he was shaken, he had been only slightly injured; he wouldn't need to visit a hospital. The three of us decided that Davidene would drive to get Lance, and I would continue with the speaking engagement. We all believed that Lance's life had been spared for a reason.

Upon arriving at the meeting, I shared our son's story, and now I share this thought with you: "Obedience has a time frame." We do not know how long we have. Eighteen people trusted Christ as their Savior that morning. They may have heard the gospel before, and other Christians may have interacted with them. They may have been thinking about this decision for a time, but hearing Lance's story inspired the sense of urgency to go ahead and follow through on their decision.

That audience had shed the false sense of security that they could wait until tomorrow. We need to do the same. We need to be sure we have accepted Christ. And we need to tell others now.

WISELY INVESTING OUR LIVES

Yes, life is fragile; invest it wisely. Remember from chapter 3 our friend Jim and his fruit trees? His desire for fruit was evident in his effort to think seriously about buying the seedlings, but the cost in time and effort seemed to him to be too great. Five years later he realized that his lack of action had cost him the goal; he had no fruit. His good intentions had produced nothing, and both he and his family missed the pleasure of having fruit. If he had invested wisely five years earlier, he would have reaped rewards.

Investment is like that. It takes planning; a cost to us of time, effort, and possibly money; care while the investment grows; and finally there's the conclusion. Of course, we desire an expected result and we want it soon, but there are times when such is not the case. Think about a man's investment in the stock market. He plans for it, using hard-earned money that he hopes will earn more. He makes the initial expenditure and follows it carefully, at times making changes, to ensure the best opportunity for his investment to grow. When the time is right, he makes his move to see his investment to a close, and rejoices in his profit.

In our Christian life, we must be committed to the long walk. We must be willing to invest our time and convenience, staying with people faithfully for as long as it takes. We are not, of course, doing this alone. God is in control. It is He who uses the Holy Spirit to woo people in His time, according to His plan. We are simply to present the gospel and model it in loving actions. As we wait for further opportunities and the Spirit's moving, we are privileged to participate in God's perfect plan.

THE JOY OF INVESTING OUR TIME

I (Davidene) learned the joy of investing with a teenage drama troupe. Many of "my kids" were with me year after year. It was a commitment—an investment—I enjoyed. The group loved Christian drama, and the kids worked tirelessly to improve their skills and present plays and programs that would bring honor to Jesus. They used drama as a ministry for evangelism, encouragement, and challenge to their audiences. The troupe and I achieved success and expertise to the point that we traveled widely. Over time, audiences responded and the troupe saw miracles happen in people's lives. But my ministry was the troupe rather than the audiences. The thrill was to see those teens grow in Christ, their faith increasing, and their dependence on God deepening as they unconsciously prepared to enter the adult world with God's leading.

When those young adults left to continue their lives in work, college, and marriage, I began another troupe. I have done this for twenty years, working with church teens, inner-city high school teens, and adults. It has not always been easy, and results have not been successful in every case, but I will tell you that the work is God's and the results are His. My job is simply to "keep on keeping on," and leave the rest to Him.

Sometimes the beginning of a commitment seems not worth it and empty of promise. But stick with it; rewards do follow. That was the case with the drama troupe. When a Christian youth organization in Oklahoma City decided to try a pilot program, a drama troupe, as an evangelistic tool, I was excited to organize and direct it. I had never done anything like that before, however, so I was nervous. I prayed for months, then started by having an announcement put over the school's public address system. The teens heard, "Anyone interested in participating in a Christian drama troupe, which will be an extracurricular activity, meet in room 205 next Tuesday at 3 o'clock."

WALKING INTO THE LIONS' DEN

I walked slowly across the parking lot that Tuesday afternoon, slightly distracted due to frantic praying going on inside my mind, when suddenly a school security policeman approached. After asking me where I was going and being told about the new endeavor, he pointed to a paper sack I was carrying.

"And what is in that?" he asked.

"Suckers," was my reply. "If their mouths are full, maybe they will listen to me."

He grinned, and as he turned to walk away, he answered, "When walking into the lions' den, take a bone."

Feeling none too comforted by that, I continued into the school, through the metal detector, up the stairs, and was finally looking at nine teenage strangers. I did not know any of the teens, and they did not know each other. Out of the nine, one had a notion about what being a Christian meant. The others were either ignorant about it or outright antagonistic.

I was facing the greatest mission field of my life. It was exciting from week to week. Scripts based on Christian principles were chosen, and the kids began asking questions. By Christmastime of that first year the troupe was performing in area churches and community centers and had become a tight-knit group of friends. But I was concerned that they did not understand what Jesus had done for them by His birth, death, and resurrection. So in December I brought the troupe over to our house for a Christmas party —and a little more.

The teens were shocked but pleased that I would have them to my house. They enjoyed the food, music, and talking to each other, but eventually I had them sit down. I told the true Christmas story and continued through the Easter story and Christ's ascension. Using the Navigators' bridge illustration on a blackboard, I explained how they could know beyond a doubt where they stood with God. My gift to each was a Bible, inscribed with the promise, "Wherever you go, God loves you and I do, too. You can always reach Him in prayer and me here. We want to stay a part of your life."

I wrote my address and phone number in each Bible, and several of those kids have stayed in touch with me through the years. One young actor, a new member, opened his gift and saw that it was a Bible and began to laugh and make rude comments. An older member, a boy who had claimed to be an atheist, hushed him by sternly admonishing, "Quiet, Sam. This is serious." Neither boy knew Jesus yet, but the one was starting to see that this subject was important, at least to me, about whom he cared.

I couldn't believe it when the troupe named themselves the "God Squad" and wore T-shirts proudly claiming the fact around school. That was quite a brave thing to do in that particular school. The next February, while preparing to perform in a local mall, Sam asked if he could take a walk around the mall until performance time arrived. Not having come from Sam's world and still being rather naive, I said yes. One of the other boys immediately took Sam around to the back of the stage, but I could hear Sam being told, "Sam, you cannot steal jewelry while you are wearing that T-shirt. Stay here where I can see you." Without saying a word to me, the teens kept tabs on each other while they were representing the troupe.

Before the first year was done, all the teens had committed their lives to Jesus, and the changes He was making were nothing short of spectacular. The Bible says, "Therefore, if anyone is in Christ, he is a new creation; the old has gone, the new has come!" (2 Corinthians 5:17). God must have been thinking about the God Squad when He inspired that verse.

WAITING ON JANE

Often your involvement with a particular person will span such a long period of time that you may think you will never know the results of your prayers and care for that person until you get to heaven. Sometimes that turns out to be true; but at other times you will receive the joy of seeing one come to Christ. Davidene and I had known Jane for ten years and interacted with her often. Highly intelligent, Jane is a hard-working person and very successful in her job. She is also a wonderful mother whose children have grown to be high achievers in life. Her husband is proud of her, with every reason. She is one of those people who is independent, strong, and kind, and has a very difficult time understanding why she would need God in her life. After all, she was handling it very well by herself. But we were concerned for her because there was no evidence that she knew Jesus as her personal Savior. We prayed that in some way God could use us to help draw her to Him, and we continued to love her and wait.

After a few years, some crises entered her life. She dealt with the loss of her father, an alcoholic mother, and the death of a very young relative in a tragic accident. Her peace was shaken, and more so as she tried to comfort other relatives. Then she began having some personality conflicts with other employees at her office and could not understand it. She had always been in control, and now she felt that she was losing her stability there.

She came to talk, and in my nonsensitive CEO-type manner, I failed to see this as the opportunity for which I had prayed. I simply reminded her that with her strong personality she could handle these people. As I drove home that evening, the Lord rebuked me the whole distance. That "still, small voice" was shouting, and when I got home it was no better. Davidene gently let me know that in her estimation I had "blown it." I had given a secular answer to a spiritual problem.

That evening I talked about it with the Lord, and He let me know that I should talk to her tomorrow. "Tomorrow, Lord? We do not see each other every day, You know." His Spirit would not let me rest until the decision was made that if she happened to come to my office the next day, I would bring it up.

God has a sense of humor, because I had hardly made myself comfortable at my desk when Jane approached it. I'm not sure she knew why she had come by, but God was arranging the details of His plan.

"Jane, I need to apologize to you," I began to explain. "I was insensitive yesterday. You had real concerns, and I did not listen to them. Please share with me what is going on in your life." She seemed pleased, and we made arrangements to go to lunch that day. A word of caution here: I do not advise men counseling women, especially not in private. Usually I call my wife and she steps in, but I believe that this was one of the very few exceptions in my life because God was using it to teach me as well as to help Jane. So we went to a public restaurant, after phoning my wife to tell her where we were going and to ask her to pray. I also asked an employee at my office, who knew both Jane and me well, to pray while I was gone. I told her in advance that I was going to share the gospel with Jane.

And so we went. En route, I prayed for God to direct the conversation. He, of course, is faithful and guided us beautifully to the plan of salvation. On a napkin, I drew a diagram that showed two sides; one where people were standing who did not know Jesus as their Savior, even though they may have tried to live good lives. On the other side was God with those who had given their lives to Him; there was a line between. When I asked Jane where she presently was, she pointed as close to the line as possible, but still on the side with those who did not know Jesus. "Would you like to be over here?" I said, pointing to God's side. Her reply was, "I really would." Jane prayed to receive Christ that day, in the car on the way back to my office.

After her prayer, I asked Jane, "If you were to die tonight and went to the gates of heaven and God wanted to know why He should let you into His heaven, what would you say?" A huge smile lit up her face as she replied, "Because I have Jesus Christ in my heart."

When we returned to my office, I invited Jane's friend to come in. There Jane told her about her new relationship with the Lord, to the great rejoicing of the friend who had spent her lunch hour praying. A new Christian joined God's family that day, and two of God's children experienced a big increase in their faith. One of us learned a life-changing lesson about taking hold of the opportunities God gives us to be bold in sharing the gospel.

DRAWING ON *HIS* STRENGTH

Spiritual investment is not possible in our own strength or with our own wisdom. Only God can change people, and in order for Him to do such work through us, we must be living in a close, daily, connected relationship with Him. Jesus challenged His disciples, "I am the vine; you are the branches. If a man remains in Me, and I in him, he will bear much fruit; apart from me you can do nothing" (John 15:5). He went on to say, "You did not choose me, but I chose you and appointed you to go and bear fruit—fruit that will last. Then the Father will give you whatever you ask in my name" (John 15:16). It was Jesus' desire that we bear fruit because we are like branches living in the vine, *drawing spiritual nourishment and strength from Him*. He never intended for us to do this ourselves; He always planned that He would supply the strength, wisdom, and creativity. We are relieved of any pressure to make anything work. That part is His; we are simply to be available, just like the branch is available to bear grapes.

Remember: A branch itself does not groan and work trying to bear grapes; having fruit just happens because the branch is part of the vine that is a grape plant. "Abide in Me" and you will bear fruit, Jesus said. What a freeing promise.

This is a unique, abiding relationship. As we seek to summarize what we have been discussing, consider with us what this ministry is not. When we show and then tell the gospel, our ministry is not about what we do, but about what we are. It is not about doing more, but about allowing Christ to do through us. It is not about just being kind, sensitive, or helpful to others, but about proclaiming Christ as the answer to all of life's problems. We are only able to serve others as we draw on His power. It is not about doing something ourselves; it is about trusting God to do something. It is not about seeking to work for God; it is about working with God.

This ministry is not about focusing primarily on people and their needs. Instead, let us focus on God. We can never meet all of the needs around us. However, as we keep our focus narrowly on Christ, He will give us insight and strength and allow us to see others from His point of view. So we shouldn't try to win the battle for the world or be the hardest working soldier, but realize that the true battle is in our own heart. As we allow our hearts to be directed to Him, He will align them with His purposes for our life and those around us.

As we show and tell others about God's love, let us remember our goal is not about seeking great things for ourselves or even about accomplishing great things for God, but to see His purposes fulfilled in us. We are not doing ministry; we are knowing Him better. We do not need to tell God what we want to do for Him, but we need to find out where He is already working and join Him there. If we strive for faithfulness rather than success, God will allow us to give Him glory in the everyday relationships and circumstances of our lives.

Finally, this life is not about reaching a goal or achieving some great end; it is about a daily walk. Oswald Chambers said, "What men call preparation and training, God calls the end."[1] It is the process that matters to God. He is not as concerned about my accomplishments as much as my obedience. We are to be like a child, depending on Him. Those around us watch how we respond to life. So although we are unsure of our next step, we must be certain about who holds our hand.

SHOW AND TELL NATURALLY

Yes, as we focus on knowing Jesus Christ and responding to His love, He gives us the power to love those around us. In the introduction to this book, we considered J.B. Phillips's translation of Colossians 1:27–28: "So, naturally, we proclaim Christ! We warn everyone we meet, and we teach everyone we can all that we know about him, so that we may bring every man up to his full maturity in Christ Jesus. This is what I am working and struggling at, with all the strength that God puts into me." We show and tell as a normal part of our daily lives. As we abide in Christ and He fills our life, He overflows through us to others.

We can be bold in our interaction with others after we realize that God has sovereignly placed us where we are and has given us our unique gifts, talents, and personalities. As we proceed on our daily walk, we desire to live in a manner that will please the Lord. Then we fulfill the apostle Paul's desire that we may "live a life worthy of the Lord and may please him in every way: bearing fruit in every good work, growing in the knowledge of God" (Colossians 1:10).

We understand that ministry is not an activity, but a part of everyday life. A biblical character who demonstrated this was Cornelius, who, as a centurion, honored God (Acts 10:22) and as one who sought God told "a large gathering of people" (verse 27). Though a man of influence and very busy, he loved God enough that when God said someone would bring a message of hope from Him, Cornelius invited many to hear the messenger, the Jewish fisherman Peter.

TO A DYING WORLD, SHARE
INTENTIONALLY AND SPONTANEOUSLY

We have come to know that we must plan and strategize to share Christ intentionally, yet be ready to respond spontaneously at any time. The Spirit of God allows us to observe others in pain and to be sensitive to them. We learn to be available and listen to their heart cries. We show our love by serving and encouraging them. And we boldly walk through open doors and share Christ verbally, revealing Him to be the answer to all of their needs.

God has given all Christians open doors so that we may represent Him to a world that is fragile; indeed, a world that is dying. Those of us who know the truth must show and tell the cure to those in great pain. Davidene and I are still in process, every day seeking new and fresh ways to share the oldest love story ever known. May it be so with you. May you find fresh ways to express your faith, new ways to spot open doors and march boldly yet sensitively through them.

"We loved you so much that we were delighted to share with you not only the gospel of God but our lives as well, because you had become so dear to us" (1 Thessalonians 2:8). Let us follow the apostles' examples in showing and sharing God's love with those around us.

> *When you think about investing for eternity . . .*
> ## Remember Daniel

Daniel had everything in life stacked against him. He was just a teenager when he was captured and taken into a pagan land to be trained in pagan practices. Yet Daniel so faithfully walked with God that he influenced the society around him rather than the reverse. He enjoyed a career that spanned seventy years and three kings.

What was the secret to his success? According to the Scripture, "He went home to his upstairs room where the windows opened toward Jerusalem. Three times a day he got down on his knees and prayed, giving thanks to his God, just as he had done before" (Daniel 6:10).

Daniel never lost his focus. He knew he was to focus on the eternal and invest in the eternal. His daily habit was to spend time with God, a practice that he kept even though he was persecuted for it. His example continued to impact those around him for all of his life. During his seventy years in Babylon, he made many eternal investments. What does your eternal investment portfolio look like?

EPILOGUE: "SHOW AND TELL THEM ...JESUS CHRIST"

The trip through Oklahoma and Texas toward Mexico had just begun, and Marci Wintz could hardly contain her excitement. She was part of a group of 135 teenagers and their chaperones who would spend their spring break in northern Mexico helping lead a vacation Bible school, telling boys, girls, and teens about Jesus.

Her thoughts drifted momentarily back three weeks, when she made an entry in her journal, part of an assignment for Mrs. Wilson's English class. She knew the ongoing journal questions were her teacher's way to help the students keep the creative juices flowing. Now Marci recalled that one question: "If I could go anywhere, where would I go and why?"

Marci's thoughtful journal entry, dated February 22, 2000, read:

I would want to go to Mexico . . . for about a week and a half. I would want to go there because I would want to go help out the people that live in the dumps there, to show them that there really is something out there for them. I would *show and tell* them that there is something exciting to wake up to every day . . . Jesus Christ. I like to lead people to Christ. I love to look at their faces as soon as they accepted Jesus Christ because they are totally clean (spiritually). . . .

Well, I guess my wish/dream came true, I will be going to Matamoros, Mexico, this spring break with my youth group. We are going to be gone for a week and we will be doing a Vacation Bible School while we are in Mexico. Not only will we help them, but in the long run, I think they will also show and teach us some things while we are there.[1]

Perhaps as Marci recalled that entry, she may have thought, *How great of God that just because of this trip, I also got to tell my English teacher about how wonderful Jesus is! God thinks of everything.*

Marci was brought back to the present by the giggling in her van. She, her friend Heather Hulsey, and four others had piled into one of the seven vans making the trip along with a busload of other youths from Henderson Hills Baptist Church of Edmond (Oklahoma).

Many hours passed, and the first driver had steered them through central Texas. Everyone took a break, and now Cindy Loehrs took over for Linda Housley. The women had met the previous September and had developed a fast friendship, so Cindy was delighted that she and Linda were paired to drive the van. The two women reminded the girls to buckle their seat belts, and Linda became the enforcer of that rule. (Fifteen-year-olds don't always think such a rule is necessary.)

When the trip resumed, Marci sat in the middle row, by the window. Marci began taking pictures of her friends in the van, who created silly poses and laughed. Marci glanced at Cindy and smiled. She loved Mrs. Loehrs, who had hosted a weekend Bible study that she had attended in January.

Less than an hour later, the van rounded a curve in the highway while passing through San Antonio. Cindy felt the vehicle start to slip onto the shoulder of the road. Her quick pull on the steering wheel corrected the situation, but the vehicle was now heading too quickly across the lane toward the median. Since the rental van's steering was unfamiliar to her before this trip, it was easy to overcorrect its trajectory. In her effort to bring the van back into line with the highway, it actually began to roll, flipped, and landed hard against the guardrail.

Marci, sitting at the point of impact with the guardrail, died instantly. Her friend Heather, whose head rested just inches from Marci's, lived.

The next day, Mrs. Wilson called Marci's parents and told them they might want to have her journal, which was at school. Soon they learned about Marci's desire for her memory. In a journal entry dated March 2, less than two weeks before Marci's death, she had responded to the journal entry question, "What kind of arrangements would you like for your funeral?"

"I would like to be thanked for the things that I had done throughout my life on earth," the teenager began. "I would like flowers surrounding me. . . . I would like to be in nice clothing and be made up really nice. . . . I would want my favorite Bible verses read. . . . I would like to have all my awards and medals . . . around the coffin as I am in front of the church."

Then the fifteen-year-old continued:

> I would want balloons and streamers hung in the church so that it would remind people that I had gone to a better place than the earth we live on today. I would want them to know this so they would not mourn over me for a long time. I want all my friends there saying their good-byes, but most of all, I would want all my family members and friends to know I loved them very much, but now I am in Heaven watching over all of them and having a great time.

At Marci's funeral days later, her parents carried out their daughter's desire. More than one hundred balloons were sent flying to unknown destinations at the end of the service. All carried the written gospel of salvation within them. Today, as Marci watches over her friends from heaven, she is aware that Heather gave her life to Christ during the accident, and that countless others have been touched by Jesus' love because of the life Marci lived.

Marci was ready to show and tell God's love in Matamoros. She was an excellent example of someone who understood what it means to show and tell God's love to other people.

Remember that God is in total control. That is why we can be "working and struggling at, with all the strength that God puts into [us]" (Colossians 1:28 Phillips). It is *His* love, shown through *His* children, using *His* strength that brings people to Him. Nothing takes Him by surprise; He knows all. He is aware of our natural strengths, weaknesses, personalities, and talents because He made us. He knows how much time we have on earth and how much time others have as well. He is God Almighty, and He is more than worthy of our lives spent to touch others with His love.

Marci knew this. She desired that her life would show and tell God's love to children and teens in Matamoros, just as it had to friends in her hometown.

We, as well, can have the same focus and passion to live a life that draws others to Jesus.

NOTES

Chapter 1: Called to Represent Him

1. Richard Halverson, "Perspective," a biweekly devotional letter of Concern Ministries, Inc., n.d.
2. Lee Yih, "Of Frogs and Lizards," *Marketplace Ministries* 3, no. 1 (winter 1990): 1.

Chapter 2: Loving God and Loving People

1. Henry Blackaby, *Experiencing God* (Nashville: Lifeway, 1990), 18.
2. Richard Halverson, "Perspective," a biweekly devotional letter of Concern Ministries, Inc., n.d.
3. *Approved Unto God,* Oswald Chambers, Christian Literature Crusade, 1946, 86.
4. *The Moral Foundations of Life,* Oswald Chambers, Christian Literature Crusade, 1966, 107.
5. Henry Blackaby, *Experiencing God,* 64–65.

6. Oswald Chambers, *My Utmost for His Highest* (Grand Rapids: Discovery House, 1992), August 30 reading.

7. Adapted from *On the Anvil,* Max Lucado (Wheaton, Ill.: Tyndale, 1985), 11–13, 17.

Chapter 4: Walking Down One Road: The Integrated Life

1. Jim Petersen, "The Gospel Travels the Trade Routes," *Worldwide,* The Navigators International, November 1995, 1.

2. Ibid., 3.

3. Paul Stanley, "Kenya Takes Missions to Heart," *Worldwide,* November 1995, 2.

Chapter 5: An Intentional and Spontaneous Life

1. Buck Jacobs, "The Power of One," *Godly Counsel* 3, no. 9: 5. *Godly Counsel* is a monthly newsletter published by The C12 Group of Apollo Beach, Florida. For more information on The C12 Group, see their web site at www.thec12group.com.

Chapter 6: Watching for Doors of Opportunity

1. As cited in *Common Ground,* a newsletter of Search Ministries, July 1998.

Chapter 8: Serving and Encouraging As You Walk

1. Adapted from the web site and speeches of Charles Plumb. You may reach him at Plumbtalk@aol.com or at www.Charlieplumb.com or by writing him at 1200 N. San Marcos Rd., Santa Barbara, CA 93111.

Chapter 9: Sharing As You Go

1. "Alan Andrews, Seeking to Be Effective," *One To One,* Fall 1999, 5; newsletter of The Navigators.

Chapter 10: Show and Tell in a Fragile World

1. Oswald Chambers, *My Utmost For His Highest,* (Burlington, Ont.: Welsh, 1935), July 28 reading.

Epilogue: "Show and Tell Them . . . Jesus Christ"

1. Journal entries provided by Marci's parents, Billy and Cynthia Wintz, during a personal interview on 9 April 2000. Used by permission. Italics added.

APPENDIX 1:
RESOURCES

Here are resources that will help as you show and tell your faith and love. Some of these publications will help you become more sensitive to others' needs and give you strategies to help. Others will be helpful to those in need, and you may want to give the resources away. The publications are organized into four categories: encouragement, grief, illness and suffering, and recovery. Book titles are indicated in italics, and other written materials are indicated as booklets (B; under 100 pages), cards (C), pamphlets (P), and tracts (T), respectively.

You can find many of the following materials at your local Christian bookstore. If you are unsuccessful or would like to obtain them all from one source, you may contact Triad Marketing at P.O. Box 271054, Oklahoma City, OK 73137-1054 (Attn: Customer Service). Or call them at 405-949-0070.

ENCOURAGEMENT

The Bible Promise Book. Barbour.

Brumfield, J.C. "Comfort for Troubled Christians." Moody (B).

Chambers, Oswald. *My Utmost for His Highest*. Barbour.

Dobson, James. *In the Arms of God*. Tyndale.

_____. *When God Does Not Make Sense*. Tyndale.

Dravecky, Dave. *Portraits in Courage*. Zondervan.

Drummond, Henry. "Love." Barbour (B).

"Family Stress" (selected Scriptures). American Bible Society (P, page 13).

God's Answers for Your Life. A. L. Gill, comp. (selected Scriptures). Word.

"The Greatest is Love." American Bible Society (C).

"The Lord Is My Shepherd." American Bible Society (C).

"The Lord Leads You" (Psalms). American Bible Society (T).

"The Lord Keeps You Safe" (Psalms). American Bible Society (T).

The Message Promise Book (selected Scriptures). NavPress.

Pritchard, Ray. *Keep Believing*. Moody.

Rice, Helen Steiner. "Love Gifts." Barbour (B).

Wilkerson, David. *Have You Felt Like Giving Up Lately?* Baker.

GRIEF

Alderman, Harry. "God of All Comfort." American Tract Society (T).

Becton, Randy. *Everyday Comfort*. Baker.

Bible Promise Book (selected Scriptures). Barbour.

Bridges, Jerry. "You Can Trust God." NavPress (P).

Carmichael, Amy. *Rose from Brier*. Christian Literature Crusade.

Christensen, N.J. "Someone Cares" (evangelistic). American Tract Society (T).

Cornils, Stanley P. "The Mourning After." R&E Publishers (B).

Cushenbery, Donald C. and Rita Crossley. *Coping with Life After Your Mate Dies.* Baker.

Elliot, Elisabeth. "Facing the Death of Someone You Love." Good News Publishers (P).

_____. "How to Overcome Loneliness." NavPress (P).

"God Cares for You" (evangelistic). Good News (T).

Graham, Billy. *Hope for the Troubled Heart.* Bantam.

Hayford, Jack. *I'll Hold You in Heaven* (for child loss by miscarriage, stillbirth, abortion, or early infant death). Regal.

Heavilin, Marilyn. *Roses in December.* Harvest House.

Lenzkes, Susan. *When Life Takes What Matters.* Barbour.

"The Lord Is Faithful" (Psalms). American Bible Society (T).

"The Lord Is My Shepherd." American Bible Society (C).

"The Lord Is Near to the Broken Heart." American Bible Society (P).

"The Lord Loves You" (Psalms). American Bible Society (T).

Martin, Elva Minette. *Sorrowing in Hope.* Barbour.

Peterson, Eugene, *Psalms,* from *The Message.* NavPress.

Robinson, Haddon W. *Grief.* Barbour (B).

Sissom, Ruth. "Instantly a Widow." Word (B).

_____. *Moving Beyond Grief.* Barbour.

Stories of Hope for a Healthy Soul, Gwen Ellis, ed. Zondervan.

Wernecke, Herbert H. *When Loved Ones Are Called Home.* Baker (B).

Wiersbe, Warren W. *When Life Falls Apart.* NavPress (B).

White, Jerry. *Harsh Grief, Gentle Hope.* NavPress.

Zonnebelt-Smeenge, Susan J. and Robert C. DeVries. *Getting to the Other Side of Grief* (for spouses). Baker.

ILLNESS AND SUFFERING

Arnold, Johann. *I Tell You a Mystery.* Plough.

Becton, Randy. *Everyday Strength* (cancer). Baker.

Bundy, Miriam and Stuart Bundy. *Restoring the Soul* (cancer).
   Moody.

Burkett, Larry with Michael Taylor. *Hope When It Hurts* (cancer).
   Moody.

DeHann, M.R. "Broken Things." Discovery House (B).

God's Promises (selected Scriptures). Word.

"Little Treasure Book of Hope." Rutledge (B).

"The Lord Protects You" (Psalms). American Bible Society (T).

"The Lord Is Near You" (Psalms). American Bible Society (T).

"Someone Cares" (evangelistic). American Tract Society (T).

Swindoll, Charles. "God Cares for You" (evangelistic). Good News
   (T).

Yancey, Phillip. *Where Is God When It Hurts?* Zondervan.

RECOVERY

Dunn, Jerry with Bernard Palmer. *God Is for the Alcoholic.* Moody.

"The Lord Hears Your Cries" (selected Scriptures; on domestic
   abuse). American Bible Society (P).

"Turning to God." American Bible Society (P).

BOXES OF CARDS

Dayspring Cards, Siloam Springs, Arkansas

Lawson Falle, Cambridge, Ontario

Purchase boxes of cards at your Christian bookstore, especially
during sales. We have had good success finding suitable cards
from the two above publishers, and we supplement these with
boxes of cards from discount stores. Look for cards with appropriate remarks inside or blank inside. It is sometimes harder
to find masculine looking cards, so we look for rugged
scenery, wildlife, hunting dogs, fishing scenes, etc.

APPENDIX 2: SUPPORT ORGANIZATIONS

"These commandments that I give you today are to be upon your hearts. Impress them on your children. Talk about them when you sit at home and when you walk along the road, when you lie down and when you get up."

DEUTERONOMY 6:6–7

Many Christian organizations offer materials and help in ministering God's love to others. Below are eight organizations that provide a variety of resources that can help you to comfort, encourage, and educate non-Christians and Christians alike.

1. American Bible Society
1865 Broadway, New York, NY 10023-9980
Phone: 212-408-1499

The American Bible Society supplies Bibles and New Testaments in many translations and languages.

2. American Tract Society
P.O. Box 462008, Garland, TX 75046-2008

Phone: 972-276-9408 or 800-548-7228, Fax: 972-276-9642
Web site: www.atstracts.org (for free catalog)

American Tract Society has been reaching the world with the life-changing gospel of Jesus Christ since 1825 by producing some of the best tracts available for evangelism.

3. Family Life Division, Campus Crusade for Christ
3900 N. Rodney Parham, Little Rock, AR 72212
Phone: 501-223-8663 or 800-FL-TODAY, Fax: 501-224-2529
Web site: www.familylife-ccc.org

Family Life Conferences are get-away weekends designed to bring God's timeless principles into marriage and family relationships. Family Life offers a variety of books, videos, and seminars on marriage and parenting.

4. Eagle Lake Camps, the Navigators
P.O. Box 6000, Colorado Springs, CO 80934
Phone: 800-US-EAGLE, Fax: 719-472-1208
Web site: www.eaglelake.org

Eagle Lake Camps are a mix of God's creation, solid biblical input, and love of a dedicated, well-trained staff. They are accredited with the American Camping Association and with Christian Camping International. The goal of Eagle Lake Camps is to inspire Christ-centered love and commitment, through counselor relationships, in the midst of exciting outdoor experiences. Eagle Lake Camps offer resident and family camps as well as horse, karate/drama, wilderness excursion, whitewater, biking, and extreme camps in a variety of locations throughout the United States.

5. Man in the Mirror
180 Wilshire Blvd., Casselberry, FL 32707
Phone: 407-331-0095 or 800-929-2536, Fax: 407-331-7839
Web site: www.maninthemirror.org or www.answers4men.com

Man in the Mirror helps local churches reach men through one-day retreats and seminars and follow-up discussion groups. Man in the Mirror teaches biblical concepts of manhood applied to everyday living. More than one hundred fifty churches will host these events during the year 2000.

6. Marketplace Ministries
12900 Preston Rd., Suite 1215, Dallas, TX 75230-1328
Phone: 972-385-7657, Fax: 972-385-7307

Marketplace Ministries is a unique proactive Employee Assistance Program. It contracts with corporations large and small, providing them with corporate chaplains and pastoral counselors who help employees and their family members with the stresses of daily life.

7. Prison Fellowship
P.O. Box 17500, Washington D.C. 20041-0500
Phone: 703-478-0100
Web site: www.prisonfellowship.org

Prison Fellowship Ministries (PF) is the largest prison outreach and criminal justice organization in the world. PF was founded by Charles W. Colson, former special counsel to President Richard Nixon, after he served seven months in prison for Watergate-related offenses. The programs of PF reach prisoners, ex-prisoners, and their families in all fifty states and in eighty-three countries. PF targets the root causes of crime by providing programs such as job training, family counseling, one-to-one counseling, and weekly Bible studies.

8. Search Ministries
Broadway Ext., Suite 202, Oklahoma City, OK 73116
Phone: 405-840-9909, 800-617-3272, Fax: 405-840-8915
E-mail: kmsearch@aol.com

Search Ministries is the home of Search Open Forum, a plan for low-key neighborhood evangelism. Held in homes and emphasizing hospitality, the forum attracts people to a discussion of life and God issues.

9. Walk Through the Bible Ministries
421 Peachtree Rd., Atlanta, GA 30341-1362
Phone: 800-763-5433
Web site: www.walkthru.org

Walk Through the Bible Ministries is an international Bible teaching ministry which offers life-changing videos, devotional publications, books, Bibles, and seminars in more than fifty languages.

Moody Press, a ministry of Moody Bible Institute,
is designed for education, evangelization, and edification.
If we may assist you in knowing more about Christ
and the Christian life, please write us without obligation:
Moody Press, c/o MLM, Chicago, Illinois 60610.

new novel, *Autumn*, Ali Smith also proves herself to be one of the country's foremost chroniclers, her finger firmly on the social and political pulse."
—*The Independent* (UK)

"It is undoubtedly Smith at her best. . . . This book sets Smith's complex creative character in stone: puckish yet elegant, angry but comforting. Long may she Remain that way."
—*The Times* (UK)

"Smith writes in a liltingly singsong prose that fizzes with exuberant punning and wordplay. . . . Compellingly contemporary. . . . [An] appeal to conscience and common humanity— intergenerational, interracial, international—in these deeply worrying times." —*The Irish Times*

"In bringing together the present and the seasons, Smith brings to contemporary politics the timeless injunction of art: to stop and look. . . . *Autumn* shows that the contemporary novel can be both timeless and timely. This may simply be what good novels always have done, but Smith reminds us how to do it, even now." —*Public Books*

of the reading. Smith's prose is seductively simple, beguiling, its effects hard-won."
—Edward T. Wheeler, *Commonweal*

"An ambitious, multilayered creation. . . . Smith is convincing as both a twelve-year-old girl proud of her new rollerblades and a man living in a care home. . . . The story is rooted in autumn, and Smith writes lyrically about the changing seasons. . . . An energising and uplifting story."
—*London Evening Standard*

"Smith is brilliant on what the referendum has done to Britain. . . . I can think of few writers—Virginia Woolf is one, James Salter another—so able to propel a narrative through voice alone. . . . This is a novel that works by accretion, appearing light and playful, surface-dwelling, while all the time enacting profound changes on the reader's heart."
—Alex Preston, *Financial Times*

"Hums with life. . . . [Smith] is indeed a writer in her prime. *Autumn* is clever and invigorating. The promise of three more books to come is something to be savored."
—*The Washington Times*

"Already acknowledged as one of the most inventive novelists writing in Britain today, with her

ali smith
Autumn

Ali Smith is the author of many works of
fiction, including the novel *Hotel World*, which
was shortlisted for both the Orange Prize and
the Man Booker Prize and won the Encore
Award and the Scottish Arts Council Book of
the Year Award, and *The Accidental*, which
won the Whitbread Award and was shortlisted
for the Man Booker Prize and the Orange
Prize for Fiction. Her most recent novel, *How
to be both*, was a Man Booker Prize finalist
and winner of the Baileys Women's Prize for
Fiction, the Goldsmiths Prize, the Costa Novel
Award, and the Saltire Society Scottish Fiction
Book of the Year Award. Born in Inverness,
Scotland, Smith lives in Cambridge, England.

Autumn

ali smith
Autumn

A Novel

PENGUN

an imprint of Penguin Canada, a division of Penguin Random House Canada Limited

Penguin Canada
320 Front Street West, Suite 1400, Toronto, Ontario M5V 3B6, Canada

First published in Hamish Hamilton hardcover by Penguin Canada, 2017. Simultaneously published in the United States by Pantheon Books, a division of Penguin Random House LLC, New York. Originally published in hardcover in Great Britain by Hamish Hamilton, an imprint of Penguin Books Ltd., a division of Penguin Random House Ltd., London, in 2016.

Published in this edition, 2017

1 2 3 4 5 6 7 8 9 10

Copyright © 2016 by Ali Smith

Grateful acknowledgment is made to the following for permission to reprint previously published material: Pan Books: Excerpt from *Talking to Women* by Nell Dunn, copyright © 1966 by Nell Dunn. Reprinted by permission of Pan Books. Penguin Books Ltd.: Excerpt from *Metamorphosis* by Ovid, translated by Mary M. Innes. Copyright © 1995 by Mary M. Innes. Reprinted by permission of Penguin Books Ltd. Wolverhampton Art Gallery & Museums: Excerpt from *Pauline Boty: Pop Artist and Woman* by Sue Tate, copyright © 2013 by Sue Tate. Reprinted by permission of Wolverhampton Art Gallery & Museums.

All rights reserved. Without limiting the rights under copyright reserved above, no part of this publication may be reproduced, stored in or introduced into a retrieval system, or transmitted in any form or by any means (electronic, mechanical, photocopying, recording or otherwise), without the prior written permission of both the copyright owner and the above publisher of this book.

Publisher's note: This book is a work of fiction. Names, characters, places and incidents either are the product of the author's imagination or are used fictitiously, and any resemblance to actual persons living or dead, events, or locales is entirely coincidental.

Printed and bound in the United States of America.

Library and Archives Canada Cataloguing in Publication data available upon request.

ISBN 978-0-14-319789-8
eBook ISBN 978-0-14-319788-1

www.penguinrandomhouse.ca

Penguin
Random House
Canada

For Gilli Bush-Bailey
see you next week

and for Sarah Margaret
Hardy perennial Wood

Spring come to you at the farthest,
In the very end of harvest!
William Shakespeare

At current rates of soil erosion, Britain has just
100 harvests left.
Guardian, 20 July 2016

Green as the grass we lay in corn, in sunlight
Ossie Clark

If I am destined to be happy with you here –
how short is the longest Life.
John Keats

Gently disintegrate me
WS Graham

1

It was the worst of times, it was the worst of times.
Again. That's the thing about things. They fall apart,
always have, always will, it's in their nature. So an
old old man washes up on a shore. He looks like a
punctured football with its stitching split, the leather
kind that people kicked a hundred years ago. The
sea's been rough. It has taken the shirt off his back;
naked as the day I was born are the words in the head
he moves on its neck, but it hurts to. So try not to
move the head. What's this in his mouth, grit? it's
sand, it's under his tongue, he can feel it, he can hear it
grinding when his teeth move against each other,
singing its sand-song: I'm ground so small, but in the
end I'm all, I'm softer if I'm underneath you when you
fall, in sun I glitter, wind heaps me over litter, put a
message in a bottle, throw the bottle in the sea, the
bottle's made of me, I'm the hardest grain to harvest

to harvest

the words for the song trickle away. He is tired.
The sand in his mouth and his eyes is the last of the
grains in the neck of the sandglass.

Daniel Gluck, your luck's run out at last.

He prises open one stuck eye. But –

Daniel sits up on the sand and the stones

– is this it? really? this? is death?

He shades his eyes. Very bright.

Sunlit. Terribly cold, though.

He is on a sandy stony strand, the wind distinctly
harsh, the sun out, yes, but no heat off it. Naked,
too. No wonder he's cold. He looks down and
sees that his body's still the old body, the ruined
knees.

He'd imagined death would distil a person, strip
the rotting rot away till everything was light as a
cloud.

Seems the self you get left with on the shore, in
the end, is the self that you were when you went.

If I'd known, Daniel thinks, I'd have made sure to
go at twenty, twenty five.

Only the good.

Or perhaps (he thinks, one hand shielding his
face so if anyone can see him no one will be
offended by him picking out what's in the lining of
his nose, or giving it a look to see what it is – it's
sand, beautiful the detail, the different array of
colours of even the pulverized world, then he rubs it

4

away off his fingertips) this *is* my self distilled. If so then death's a sorry disappointment.

Thank you for having me, death. Please excuse me, must get back to it, life.

He stands up. It doesn't hurt, not so much, to.

Now then.

Home. Which way?

He turns a half circle. Sea, shoreline, sand, stones. Tall grass, dunes. Flatland behind the dunes. Trees past the flatland, a line of woods, all the way back round to the sea again.

The sea is strange and calm.

Then it strikes him how unusually good his eyes are today.

I mean, I can see not just those woods, I can see not just that tree, I can see not just that leaf on that tree. I can see the stem connecting that leaf to that tree.

He can focus on the loaded seedhead at the end of any piece of grass on those dunes over there pretty much as if he were using a camera zoom. And did he just look down at his own hand and see not just his hand, in focus, and not just a scuff of sand on the side of his hand, but several separate grains of sand so clearly delineated that he can see their edges, and (hand goes to his forehead) *no glasses*?

Well.

He rubs sand off his legs and arms and chest then

off his hands. He watches the flight of the grains of it as it dusts away from him in the air. He reaches down, fills his hand with sand. Look at that. So many.

Chorus:

How many worlds can you hold in a hand.

In a handful of sand.

(Repeat.)

He opens his fingers. The sand drifts down.

Now that he's up on his feet he is hungry. Can you be hungry *and* dead? Course you can, all those hungry ghosts eating people's hearts and minds. He turns the full circle back to the sea. He hasn't been on a boat for more than fifty years, and that wasn't really a boat, it was a terrible novelty bar, party place on the river. He sits down on the sand and stones again but the bones are hurting in his, he doesn't want to use impolite language, there's a girl there further up the shore, are hurting like, he doesn't want to use impolite –

A girl?

Yes, with a ring of girls round her, all doing a wavy ancient Greek looking dance. The girls are quite close. They're coming closer.

This won't do. The nakedness.

Then he looks down again with his new eyes at where his old body was a moment ago and he knows he is dead, he must be dead, he is surely dead, because his body looks different from the last time he looked down at it, it looks better, it looks rather good as bodies go. It looks very familiar, very like his own body but back when it was young.

A girl is nearby. Girls. Sweet deep panic and shame flood through him.

He makes a dash for the long grass dunes (he can run, really run!), he puts his head round the side of a grass tuft to check nobody can see him, nobody coming, and up and off (again! not even breathless) across the flatland towards those woods.

There will be cover in the woods.

There will maybe be something too with which to cover himself up. But pure joy! He'd forgotten what it feels like, to feel. To feel even just the thought of one's own bared self near someone else's beauty.

There's a little copse of trees. He slips into the copse. Perfect, the ground in the shade, carpeted with leaves, the fallen leaves under his (handsome, young) feet are dry and firm, and on the lower branches of the trees too a wealth of leaves still bright green, and look, the hair on his body is dark black again all up his arms, and from his chest down to the groin where it's thick, ah, not just the hair, everything is thickening, look.

This is heaven all right.

Above all, he doesn't want to offend.

He can make a bed here. He can stay here while he gets his bearings. Bare-ings. (Puns, the poor man's currency; poor old John Keats, well, poor all right, though you couldn't exactly call him old. Autumn poet, winter Italy, days away from dying he found himself punning like there was no tomorrow. Poor chap. There really was no tomorrow.) He can heap these leaves up over himself to keep him warm at night, if there's such a thing as night when you're dead, and if that girl, those girls, come any closer he'll heap a yard of them over his whole self so as not to dishonour.

Decent.

He had forgotten there is a physicality in not wanting to offend. Sweet the feeling of decency flooding him now, surprisingly like you imagine it would be to drink nectar. The beak of the hummingbird entering the corolla. That rich. That sweet. What rhymes with nectar? He will make a green suit for himself out of leaves, and – as soon as he thinks it, a needle and some kind of gold coloured threading stuff on a little bobbin appears here in his hand, look. He *is* dead. He must be. It is perhaps rather fine, after all, being dead. Highly underrated in the modern western world. Someone should tell them. Someone should let them know. Someone should be sent, scramble back to, wherever it is. Recollect her. Affect her. Neglect her. Lie detector. Film projector. Director. Collector. Objector.

He picks a green leaf off the branch by his head.

He picks another. He puts their edges together. He stitches one to the other with a neat, what is it, running stitch? blanket stitch? Look at that. He can sew. Not something he could do while he was alive. Death. Full of surprises. He picks up a layering of leaves. He sits down, matches an edge to an edge and sews. Remember that postcard he bought off a rack in the middle of Paris in the 1980s, of the little girl in one of the parks? She looked like she was dressed in dead leaves, black and white photo dated not long after the war ended, the child from behind, dressed in the leaves, standing in the park looking at scattered leaves and trees ahead of her. But it was a tragic as well as a fetching picture. Something about the child plus the dead leaves, terrible anomaly, a bit like she was wearing rags. Then again, the rags weren't rags. They were leaves, so it was a picture about magic and transformation too. But then again *again*, a picture taken not long after, in a time when a child just playing in leaves could look, for the first time to the casual eye, like a rounded-up and offed child (it hurts to think it)

or maybe also a nuclear after-child, the leaves hanging off her looked like skin become rags, hanging to one side as if skin *is* nothing but leaves.

So it was fetching in the other sense of fetch too, the picture, like a picture of your *fetch*, the one who comes to fetch you off to the other world. One blink of a camera eye (can't quite put his finger on the name of the photographer) and that child dressed in leaves became all these things: sad, terrible, beautiful, funny, terrifying, dark, light, charming, fairystory, folkstory, truth. The more mundane truth was, he'd bought that postcard (Boubat! *he* took it) when he visited the city of love with yet another woman he wanted to love him but she didn't, course she didn't, a woman in her forties, a man in his late sixties, well, be honest, nearer seventy, and anyway he didn't love her either. Not truly. Matter of profound mismatch nothing to do with age, since at the Pompidou Centre he'd been so moved by the wildness in a painting by Dubuffet that he'd taken his shoes off and knelt down in front of it to show respect, and the woman, her name was Sophie something, had been embarrassed and in the taxi to the airport told him he was too old to take off his shoes in an art gallery, even a modern one.

In fact all he can remember of her is that he sent her a postcard he wished afterwards he'd kept for himself.

He wrote on the back of it, *with love from an old child*.

He is always looking out for that picture.

He has never found it again.

He has always regretted not keeping it.

Regrets when you're dead? A past when you're

dead? Is there never any escaping the junkshop of the self?

He looks out from the copse at the edge of the land, the sea.

Well, wherever it is I've ended, it's given me this very swanky green coat.

He wraps it around him. It's a good fit, it smells leafy and fresh. He would make a good tailor. He has made something, made something of himself. His mother would be pleased at last.

Oh God. Is there still mother after death?

He is a boy collecting chestnuts from the ground under the trees. He splits the bright green prickly cauls and frees them brown and shining from the waxy pith. He fills his cap with them. He takes them to his mother. She is over here with the new baby.

Don't be stupid, Daniel. She can't eat these. Nothing eats these, not even horses, far too bitter.

Daniel Gluck, seven years old, in good clothes he's always being told how lucky he is to have in a world where so many have so little, looks down at the conkers he should never have sullied his good cap with and sees the brown shine on them go dull.

Bitter memories, even when you're dead.

How very disheartening.

Never mind. Hearten up.

He's on his feet. He is his respectable self again. He scouts around him, finds some large rocks and a couple of good-sized sticks with which he marks the door of his copse so he'll find it again.

In his bright green coat he comes out of the woods, across the plain and back towards the shore.

But the sea? Silent, like sea in a dream.

The girl? No sign. The ring of dancers round her? Gone. On the shore, though, there's a washed-up body. He goes to look. Is it his own?

No. It is a dead person.

Just along from this dead person, there is another dead person. Beyond it, another, and another.

He looks along the shore at the dark line of the tide-dumped dead.

Some of the bodies are of very small children. He crouches down near a swollen man who has a child, just a baby really, still zipped inside his jacket, its mouth open, dripping sea, its head resting dead on the bloated man's chest.

Further up the beach there are more people. These people are human, like the ones on the shore, but these are alive. They're under parasols. They are holidaying up the shore from the dead.

There is music coming out of a screen. One of the people is working on a computer. Another is sitting in the shade reading a little screen. Another is dozing under the same parasol, another is rubbing suncream into his shoulder and down his arm.

A child squealing with laughter is running in and out of the water, dodging the bigger waves.

Daniel Gluck looks from the death to the life, then back to the death again.

The world's sadness.

Definitely still in the world.

He looks down at his leaf coat, still green.

He holds out a forearm, still miraculous, young.

It will not last, the dream.

He takes hold of one leaf at the corner of his coat. He holds it hard. He will take it back with him if he can. Proof of where he's been.

What else can he bring?

How did that chorus go, again?

How many worlds

Handful of sand

It is a Wednesday, just past midsummer. Elisabeth Demand – thirty two years old, no-fixed-hours casual contract junior lecturer at a university in London, living the dream, her mother says, and she is, if the dream means having no job security and almost everything being too expensive to do and that you're still in the same rented flat you had when you were a student over a decade ago – has gone to the main Post Office in the town nearest the village her mother now lives in, to do Check & Send with her passport form.

Apparently this service makes things quicker. It means your passport can be issued in half the time, if you've gone in with your form filled out and with your old passport and your new photographs, and had a certified Post Office official check it through with you before it goes to the Passport Office.

The Post Office ticket machine gives her a ticket with number 233 on it for counter service. The place isn't busy, apart from the queue of angry people stretching out the door for the self-service weighing machines, for which there's no ticketing system. But the number she's been given is so far ahead of the numbers highlighted on the boards above everybody's heads as *coming up next* (156, 157, 158), and it takes so long anyway for the lone two people behind the twelve counters to serve the people who are presumably numbers 154 and 155 (she's been here twenty minutes and they're still the same two customers) that she leaves the Post Office, crosses the green, goes to the second-hand bookshop on Bernard Street.

When she gets back ten minutes later the same two lone people behind the counters are still the only people serving. But the screen now says that the numbers *coming up next* for counter service will be 284, 285 and 286.

Elisabeth presses the button on the machine and takes another ticket (365). She sits down on the circular communal seating unit in the middle of the room. Something inside it is broken, so that when she does this something clanks inside its structure and the person sitting along from her is jerked an inch into the air. Then that person shifts position, the seat clanks again and Elisabeth jolts an inch or so downwards.

Through the windows, there on the other side of the road, she can see the grand municipal building that used to be the town Post Office. It's now a row of designer chainstores. Perfume. Clothes. Cosmetics. She looks round the room again. The people sitting on the communal seat are almost all exactly the same people who were here when she first came in. She opens the book in her hand. Brave New World. Chapter One. *A squat grey building of only thirty-four storeys. Over the main entrance the words, CENTRAL LONDON HATCHERY AND CONDITIONING CENTRE, and, in a shield, the World State's motto, COMMUNITY, IDENTITY, STABILITY.* An hour and forty five minutes later, when she's quite far through the book, most of the people round her are still those same people. They're still staring into space. They occasionally clank the chair. Nobody talks to anyone else. Nobody has said a single word to her the whole time she's been here. The only thing that changes is the queue snaking towards the self-service weighing machines. Occasionally someone crosses the room to look at the commemorative coins in the plastic display unit. There's a set, she can see from here, for Shakespeare's birthday or deathday anniversary. There's a skull on one of the coins. Presumably deathday, then.

Elisabeth goes back to the book and by chance

the page she's on happens to be quoting Shakespeare. *'O brave new world!' Miranda was proclaiming the possibility of loveliness, the possibility of transforming even the nightmare into something fine and noble. 'O brave new world!' It was a challenge, a command.* To look up from it and see the commemorative money at the very second when the book brings Shakespeare and itself properly together – that's really something. She shifts in her seat and clanks the chair by mistake. The woman along from her jumps slightly in the air but gives no sign at all that she knows or cares that she has.

It's funny to be sitting on such an uncommunal communal chair.

There's no one Elisabeth can exchange a look with about that, though, let alone tell the thing she's just thought about the book and the coins.

In any case, it's one of those coincidences that on TV and in books might mean something but in real life mean nothing at all. What would they put on a commemorative coin to celebrate Shakespeare's *birth*day? O brave new world. That'd be good. That's a bit like what it's like, presumably, to be born. If anyone could ever remember being born.

The board says 334.

Hello, Elisabeth says to the man behind the counter forty or so minutes later.

The number of days in the year, the man says.

I'm sorry? Elisabeth says.

Number 365, the man says.

I've read nearly a whole book while I've been waiting here this morning, Elisabeth says. And it struck me that maybe it'd be a good idea to have books available here so all the people who end up waiting could have a read too, if they'd like to. Have you ever thought of opening or installing a small library?

Funny you should say that, the man says. Most of those people aren't here for Post Office services at all. Since the library closed this is where they come if it's raining or intemperate.

Elisabeth looks back at where she was sitting. The seat she's just left has been taken by a very young woman breastfeeding a baby.

Anyway, thank you for your query, and I hope we've answered it to your full satisfaction, the man is saying.

He is about to press the button next to him to call 366 to the counter.

No! Elisabeth says.

The man creases up. It seems he was joking; his shoulders go up and down but no sound comes out of him. It's like laughter, but also like a parody of laughter, and simultaneously a bit like he's having an asthma attack. Maybe you're not allowed to laugh out loud behind the counter of the main Post Office.

I'm only here once a week, Elisabeth says. I'd

have had to come back next week if you'd
done that.

The man glances at her Check & Send form.

And you may well have to come back next week
anyway, he says. It's a nine times out of ten-er that
something's not going to be right with this.

Very funny, Elisabeth says.

I'm not joking, the man says. You can't joke
about passports.

The man empties all the papers out of her
envelope on his side of the divide.

I just have to make it clear to you first up before
we check anything, he says, that if I go ahead now
and check your Check & Send form today it'll cost
you £9.75. I mean £9.75 today. And if by chance
something isn't correct in it today, it'll still cost you
£9.75 today, and you'll need to pay me that money
anyway even if we can't send it off because of
whatever incorrect thing.

Right, Elisabeth says.

But. Having said that, the man says. If something's
not correct and you pay the £9.75 today, which you
have to do, and you correct the thing that's not
correct and bring it back here within one month,
provided you can show your receipt, then you won't
be charged another £9.75. However. If you bring it
back *after* one month, or *without* your receipt,
you'll be charged another £9.75 for another
Check & Send service.

Got it, Elisabeth says.

Are you sure you still want to go ahead with today's Check & Send? the man says.

Uh huh, Elisabeth says.

Could you say the word yes, rather than just make that vaguely affirmative sound you're making, please, the man says.

Uh, Elisabeth says. Yes.

Though you'll have to pay even if the Check & Send isn't successful today?

I'm beginning to hope it won't be, Elisabeth says. There's a few old classics I haven't read yet.

Think you're funny? the man says. Would you like me to fetch you a complaints form and you can fill it in while you wait? If you do, though, I have to advise you that you'll need to leave the counter while I serve someone else and because I'm shortly due my lunch break you'll lose your consecutive place and will have to take a new counter service ticket from the machine and wait your turn.

I've absolutely no wish to complain about anything, Elisabeth says.

The man is looking at her filled-in form.

Is your surname really Demand? he says.

Uh huh, Elisabeth says. I mean yes.

A name you live up to, he says. As we've already ascertained.

Uh, Elisabeth says.

Only joking, the man says.

21

His shoulders go up and down.

And you're sure you've spelt your Christian name correctly? he says.

Yes, Elisabeth says.

That's not the normal way of spelling it, the man says. The normal way of spelling it is with a z. As far as I'm aware.

Mine is with an s, Elisabeth says.

Fancy way, the man says.

It's my name, Elisabeth says.

It's people from other countries that spell it like that, generally, isn't it? the man says.

He flicks through the outdated passport.

But this does say you're UK, he says.

I am, Elisabeth says.

Same spelling in here, the s and all, he says.

Amazingly, Elisabeth says.

Don't be sarky, the man says.

Now he's comparing the photograph inside the old passport with the new sheet of booth shots Elisabeth has brought with her.

Recognizable, he says. Just. (Shoulders.) And that's just the change from twenty two to thirty two. Wait till you see the difference when you come back in here for a new passport in ten years' time. (Shoulders.)

He checks the numbers she's written on the form against the ones in the outdated passport.

Going travelling? he says.

Probably, Elisabeth says. Just in case.

Where you thinking of going? he says.

Lots of places, I expect, Elisabeth says. Who knows? World. Oyster.

Seriously allergic, the man says. Don't even say the word. If I die this afternoon, I'll know who to tell them to blame.

Shoulders. Up, down.

Then he puts the booth photographs down in front of him. He screws his mouth over to one side. He shakes his head.

What? Elisabeth says.

No, I think it's all right, he says. The hair. It has to be completely clear of your eyes.

It *is* completely clear of my eyes, Elisabeth says. It's nowhere near my eyes.

It also can't be anywhere near your face, the man says.

It's on my head, Elisabeth says. That's where it grows. And my face is also attached to my head.

Witticism, the man says, will make not a jot of difference to the stipulations which mean you can, in the end, be issued a passport, which you will need before you are permitted to go anywhere not in this island realm. In other words. Will get you. Nowhere.

Right, Elisabeth says. Thanks.

I think it's all right, the man says.

Good, Elisabeth says.

Wait, the man says. Wait a minute. Just a.

23

He gets up off his chair and ducks down behind the divide. He comes back up with a cardboard box. In it are various pairs of scissors, rubbers, a stapler, paperclips and a rolled-up measuring tape. He takes the tape in his hands and unrolls the first centimetres of it. He places the tape against one of the images of Elisabeth on the booth sheet.

Yes, he says.

Yes? Elisabeth says.

I thought so, he says. 24 millimetres. As I thought.

Good, Elisabeth says.

Not good, the man says. I'm afraid not good at all. Your face is the wrong size.

How can my face be a wrong size? Elisabeth says.

You didn't follow the instructions about filling the facial frame, that's if the photobooth you used is fitted with passport instructions, the man says. Of course, it's possible the booth you used wasn't passport-instruction-fitted. But that doesn't help here either way I'm afraid.

What size is my face meant to be? Elisabeth says.

The correct size for a face in the photograph submitted, the man says, is between 29 millimetres and 34 millimetres. Yours falls short by 5 millimetres.

Why does my face need to be a certain size? Elisabeth says.

Because it's what is stipulated, the man says.

Is it for facial recognition technology? Elisabeth says.

The man looks her full in the face for the
first time.

Obviously I can't process the form without the
correct stipulation, he says.

He takes a piece of paper off a pile to the right
of him.

You should go to Snappy Snaps, he says as he
stamps a little circle on the piece of paper with a
metal stamp. They'll do it there for you to the
correct specification. Where are you planning to
travel to?

Well, nowhere, till I get the new passport,
Elisabeth says.

He points to the unstamped circle next to the
stamped one.

If you bring it back within a month of this date,
provided everything's correct, you won't have to pay
£9.75 for another Check & Send, he says. Where did
you say you were thinking of going, again?

I didn't, Elisabeth says.

Hope you won't take it the wrong way if I write
in this box that you're wrong in the head, the
man says.

His shoulders aren't moving. He writes in a box next
to the word *Other*: HEAD INCORRECT SIZE.

If this were a drama on TV, Elisabeth says, you
know what would happen now?

It's largely rubbish, TV, the man says. I prefer
box sets.

What I'm saying is, Elisabeth says, in the next shot you'd be dead of oyster poisoning and I'd be being arrested and blamed for something I didn't do.

Power of suggestion, the man says.

Suggestion of power, Elisabeth says.

Oh, very clever, the man says.

And also, this notion that my head's the wrong size in a photograph would mean I've probably done or am going to do something really wrong and illegal, Elisabeth says. And because I asked you about facial recognition technology, because I happen to know it exists and I asked you if the passport people use it, that makes me a suspect as well. And there's the notion, too, in your particular take on our story so far, that I might be some kind of weirdo because there's an s in my name instead of a z.

I'm sorry? the man says.

Like if a child cycles past in a drama or a film, Elisabeth says, like the way if you're watching a film or a drama and there's a child cycling away on a bicycle and you see the child going, getting further away, and especially if you watch this happen from a camera position behind that child, well, something terrible's bound to be about to happen to that child, for sure it'll be the last time you'll see that child, that child still innocent, anyway. You can't just be a child and cycle away because you're off to the shops any more. Or if there's a happy man or woman driving a car, just out driving, enjoying it, nothing else happening – and especially if this is edited into someone else's waiting for that person to come home – then he or she is probably definitely about to crash and die. Or, if it's a woman, to be abducted and come to a gruesome sex-crime end, or to disappear. Probably definitely he or she one way or another is driving to his or her doom.

The man folds the Check & Send receipt and tucks it into the envelope Elisabeth gave him with the form, the old passport and the unsuitable photographs. He hands it back to her across the divide. She sees terrible despondency in his eyes. He sees her see it. He hardens even more. He opens a drawer, takes a laminated sheet out of it and places it at the front of the divide.

Position Closed.

This isn't fiction, the man says. This is the Post Office.

Elisabeth watches him go through the swing door at the back.

She pushes her way through the self-service queue and out of the non-fictional Post Office.

She crosses the green to the bus station.

She's going to The Maltings Care Providers plc to see Daniel.

Daniel is still here.

The last three times Elisabeth's been, he's been asleep. He'll be asleep this time too, when she gets there. She'll sit on the chair next to the bed and get the book out of her bag.

Brave old world.

Daniel will be so asleep that he'll look like he's never going to wake up.

Hello Mr Gluck, she'll say if he does. Sorry I'm late. I was having my face measured and rejected for being the wrong specification.

But there's no point in thinking this. He won't.

If he were to wake, the first thing he'd do is he'd tell her some fact from whichever fruitful place in his brain he'd been down deep in.

Oh a long queue of them, Daniel'd say, all the

way up the mountain. A line of tramps from the foot to the peak of one of the Sacramento mountains.

Sounds serious, she'd say.

It was, he'd say. Nothing comic isn't serious. And he was the greatest comedian of all. He hired them, hundreds and hundreds of them, and they were real, the real thing, real tramps to his movie star tramp, real loners, real lost and homeless men. He wanted it to look like the real gold rush. The local police said the tramps weren't to be paid any money by the producers till they'd all been rounded up and taken back to Sacramento City. They didn't want them going all over the district. And when he was a boy – the boy who ended life as one of the richest, the most famous men in the world – when he was a boy in the poorhouse for children, the orphanage, when his mother was taken to the asylum, he got given a bag of sweets and an orange at Christmas time, all the kids in the place got the same. But the difference, here's the difference. He made that December bag of sweets last all the way to October.

He'd shake his head.

Genius, he'd say.

Then he'd squint at Elisabeth.

Oh, hello, he'd say.

He'd look at the book in her hands.

What you reading? he'd say.
Elisabeth would hold it up.
Brave New World, she'd say.
Oh, that old thing, he'd say.
It's new to me, she'd say.

That moment of dialogue? Imagined.

Daniel is now in an increased sleep period.
Whichever care assistant chances to be on duty
always makes a point of explaining, when Elisabeth
sits with him, that the increased sleep period
happens when people are close to death.

He is beautiful.

He is so tiny in the bed. It is like he is just a head.
He's small and frail now, thin as the skeleton of a
cartoon fish left by a cartoon cat, his body so near-
nothing under the covers that it hardly makes any
impression, just a head by itself on a pillow, a head
with a cave in it and the cave is his mouth.

His eyes are closed and watery. There's a long
time between each breath in and out. In that long
time there's no breathing at all, so that every time
he breathes out there's the possibility that he might

not breathe in again, it doesn't seem quite possible that someone could be able not to breathe for so long and yet still be breathing and alive.

A good old age, he's done very well, the care assistants say.

He's had a good innings, the care assistants say, as if to say, it won't be long now.

Oh really?

They don't know Daniel.

Are you next of kin? Because we've been trying to contact Mr Gluck's next of kin with no success, the receptionist said the first time Elisabeth came. Elisabeth lied without even pausing. She gave them her mobile number, her mother's home number and her mother's home address.

We'll need further proof of identity, the receptionist said.

Elisabeth got out her passport.

I'm afraid this passport has expired, the receptionist said.

Yes, but only a month ago. I'm going to renew it. It's obviously still clearly me, Elisabeth said.

The receptionist started a speech about what was and what wasn't permitted. Then something happened at the front door, a wheelchair wheel jammed in a groove between the ramp and the edge of the door, and the receptionist went to find someone to free the wheelchair up. An assistant came through from the back. This assistant, seeing

Elisabeth putting her passport back into her bag, assumed that the passport had been checked and printed out a visitor card for Elisabeth.

Now, when Elisabeth sees the man whose wheelchair wheel got caught in the groove, she smiles at him. He looks back at her like he doesn't know who she is. Well, it's true. He doesn't.

She brings a chair in from the corridor and puts it next to the bed.

Then, in case Daniel opens his eyes (he dislikes attention), she gets out whatever book she's got with her.

With the book open in her hands, Brave New World, she looks at the top of his head. She looks at the darker spots in the skin beneath what's left of his hair.

Daniel, as still as death in the bed. But still. He's still here.

Elisabeth, at a loss, gets her phone out. She keys in the word *still* on her phone, just to see what'll come up.

The internet provides her instantly with a series of sentences to show usage of the word.

How still everything was!
She still held Jonathan's hand.
When they turned around, Alex was still
    on the horse.
Still, it did look stylish.

The throng stood still and waited.
Then Psammetichus tried still another plan.
When he still didn't respond, she continued.
People were still alive who knew the Wright
        Brothers.

Ah yes, Orville and Will, the two flighty boys
who started it all, Daniel, lying there so still, says
without saying. The boys who gave us the world in
a day, and air warfare, and every bored and restless
security queue in the world. But I will lay you a
wager (he says/doesn't say) that they don't have the
kind of *still* on that list which forms part of the
word di*still*ery.

Elisabeth scrolls down to check.

And that word scroll, Daniel says without saying,
it makes me think of all the scrolls still rolled up,
unread for two millennia, still waiting to be
unfurled in the still-unexcavated library in
Herculaneum.

She scrolls to the bottom of the page.

You're right, Mr Gluck. No whisky still.

Still, Daniel says/doesn't say. I *do* look stylish.

Daniel lies there very still in the bed, and the cave
of his mouth, its unsaying of these things, is the
threshold to the end of the world as she knows it.

Elisabeth is staring up at an old tenement rooming house, the kind you see being bulldozed and crashing down into themselves on old footage from when they modernized British cities in the 1960s and 70s.

It is still standing, but in a ravaged landscape. All the other houses have been pulled out of the street like bad teeth.

She pushes the door open. Its hall is dark, its wallpaper stained and dark. The front room is empty, no furniture. Its floor has boards broken where whoever was living or squatting here ripped them up to burn in the hearth, above the old mantel of which a shock of soot-grime shoots almost to the ceiling.

She imagines its walls white. She imagines everything in it painted white.

Even the holes in the floor, through the white broken boards, are painted white inside.

The house's windows look out on to high privet hedge. Elisabeth goes outside to paint that high hedge white too.

Inside, sitting on a white-painted old couch, the stuffing coming out of it also stiff with white emulsion, Daniel laughs at what she's doing. He laughs silently but like a child with his feet in his hands as she paints one tiny green leaf white after another.

He catches her eye. He winks. That does it.

They're both standing in pure clean white space.

Yes, she says. Now we can sell this space for a fortune. Only the very rich can afford to be this minimalist these days.

Daniel shrugs. Plus ça change.

Will we go for a walk, Mr Gluck? Elisabeth says.

But Daniel's off on his own already, crossing the white desert at a fair rate. She tries to catch him up. She can't quite. He's always just too far ahead. The whiteness goes on forever ahead of them. When she looks over her shoulder it's forever behind them too.

Someone killed an MP, she tells Daniel's back as she struggles to keep up. A man shot her dead and came at her with a knife. Like shooting her wouldn't be enough. But it's old news now. Once it would have been a year's worth of news. But news right now is like a flock of speeded-up sheep running off the side of a cliff.

The back of Daniel's head nods.

Thomas Hardy on speed, Elisabeth says.

Daniel stops and turns. He smiles benignly.

His eyes are closed. He breathes in. He breathes out. He is dressed in clothes made of hospital sheets. They've got the hospital name stamped on the corners, occasionally she can see it, pink and blue writing on a cuff or at the corner in the lining at the bottom of the jacket. He is peeling a white orange with a white penknife. The scroll of peel falls into the whiteness like into deep snow and disappears. He watches this happen and he makes an annoyed noise, tch. He looks at the peeled orange in his hand. It's white. He shakes his head.

He pats his pockets, chest, trousers, as if he's looking for something. Then he pulls, straight out of his chest, of his collarbone, like a magician, a free-floating mass of the colour orange.

He throws it like a huge cloak over the whiteness ahead of them. Before it settles away from him he twists a little of it round a finger and binds it round the too-white orange he's still holding.

The white orange in his hand becomes its natural colour.

He nods.

He pulls the colours green and blue like a string of handkerchiefs out of the centre of himself. The orange in his hand turns Cézanne-colours.

People crowd round him, excited.

People queue up, bring him their white things, hold them out.

Anonymous people start to add tweet-sized comments about Daniel beneath Daniel. They are commenting on his ability to change things.

The comments get more and more unpleasant.

They start to make a sound like a hornet mass and Elisabeth notices that what looks like liquid excrement is spreading very close to her bare feet. She tries not to step in any of it.

She calls to Daniel to watch where he steps too.

Having a bit of time out? the care assistant says. All right for some, huh?

Elisabeth comes to, opens her eyes. The book falls off her lap. She picks it up.

The care assistant is tapping the rehydration bag.

Some of us have to work for a living, she says.

She winks in the general direction of Elisabeth.

I was miles away, Elisabeth says.

Him too, the care assistant says. A very nice polite gentleman. We miss him now. Increased sleep period. It happens when things are becoming more (slight pause before she says it) final.

The pauses are a precise language, more a language than actual language is, Elisabeth thinks.

Please don't talk about Mr Gluck as if he can't hear you, she says. He can hear you as well as I can. Even if it looks like he's asleep.

The care assistant hooks the chart she's been looking at back on the rail at the end of the bed.

One day I was giving him a wash, she says as if Elisabeth's not there either and as if she's quite used to people not being there, or equally to having to function as if people aren't.

And the TV was on in the lounge, loud, and his door was open. He opens his eyes and sits straight up in the bed in the middle of. Advert, a supermarket. A song starts above the people's heads in the shop and all the people buying the things, dropping them on the floor instead and are dancing everywhere in the shop, and he sat straight up in the bed, he said this one is me, I wrote this one.

Old queen, Elisabeth's mother said under her breath.

Why him? she said at the more normal level of voice.

Because he's our neighbour, Elisabeth said.

It was a Tuesday evening in April in 1993. Elisabeth was eight years old.

But we don't know him, her mother said.

We're supposed to talk to a neighbour about what it means to be a neighbour, then make a portrait in words of a neighbour, Elisabeth said. You're meant to come with me, I'm meant to make up two or three questions and ask them to a neighbour for the portrait and you're meant to accompany me. I *told* you. I told you on Friday. You said we would. It's for school.

Her mother was doing something to the make-up on her eyes.

About what? her mother said. About all the arty art he's got in there?

We've got pictures, Elisabeth said. Are they arty art?

She looked at the wall behind her mother, the picture of the river and the little house. The picture of the squirrels made from bits of real pinecone. The poster of the dancers by Henri Matisse. The poster of the woman and her skirt and the Eiffel Tower. The blown-up real photographs of her grandmother and grandfather from when her mother was small. The ones of her mother when her mother was a baby. The ones of herself as a baby.

The stone with the hole through the middle of it. In the middle of his front room, her mother was saying. That's very arty art. I wasn't being nosy. I was passing. The light was on. I thought you were supposed to be collecting and identifying fallen leaves.

That was like three weeks ago, Elisabeth said. Are you going out?

Can't we phone Abbie and ask her the questions over the phone? her mother said.

But we don't live next to Abbie any more, Elisabeth said. It's supposed to be someone who's a neighbour *right now*. It's supposed to be in person, an in-person interview. And I'm supposed to ask about what it was like where the neighbour grew up and what life was like when the neighbour was my age.

People's lives are private, her mother said. You can't just go traipsing into their lives asking all sorts of questions. And anyway. Why does the school want to know these things about our neighbours?

They just do, Elisabeth said.

She went and sat on the top step of the stairs. She'd end up being the new girl who hasn't done the right homework. Her mother was going to say any minute now that she was off to do shopping at the late-night Tesco's and that she'd be back in half an hour. In reality she'd be back in two hours. She would smell of cigarettes. There'd be nothing brought back from Tesco's.

It's about history, and being neighbours, Elisabeth said.

He probably can't speak very good English, her mother said. You can't just go bothering old frail people.

He's not frail, Elisabeth said. He's not foreign. He's not old. He doesn't look in the least imprisoned.

He doesn't look what? her mother said.

It has to be done for tomorrow, Elisabeth said.

I've an idea, her mother said. Why don't you make it up? Pretend you're asking him the questions. Write down the answers you think he'd give.

It's supposed to be true, Elisabeth said. It's for News.

They'll never know, her mother said. Make it up. The real news is always made up anyway.

The real news is *not* made up, Elisabeth said. It's the *news*.

That's a discussion we'll have again when you're a bit older, her mother said. Anyway. It's much harder to make things up. I mean, to make them up really well, well enough so that they're convincing. It requires much more skill. Tell you what. If you make it up and it's convincing enough to persuade Miss Simmonds that it's true, I'll buy you that Beauty and the Beast thing.

The video? Elisabeth said. Really?

Uh huh, her mother said, pivoting on one foot to look at herself from the side.

In any case our video player is broken, Elisabeth said.

If you persuade her, her mother said. I'll splash out on a new one.

Do you mean it? Elisabeth said.

And if Miss Simmonds gives you a hard time because it's made up, I'll ring the school and assure her that it's not made up, it's true, her mother said. Okay?

Elisabeth sat down at the computer desk.

If he *was* very old, the neighbour, he didn't look anything like the people who were meant to be it on

TV, who always seemed as if they were trapped inside a rubber mask, not just a face-sized mask, but one that went the length of the body from head to foot, and if you could tear it off or split it open it was like you'd find an untouched unchanged young person inside, who'd simply step cleanly out of the old fake skin, like the skin after you take out the inner banana. When they were trapped inside that skin, though, the eyes of people, at least the people in all the films and comedy programmes, looked desperate, like they were trying to signal to outsiders without giving the game away that they'd been captured by empty aged selves which were now keeping them alive inside them for some sinister reason, like those wasps that lay eggs inside other creatures so their hatchlings will have something to eat. Except the other way round, the old self feeding off the young one. All that was left would be the eyes, pleading, trapped behind the eyeholes.

Her mother was at the front door.

Bye, she called. Back soon.

Elisabeth ran through to the hall.

If I want to write the word elegant how do I spell it?

The front door closed.

Next evening after supper her mother folded the Newsbook jotter open at the page and went out the back door and down the garden to the still-sunny back fence, where she leaned over and waved the jotter in the air.

Hi, she said.

Elisabeth watched from the back door. The neighbour was reading a book and drinking a glass of wine in what was left of the sun. He put his book down on the garden table.

Oh hello, he said.

I'm Wendy Demand, she said. I'm your next door neighbour. I've been meaning to come and say hi since my daughter and I moved in.

Daniel Gluck, he said from the chair.

Lovely to meet you, Mr Gluck, her mother said.

Daniel, please, he said.

He had a voice off old films where things happen to well-dressed warplane pilots in black and white.

And, well, I really don't want to bother you, her mother said. But it suddenly struck me, and I hope you don't mind, and you don't think it's cheeky. I thought you might like to read this little piece that my daughter wrote about you for a school exercise.

About me? the neighbour said.

It's lovely, her mother said. A Portrait In Words Of Our Next Door Neighbour. Not that I come out of it very well myself. But I read it and then I saw you were out in the garden, and I thought, well. I mean it's charming. I mean it puts me to shame. But it's very fetching about you.

Elisabeth was appalled. She was appalled from head to foot. It was like the notion of appalled had opened its mouth and swallowed her whole, exactly like an old-age rubberized skin would.

She stepped back behind the door where she couldn't be seen. She heard the neighbour scraping his chair on the flagstone. She heard him coming over to her mother at the fence.

When she came home from school next day the neighbour was sitting crosslegged on his garden wall right next to the front gate she needed to go through to get into the house.

She stopped stock still at the corner of the road.

She would walk past and pretend she didn't live in the house they lived in.

He wouldn't recognize her. She would be a child from another street altogether.

She crossed the road as if she were walking past. He unfolded his legs and he stood up.

When he spoke, there was nobody else in the road, so it was definitely to her. There was no getting out of it.

Hello, he said from his own side of the road. I was hoping I might run into you. I'm your neighbour. I'm Daniel Gluck.

I am not actually Elisabeth Demand, she said.

She kept walking.

Ah, he said. You're not. I see.

I am someone else, she said.

She stopped on the other side of the street and turned.

It was my sister who wrote it, she said.

I see, he said. Well, I had something I wanted to tell you, regardless.

What? Elisabeth said.

It's that I think your surname is originally French, Mr Gluck said. I think it comes from the French words de and monde, put together, which means, when you translate it, of the world.

Really? Elisabeth said. We always thought it meant like the asking kind of demand.

Mr Gluck sat down on the kerb and wrapped his arms round his knees. He nodded.

Of the world, or in the world, I think so, yes, he said. It might also mean of the people. Like Abraham Lincoln said. Of the people, by the people, for the people.

(He wasn't old. She was right. Nobody truly old sat with their legs crossed or hugged their knees like that. Old people couldn't do anything except sit in front rooms as if they'd been stunned by stun guns.)

I know that my – my sister's – Christian name, I mean the name Elisabeth, is meant to mean something about making promises to God, Elisabeth said. Which is a little difficult, because I'm not completely sure I believe in one, I mean, *she* does. I mean, doesn't.

Something else we have in common, he said, she and I. In fact, according to the history I've happened to live through, I'd say that her first name, Elisabeth, means that one day she'll probably, quite unexpectedly against the odds, find herself being made queen.

A queen? Elisabeth said. Like you?

Um –, the neighbour said.

I myself think it would be really good, Elisabeth said, because of all the arty art you get to have all round you all the time.

Ah, the neighbour said. Right.

But does the name Elisabeth still mean that thing even if it's spelt with an s not a z? Elisabeth said.

Oh yes, indubitably, he said.

Elisabeth crossed to the same side of the road as the neighbour. She stood a little distance away.

What does your name mean? she said.

It means I'm lucky and happy, he said. The Gluck part. And that if I'm ever thrown into a pit that's full of hungry lions I'll survive. That's the first name. And if you ever have a dream and you don't know what it means you can ask me. My first name also designates an ability to interpret dreams.

Can you? Elisabeth said.

She sat down on her own piece of kerb only slightly along from the neighbour.

Actually I'm extremely bad at it, he said. But I can make up something useful, entertaining, perspicacious and kind. We have this in common, you and I. As well as the capacity to become someone else, if we so choose.

You mean you have it in common with my sister, Elisabeth said.

I do, the neighbour said. Very pleased to meet you both. Finally.

How do you mean, finally? Elisabeth said. We only moved here six weeks ago.

The lifelong friends, he said. We sometimes wait a lifetime for them.

He held his hand out. She got up, crossed the distance and held her own hand out. He shook her hand.

See you later, unexpected queen of the world. Not forgetting the people, he said.

It is just over a week since the vote. The bunting in the village where Elisabeth's mother now lives is up across the High Street for its summer festival, plastic reds and whites and blues against a sky that's all threats, and though it's not actually raining right now and the pavements are dry, the wind rattling the plastic triangles against themselves means it sounds all along the High Street like rain is hammering down.

The village is in a sullen state. Elisabeth passes a cottage not far from the bus stop whose front, from the door to across above the window, has been painted over with black paint and the words GO and HOME.

People either look down, look away or stare her out. People in the shops, when she buys some fruit, some ibuprofen and a newspaper for her mother, speak with a new kind of detachment. People she passes on the streets on the way from the bus stop to her mother's house regard her, and each other, with a new kind of loftiness.

Her mother, who tells her when she gets there that half the village isn't speaking to the other half of the village, and that this makes almost no difference to her since no one in the village speaks to her anyway or ever has though she's lived here nearly a decade now (in this her mother is being a touch melodramatic), is doing some hammering herself, nailing to the kitchen wall an old Ordnance Survey map of where she now lives, which she bought yesterday in a shop that used to be the local electrician's business and electrical appliances store and is now a place selling plastic starfish, pottery looking things, artisan gardening tools and canvas gardening gloves that look like they've been modelled on a 1950s utilitarian utopia.

The kind of shop with the kinds of things that look nice, cost more than they should and persuade you that if you buy them you'll be living the right kind of life, her mother says between lips still holding two little nails.

The map is from 1962. Her mother has drawn a red line with a Sharpie all round the coast marking where the new coast is.

She points to a spot quite far inland, on the new red line.

That's where the World War II pillbox fell into the sea ten days ago, she says.

She points to the other side of the map, furthest from the coast.

That's where the new fence has gone up, she says. Look.

She is pointing to the word *common* in the phrase *common land*.

Apparently a fence three metres high with a roll of razorwire along the top of it has been erected across a stretch of land not far from the village. It has security cameras on posts all along it. It encloses a piece of land that's got nothing in it but furze, sandy flats, tufts of long grass, scrappy trees, little clumps of wildflower.

Go and see it, her mother says. I want you to do something about it.

What can I do about it? Elisabeth says. I'm a lecturer in history of art.

Her mother shakes her head.

You'll know what to do, she says. You're young. Come on. We'll both go.

They walk along the single-track road. The grass is high on either side of them.

Can't believe he's still alive, your Mr Gluck, her mother is saying.

That's what everybody in The Maltings Care Providers plc pretty much says too, Elisabeth says.

He was so old back *then*, her mother says. He

must be more than a hundred. He must be. He was eighty back in the 90s. He used to walk up the street, remember, all bowed with age.

I don't remember that at all, Elisabeth says.

Like he carried the weight of the world on his back, her mother says.

You always said he was like a dancer, Elisabeth says.

An old dancer, her mother says. He was all bent over.

You used to say he was lithe, Elisabeth says.

Then she says,

oh dear God.

In front of them, slicing straight across a path Elisabeth's walked several times since her mother came to live here, and blocking the way as far as the eye can see no matter which way she turns her head, is a mass of chainlink metal.

Her mother sits down on the churned-up ground near the fence.

I'm tired, she says.

It's only two miles, Elisabeth says.

That's not what I mean, she says. I'm tired of the news. I'm tired of the way it makes things spectacular that aren't, and deals so simplistically with what's truly appalling. I'm tired of the vitriol. I'm tired of the anger. I'm tired of the meanness. I'm tired of the selfishness. I'm tired of how we're doing nothing to stop it. I'm tired of how we're encouraging it. I'm tired of the violence there is and I'm tired of the violence that's on its way, that's coming, that hasn't happened yet. I'm tired of liars. I'm tired of sanctified liars. I'm tired of how those liars have let this happen. I'm tired of having to wonder whether they did it out of stupidity or did it on purpose. I'm tired of lying governments. I'm tired of people not caring whether they're being lied to any more. I'm tired of being made to feel this fearful. I'm tired of animosity. I'm tired of pusillanimosity.

I don't think that's actually a word, Elisabeth says.

I'm tired of not knowing the right words, her mother says.

Elisabeth thinks of the bricks of the old broken-up pillbox under the water, the air bubbles rising from their pores when the tide covers them.

I'm a brick under water, she thinks.

Her mother, sensing her daughter's attention wandering, sags momentarily towards the fence.

Elisabeth, who is tired of her mother (already, and she's only an hour and a half into the visit) points to the little clips placed at different positions along the wire.

Careful, she says. I think it's electrified.

All across the country, there was misery and rejoicing.

All across the country, what had happened whipped about by itself as if a live electric wire had snapped off a pylon in a storm and was whipping about in the air above the trees, the roofs, the traffic.

All across the country, people felt it was the wrong thing. All across the country, people felt it was the right thing. All across the country, people felt they'd really lost. All across the country, people felt they'd really won. All across the country, people felt they'd done the right thing and other people had done the wrong thing. All across the country, people looked up Google: *what is EU?* All across the country, people looked up Google: *move to Scotland*. All across the country, people looked up Google: *Irish passport applications*. All across the country, people called each other cunts. All across the country, people felt unsafe. All across the country, people were laughing their heads off. All across the country, people felt legitimized. All across the country, people felt bereaved and shocked. All across the country, people felt righteous. All across the country, people felt sick. All across the country, people felt history at their shoulder. All across the country, people felt history meant nothing. All across the country, people felt like they counted for nothing. All across the country, people had pinned their hopes on it. All across the country, people waved flags in the rain. All across the country, people drew swastika graffiti. All across the country, people threatened other people. All across the country, people told people to leave. All across the country, the media was insane. All across the country, politicians lied. All across the country, politicians fell apart. All across the country, politicians vanished. All across the country, promises vanished. All across the country, money vanished. All across the country, social media did the job. All across the country, things got nasty. All across the country, nobody spoke about it. All across the country, nobody spoke about anything else. All across the country, racist bile was general. All across the country, people said it wasn't that they didn't like immigrants. All across the country, people said it was about control. All across the country, everything changed overnight. All across the country, the haves and the have nots stayed the same. All across the country, the usual tiny per cent of the people made their money out of the usual huge per cent of the people. All across the country, money money money money. All across the country, no money no money no money no money.

All across the country, the country split in pieces. All across the country, the countries cut adrift.

All across the country, the country was divided, a fence here, a wall there, a line drawn here, a line crossed there,

a line you don't cross here,
a line you better not cross there,
a line of beauty here,
a line dance there,
a line you don't even know exists here,
a line you can't afford there,
a whole new line of fire,
line of battle,
end of the line,
here/there.

It was a typically warm Monday in late September 2015, in Nice, in the south of France. People out on the street were staring at the exterior of the Palais de la Préfecture where a long red banner with a swastika at the top of it had just coursed down the length of the front of the building and was settling itself against the balconies. Some people screamed. There was a flurry of shouting and pointing.

It was just a film production unit filming an adaptation of a memoir, using the Palais to recreate the Hôtel Excelsior, where Alois Brunner, the SS officer, had had his office and living quarters after the Italians surrendered to the Allies and the Gestapo had taken over in their place.

The Daily Telegraph reported next day on how the local authorities were apologizing for not having given enough notice about the film unit's plans to people who lived in the city, and how public confusion and offence had soon shifted to a mass taking of selfies.

It ran an online survey at the end of the news story. Were locals right to be angry about the banner: Yes or No?

Nearly four thousand people voted. Seventy per cent said no.

It was a typically warm Friday in late September 1943, in Nice, in the south of France. Hannah Gluck, who was twenty two years old (and whose real name wasn't on her identity papers, which stated that her name was Adrienne Albert), was sitting on the floor in the back of a truck. They'd picked up nine so far, all women, Hannah didn't know any of them. She and the woman opposite her exchanged looks. The woman looked down, then she looked back up, exchanged the look with Hannah one more time. Then they both lowered their eyes and looked down at the metal floor of the truck.

There were no accompanying vehicles. There were, in total, a driver plus a guard and a single quite young officer up front, and the two at the back, both even younger. The truck was part-open, part-roofed with canvas. The people on the streets could see their heads and the guards as they went past. Hannah had heard the officer saying to one of the men at the back as she climbed into the truck, keep it calm.

But the people on the street were oblivious, or made themselves it. They looked and looked away. They looked. But they weren't looking.

The streets were bright and splendid. The sun sent shockingly beautiful light off the buildings into the back of the truck.

When they stopped up a sidestreet to pick up two more, Hannah's eyes met again the eyes of the woman opposite. The woman moved her head with near-invisible assent.

The truck jolted to a stop. Traffic snarl-up. They'd taken the stupidest route. Good, and her sense of smell told her, the Friday fishmarket, busy.

Hannah stood up.

One of the guards told her to sit down.

The woman opposite stood up. One by one all the other women in the truck took their cue and stood up. The guard yelled at them to sit down. Both guards yelled. One waved a gun in the air at them.

This city isn't used to it yet, Hannah thought.

Get out of the way, the woman who'd nodded to Hannah said to the men. You can't kill us all.

Where are you taking them?

A woman had come over to the side of the truck and was looking in. A small gathering of women from the market, elegant women, headscarfed fish-seller girls and older women, formed behind her.

Then the officer got out of the truck and pushed the woman who'd asked where they were taking the women in the face. She fell and hit her head against a stone bollard. Her elegant hat fell off.

The women in that small gathering on the side of the road moved closer together. Their hush was audible. It spread back across the market like shadow, like cloud-cover.

It was a hush, Hannah thought, related to the quiet that comes over wildlife, happens to the birdsong, in an eclipse of the sun when something like night happens but it's the middle of the day.

Excuse me, ladies, Hannah said. This is where I get off.

The body of women on the truck huddled aside, let her through, let her go first.

It was another Friday in the October holidays in 1995. Elisabeth was eleven years old.

Mr Gluck from next door is going to look after you today, her mother said. I have to go to London again.

I don't need Daniel to look after me, Elisabeth said.

You are eleven years old, her mother said. You don't get a choice here. And don't call him Daniel. Call him Mr Gluck. Be polite.

What would you know about politeness? Elisabeth said.

Her mother gave her a hard look and said the thing about her being like her father.

Good, Elisabeth said. Because I wouldn't want to end up being anything like you.

Elisabeth locked the front door after her mother.

She locked the back door too. She drew the curtains in the front room and sat dropping lit matches on to the sofa to test how fireproof the new three piece suite really was.

She saw through a crack in the curtains Daniel coming up the front path. She opened the door even though she'd decided she wasn't going to.

Hello, he said. What you reading?

Elisabeth showed him her empty hands.

Does it look like I'm reading anything? she said.

Always be reading something, he said. Even when we're not physically reading. How else will we read the world? Think of it as a constant.

A constant what? Elisabeth said.

A constant constancy, Daniel said.

They went for a walk along the canal bank. Every time they passed someone, Daniel said hello. Sometimes the people said hello back. Sometimes they didn't.

It's really not all right to talk to strangers, Elisabeth said.

It is when you're as old as I am, Daniel said. It's not all right for a personage of your age.

I am tired of being a personage of my age and of having no choices, Elisabeth said.

Never mind that, Daniel said. That'll pass in the blink of an eye. Now. Tell me. What you reading?

The last book I read was called Jill's Gymkhana, Elisabeth said.

Ah. And what did it make you think about? Daniel said.

Do you mean, what was it about? Elisabeth said.

If you like, Daniel said.

It was about a girl whose father has died, Elisabeth told him.

Curious, Daniel said. It sounded like it might be more about horses.

There's a lot of horse stuff *in* it, obviously, Elisabeth said. In fact, the father who dies isn't actually in it. He isn't in it at all. Except that him not being there is the reason they move house, and her mother has to work, and the daughter gets interested in horses, and a gymkhana happens, and so on.

Your father's not dead, though? Daniel said.

No, Elisabeth said. He's in Leeds.

The word gymkhana, Daniel said, is a wonderful word, a word grown from several languages.

Words don't get grown, Elisabeth said.

They do, Daniel said.

Words aren't plants, Elisabeth said.

Words are themselves organisms, Daniel said.

Oregano-isms, Elisabeth said.

Herbal and verbal, Daniel said. Language is like poppies. It just takes something to churn the earth round them up, and when it does up come the sleeping words, bright red, fresh, blowing about. Then the seedheads rattle, the seeds fall out. Then there's even more language waiting to come up.

Can I ask you a question that's not about me or my life in any way or about my mother's life in any way either? Elisabeth said.

You can ask me anything you like, Daniel said. But I can't promise to answer what you ask unless I know a good enough answer.

Fair enough, Elisabeth said. Did you ever go to hotels with people and at the same time pretend to a child you were meant to be being responsible for that you were doing something else?

Ah, Daniel said. Before I answer that, I need to know whether there's an implicit moral judgement in your question.

If you don't want to answer the question I asked you, Mr Gluck, you should just say so, Elisabeth said.

Daniel laughed. Then he stopped laughing.

Well, it depends on what your question really is, he said. Is it about the act of going to the hotel? Or is it about the people who do or don't go to the hotel? Or is it about the pretending? Or is it about the act of pretending something to a child?

Yes, Elisabeth said.

In which case, is it a personal question to me, Daniel said, about whether I myself ever went to a hotel with someone? And in doing so chose to pretend to someone else that I wasn't doing what I was doing? Or is it about whether it matters that the person I may or may not have pretended to was a child rather than an adult? Or is it more general than that, and you want to know whether it's wrong to pretend anything to a child?

All of the above, Elisabeth said.

You are a very smart young person, Daniel said.

I am planning to go to college when I leave school, Elisabeth said. If I can afford it.

Oh, you don't want to go to college, Daniel said.

I do, Elisabeth said. My mother was the first in my family ever to go, and I will be the next.

You want to go to collage, Daniel said.

I want to go to college, Elisabeth said, to get an education and qualifications so I'll be able to get a good job and make good money.

Yes, but to study what? Daniel said.

I don't know yet, Elisabeth said.

Humanities? Law? Tourism? Zoology? Politics? History? Art? Maths? Philosophy? Music? Languages? Classics? Engineering? Architecture? Economics? Medicine? Psychology? Daniel said.

All of the above, Elisabeth said.

That's why you need to go to collage, Daniel said.

You're using the wrong word, Mr Gluck, Elisabeth said. The word you're using is for when you cut out pictures of things or coloured shapes and stick them on paper.

I disagree, Daniel said. Collage is an institute of education where all the rules can be thrown into the air, and size and space and time and foreground

71

and background all become relative, and because of these skills everything you think you know gets made into something new and strange.

Are you still using avoidance tactics about the question about the hotel? Elisabeth said.

Truthfully? Daniel said. Yes. Which game would you rather play? I'll give you a choice of two. One. Every picture tells a story. Two. Every story tells a picture.

What does every story tells a picture mean? Elisabeth said.

Today it means that I'll describe a collage to you, Daniel said, and you can tell me what you think of it.

Without actually seeing it? Elisabeth said.

By seeing it in the imagination, as far as you're concerned, he said. And in the memory, as far as I'm concerned.

They sat down on a bench. A couple of kids were fishing off the rocks ahead of them. Their dog was standing on the rocks and shaking canal water off its coat. The boys squealed and laughed when the water fanned out into the air off the dog and hit them.

Picture or story? Daniel said. You choose.

Picture, she said.

Okay, Daniel said. Close your eyes. Are they closed?

Yes, Elisabeth said.

The background is rich dark blue, Daniel said. A blue much darker than sky. On top of the dark blue, in the middle of the picture, there's a shape made of pale paper that looks like a round full moon. On top of the moon, bigger than the moon, there's a cut-out black and white lady wearing a swimsuit, cut from a newspaper or fashion magazine. And next to her, as if she's leaning against it, there's a giant human hand. And the giant hand is holding inside it a tiny hand, a baby's hand. More truthfully, the baby's hand is also holding the big hand, holding it by its thumb. Below all this, there's a stylized picture of a woman's face, the same face repeated several times, but with a different coloured curl of real hair hanging over its nose each time –

Like at the hairdresser? Like colour samples? Elisabeth said.

You've got it, Daniel said.

She opened her eyes. Daniel's were shut. She shut her own eyes again.

And way off in the distance, in the blue at the bottom of the picture, there's a drawing of a ship with its sails up, but it's small, it's the smallest thing in the whole collage.

Okay, Elisabeth said.

Finally, there's some pink lacy stuff, by which I mean actual material, real lace, stuck on to the picture in a couple of places, up near the top, then further down towards the middle too. And that's it. That's all I can recall.

Elisabeth opened her eyes. She saw Daniel open his eyes a moment later.

Later that night, when she was home and falling asleep on the couch in front of the TV, Elisabeth would remember seeing his eyes open, and how it was like that moment when you just happen to see the streetlights come on and it feels like you're being given a gift, or a chance, or that you yourself've been singled out and chosen by the moment.

What do you think? Daniel said.

I like the idea of the blue and the pink together, Elisabeth said.

Pink lace. Deep blue pigment, Daniel said.

I like that you could maybe touch the pink, if it was made of lace, I mean, and it would feel different from the blue.

Oh, that's good, Daniel said. That's very good.

I like how the little hand is holding the big hand as much as the big hand is holding the little hand, Elisabeth said.

Today I myself particularly like the ship, Daniel said. The galleon with the sails up. If I'm remembering rightly. If it's even there.

Does that mean it's a real picture? Elisabeth said. Not one you made up?

It's real, Daniel said. Well, it was once. A friend

of mine did it. An artist. But I'm making it up from memory. How did it strike your imagination?

Like it would be if I was taking drugs, Elisabeth said.

Daniel stopped on the canal path.

You've never taken drugs, he said. Have you?

No, but if I did, and everything was in my head all at once, all sort of crowding in, it would be a bit like it, Elisabeth said.

Dear God. You'll tell your mother we've been taking drugs all afternoon, Daniel said.

Can we go and see it? Elisabeth said.

See what? Daniel said.

The collage? Elisabeth said.

Daniel shook his head.

I don't know where it is, he said. It might be long gone by now. Goodness knows where those pictures are now in the world.

Where did you see it in the first place? Elisabeth said.

I saw it in the early 1960s, Daniel said.

He said it as if a time could be a place.

I was there the day she made it, he said.

Who? Elisabeth said.

The Wimbledon Bardot, Daniel said.

Who's that? Elisabeth said.

Daniel looked at his watch.

Come on, art student, he said. Pupil of my eye. Time to go.

Time flies, Elisabeth said.

Well, yes. It can do, Daniel said. Literally. Watch this.

Elisabeth doesn't remember much of the above.

She does remember, though, the day they were walking along the canal bank when she was small and Daniel took his watch off his wrist and threw it into the water.

She remembers the thrill, the absolute not-doneness of it.

She remembers there were two boys down on the rocks and they turned their heads as the watch arced through the air over them and hit the canal, and she remembers knowing that it was a watch, Daniel's watch, not just any old stone or piece of litter, flying through the air, and knowing too that there was no way those boys could know this, that only she and Daniel knew the enormity of what he'd just done.

She remembers that Daniel had given her the choice, *to throw or not to throw.*

She remembers she chose *to throw.*

She remembers coming home with something amazing to tell her mother.

Here's something else from another time, from when Elisabeth was thirteen, that she also only remembers shreds and fragments of.

And anyway, why else are you always hanging round an old gay man?

(That was her mother.)

I don't *have* a father fixation, Elisabeth said. And Daniel's not gay. He's European.

Call him Mr Gluck, her mother said. And how do you know he's not gay? And if that's true, and he's not gay, then what does he want with you?

Or if he is, Elisabeth said, then he's not *just* gay. He's not *just* one thing or another. Nobody is. Not even you.

Her mother was ultra-sensitive and ultra-irritating right now. It was something to do with

Elisabeth being thirteen, not twelve. Whatever it was about, it was ultra-annoying.

Don't be rude, her mother said. And what you are is thirteen years old. You've got to be a bit careful of old men who want to hang around thirteen year old girls.

He's my friend, Elisabeth said.

He's eighty five, her mother said. How is an eighty five year old man your friend? Why can't you have normal friends like normal thirteen year olds?

It depends on how you'd define normal, Elisabeth said. Which would be different from how I'd define normal. Since we all live in relativity and mine at the moment is not and I suspect never will be the same as yours.

Where are you learning to talk like this? her mother said. Is that what you do on those walks?

We just walk, Elisabeth said. We just talk.

About what? her mother said.

Nothing, Elisabeth said.

About me? her mother said.

No! Elisabeth said.

What, then? her mother said.

About stuff, Elisabeth said.

What stuff? her mother said.

Stuff, Elisabeth said. He tells me about books and things.

Books, her mother said.

Books. Songs. Poets, Elisabeth said. He knows about Keats. Season of mists. Opening an opiate.

He opened a what? her mother said.

He knows about Dylan, Elisabeth said.

Bob Dylan? her mother said.

No, the other Dylan, Elisabeth said. He knows it off by heart, a lot of it. Though he did meet the singer Bob Dylan once, when Bob Dylan was staying with his friend.

He told you he's friends with Bob Dylan? her mother said.

No. He met him. It was one winter. He was sleeping on a friend's floor.

Bob Dylan? On a *floor*? her mother said. I don't think so. Bob Dylan has always been a huge international star.

And he knows about that poet you like who killed herself, Elisabeth said.

Plath? her mother said. About suicide?

You so don't get it, Elisabeth said.

What exactly don't I get about an old man putting ideas about suicide and a lot of lies about Bob Dylan into my thirteen year old daughter's head? her mother said.

And anyway, Daniel says it doesn't matter how she died so long as you can still say or read her words. Like the line about no longer grieving, and the one about daughters of the darkness still flaming like Guy Fawkes, Elisabeth said.

That doesn't sound like Plath, her mother said. No, I'm almost completely sure I've never come across that line in any Plath I've read, and I've read it all.

It's Dylan. And the line about how love is evergreen, Elisabeth said.

What else does Mr Gluck tell you about love? her mother said.

He doesn't. He tells me about paintings, Elisabeth said. Pictures.

He shows you pictures? her mother said.

By a tennis player he knew, Elisabeth said. They're pictures people can't actually go and see. So he tells me them.

Why can't people see them? her mother said.

They just can't, Elisabeth said.

Private pictures? her mother said.

No, Elisabeth said. They're, like. Ones he knows.

Of tennis players? her mother said. Tennis players doing what?

No, Elisabeth said.

Oh God, her mother said. What have I done?

What you've done is used Daniel as my unofficial babysitter for years, Elisabeth said.

I told you. Call him *Mr Gluck*, her mother said. And I haven't been using him. That's just not true. And I want to know. I want to know in detail. Pictures of what?

Elisabeth made an exasperated sound.

I don't know, she said. People. Things.

What are the people doing in these pictures? her mother said.

Elisabeth sighed. She shut her eyes.

Open your eyes right now Elisabeth, her mother said.

I have to close my eyes or I can't see them, Elisabeth said. Okay? Right. Marilyn Monroe surrounded by roses, and then bright pink and green and grey waves painted all round her. Except that the picture isn't literally of literal Marilyn, it's a picture of a picture of her. That's important to remember.

Oh is it? her mother said.

Like if I was to take a photo of you and then paint a picture of the photo, not you. And the roses look a bit like flowery wallpaper rather than roses. But the roses have also come out of the wallpaper and have curled up round her collarbone, like they're embracing her.

Embracing, her mother said. I see.

And someone French, someone famous in France once, a man, he's wearing a hat and sunglasses, and the top of the hat is a pile of red petals like a huge red flower, and he's grey and black and white like a picture in a paper, and behind him is all bright orange, partly like a cornfield or golden grass, and above him is a row of hearts.

Her mother had her hands over her own eyes at the kitchen table.

Keep going, she said.

Elisabeth shut her eyes again.

One with a woman, not a famous person, she's just any woman and she's laughing, she's sort of throwing her arms up in a blue sky, and behind her at the foot of the picture there are alps, but very small, and a lot of zigzags in colours. And instead of having a body or clothes, the woman's insides are made up of pictures, pictures of other things.

He told you about a woman's body, a woman's insides, her mother said.

No, Elisabeth said. He told me about a woman whose body is made up of pictures instead of body. It's perfectly clear.

What pictures? Pictures of what? her mother said.

Things. Things that happen in the world, Elisabeth said. A sunflower. A man with a machine gun like out of a gangster film. A factory. A Russian looking politician. An owl, an exploding airship –

And Mr Gluck makes these pictures up in his head and puts them inside a woman's body? her mother said.

No, they're real, Elisabeth said. There's one called It's a Man's World. It's got a stately home in it, and the Beatles and Elvis Presley and a president in the back of a car getting shot.

That was when her mother started really yelling.

So she decided not to tell her mother about the collages with the children's heads being snipped off with the giant secateurs, and the massive hand coming out of the roof of the Albert Hall.

She decided not to mention the painting of a woman sitting on a backwards-turned chair with no clothes on, who brought a government down, and all the red paint and the black smudges through the red, that look, Daniel says, like *nuclear fallout*.

Even so, her mother still said it at the end of their talk

(and this is what Elisabeth does remember, verbatim, nearly two decades later, of the above conversation):

Unnatural.

Unhealthy.

You're not to.

I forbid it.

That's enough.

A minute ago it was June. Now the weather is
September. The crops are high, about to be cut,
bright, golden.

November? unimaginable. Just a month away.

The days are still warm, the air in the shadows
sharper. The nights are sooner, chillier, the light a
little less each time.

Dark at half past seven. Dark at quarter past
seven, dark at seven.

The greens of the trees have been duller since
August, since July really.

But the flowers are still coming. The hedgerows
are still humming. The shed is already full of apples
and the tree's still covered in them.

The birds are on the powerlines.

The swifts left weeks ago. They're hundreds of
miles from here by now, somewhere over the ocean.

2

But now? The old man (Daniel) opens his eyes to find he can't open his eyes.

He seems to be shut inside something remarkably like the trunk of a Scots pine.

At least, it smells like a pine.

He's got no real way of telling. He can't move. There's not much room for movement inside a tree. His mouth and eyes are resined shut.

There are worse tastes to have in a mouth though, truth be told, and the trunks of Scots pines do tend to be narrow. Straight and tall, because this is the kind of tree good for telegraph poles, for the props that pit builders used in the days when industry relied on people working in pits and pits relied on pitprops to hold the ceilings of the tunnels up safely over their heads.

If you have no choice but to go underground, go in the form of something useful. If you have to be cut down, good to spend the afterlife as messenger between people across landscapes. Pines are tall. It's a lot better than being confined in a dwarf conifer.

From the top of a Scots pine it's possible to see quite a distance.

Daniel in the bed, inside the tree, isn't panicking. He isn't even claustrophobic. It's reasonable in here, excepting the paralysis, and perhaps it won't last. Let's be hopeful. No, in actual fact he's pleased to be being held immobile inside not just any old tree but such an ancient and adaptable and noble species, the kind of tree that pre-dates by quite a long way the sorts of trees with leaves; a versatile tree, the Scots pine doesn't need much soil depth, is remarkably good at long life, a tree that can last for many centuries. But the best thing of all about being inside this of all trees is the fact that it's more versatile, when it comes to colour, than your average general tree. The green of a forest of Scots pines can verge towards blue. And then in the spring there's the pollen, as yellow as bright paint pigment in an artist's jar, plentiful, pervasive, scene-stealing like the smoke round a conjuring trick. Back in the old days, the primeval days, the people who wanted others to think they had special powers used to fling such pollen about in the air around them. They would come to the woods and collect it to take home and use it as part of their act.

One might imagine it'd be unpleasant, being sealed inside a tree. One might imagine, ah, pining. But the scent lightens despair. It's perhaps a little like wearing a coat of armour except much nicer, because the armour is made of a substance through which the years themselves, formative, have run.

Oh.

A girl.

Who's she?

She vaguely resembles all the pictures in the papers, back then, of,

what's her name,

Keeler. Christine.

Yes. It's her.

Probably nobody knows who she is any more. Probably what was history then is nothing but footnote now, and on that note, he notes she's barefoot, alone in the summer night light of the hall of the great stately house where, by coincidence (history, footnote), he happens to know that the song Rule Britannia was first ever sung. She is standing next to a tapestried wall and she is slipping out of her summer dress.

It falls to the floor. Up go all his pinecones. He groans. She doesn't hear a thing.

She unhooks the armour off its stand and sorts it

into pieces on the parquet floor. She fits the breastplate over her (quite magnificent, it's all true) chest. She puts her arms through the armholes. There's no metal cover at all at the place where her, ah, lower underwear is. She puts her hands down to the space in the metal there as if she's just realized how she's likely to reveal herself, through this gap, when fully armoured.

She wriggles herself out of what's left of her underwear.

It falls to the floor.

He groans.

She steps out of it, leaves it on the carpet runner. It lies there. It looks like a boned blackbird.

She fits one leg-piece to a thigh, then the next. She yelps and swears – sharp edge maybe, inside the second of the leg-pieces? She straps the leg-pieces to the backs of her thighs and slips a bare foot inside the first huge boot. She slips her arms inside the metal arm-pieces, lifts the helmet and fits it over her hair. Through the slits in its front she looks around for the gauntlets. One on. Now the next.

She pushes up the visor with her metal hand and her eyes look out.

She goes and stands in front of a huge old mirror hung on the wall. Her laugh comes tinnily out through the helmet. She knocks the visor down again with the gauntlet edge. The only thing visible of her is her privates.

Then she sets off, but delicately, so anything loosely strapped won't fall off. She clinks her way down the corridor quite as if a suit of armour isn't nearly as heavy as it looks.

When she comes to a door she turns and pushes it. It opens. She disappears.

The room she's just entered explodes into raucous laughter.

Can laughter be well-heeled?

Is powerful laughter different from ordinary laughter?

That type of laughter is always powerful.

There's a song in this, Daniel thinks.

Ballad of Christine Keeler.

Well-heel-er. Dealer. Feeler. Squealer. Conceal her. Steal her. Mrs Peel her.

Ah, no. The fictional creation Mrs Peel came later, a couple of years after this creation.

But probably the Peel of Mrs is based, partly at least, on the Keel of Keeler, a suggestive little gift to the ear of the beholder.

Right now he's pressed so close between all the people up in the public gallery that – where now?

A courtroom.

The Old Bailey.

That summer.

He only imagined Keeler trying on the armour. He dreamed it, though it's rumoured to have happened.

But this, this below, about to happen, he witnessed.

First up, Keeler versus Ward, her friend, Stephen the osteopath, the portraitist. No suit of armour but nonetheless she's armoured here, sheet-metal listless. Impervious. Masked. Perfectly made-up. Dead with a hint of exotic.

She puts the place into a trance by speaking like someone in a trance might speak. Clever. Empty. Sexy automaton. Living doll. Sensational, the public gallery turns pubic gallery. No one can think of anything else, except her friend Stephen, down at the front, who every day picks up his pencil and sketches what he's seeing.

Meanwhile, days pass.

Down in the witness box, someone else now, a woman, a different one, a Miss Ricardo, truth be told she's even lower-class than poor Keeler, young, coiffed, roughed at the edges, her hair piled red and high on her head, a dancer, *I earn money by visiting men and being paid by them.*

She has just announced to the courtroom that the statements that she first made to the police about this case were untrue.

The crowd in the gallery presses forward even harder. Scandal and lies. What prostitutes do. But Daniel sees the woman, just a girl really, fighting to hold herself straight. He sees how her face, her whole demeanour, have gone something like pale green with the fear.

Red hair.

Green girl.

I didn't want my young sister to go to a remand home, the girl says. My baby taken away from me. The chief inspector told me they would take my sister and my baby if I didn't make the statements. He also threatened to have my brother nicked. I believed him and so I made the statements. But I have decided I don't want to give false evidence at the Old Bailey. I told The People newspaper. I want everyone to know why I lied.

Oh dear God.

She's green all right.

The prosecuting lawyer has an air of foxhound. He makes fun of her. He asks her why on earth she'd sign a statement in the first place if the statement she was signing wasn't true.

She tells him she wanted the police to leave her alone.

The prosecuting lawyer worries at her. Why has she never complained about any of this before now?

Who could I complain to? she says.

A deliberate liar, then, is she?

Yes, she says.

Daniel in the gallery sees one of her hands, the one on the rail of the witness box, cover itself in little shoots and buds. The buds split open. There are leaves coming out of her fingers.

The Judge advises her to take the time overnight very carefully to consider the version of things she's choosing to tell to the court today.

Blink of an eye.

Next day.

The girl's in the box again. Today she is almost all young tree. Now only her face and her hair are unleafy. Overnight, like a girl in a myth being hunted by a god who's determined to have his way with her, she has altered herself, remade herself so she can't be had by anyone.

The same men shout at her again. They're angry with her for not lying about lying. The prosecutor asks her why she told her story about lying to a newspaper reporter, not to the police. He suggests this was improper, an improper thing to do, the sort of thing an improper woman like this woman *would* do.

What would be the point, she says, in me going to tell the truth to the very people who've told me to lie?

The Judge sighs. He turns to the jury.

Dismiss this evidence from your minds, he says. I instruct you to disregard it altogether.

There's a song in this too, Daniel thinks as he watches the white bark rise up and cover her mouth, her nose, her eyes.

Ballad of the Silver Birch.

High church. Lurch. Besmirch. Soul search.

Himself, he goes straight from that courtroom to the house of the girl he's in love with.

(He's in love with her. He can hardly say her name to himself. He's in love with her so much.

She isn't in love with him. Only a few weeks back she married someone else. He can say her husband's name all right. His name's Clive.

But he's just seen a miraculous thing, hasn't he?

He's seen something that changes the nature of things.)

He stands in the rain in the back yard. It's dark now. He is looking up at the windows of the house. His hands and forearms, his face, his good shirt and suit are smeared from the dustbins and climbing the fence, as if he's still young enough to.

There is a famous short story, The Dead, by James Joyce, in which a young man stands at the back of a house and sings a song on a freezing night to a woman he loves. Then this young man, pining for the woman, dies. He catches a chill in the snow, he dies young. Height of romanticism! That woman in that story, for the rest of her life, has that young man's song always riddling through her like woodworm.

Well, Daniel himself's not a young man. That's partly the problem. The woman he's pretty much sure he loves more than anyone he's ever, the woman he will pine away to nothing without the love of, is twenty years younger than him, and, yes, not that long ago, there *is* that, married Clive.

And then there's the extra other matter, the matter of not being able to sing. Well, not in tune.

But he can shout a song. He can shout the words. And they're *his* words, not just any old words.

And she only knew him for ten days before she married him, Clive, that is. There's always hope, with this particular girl.

The Ballad of the Girl Who Keeps Telling Me No.

Fast little number, witty, to meet her wit.

Throaty. Gloaty. Wild oat(y). Grace-note(y). Misquote(y). Anecdote(y). Casting vote(y). Furcoat(y). Petticoat(y). Torpedo boat(y).

(Terrible.)

I'm billy goaty.

Don't be haughty.

But no light comes on in any of the windows. It takes about half an hour of standing in the rain for him to admit there's nobody in, that he's been standing in a yard shouting bad rhymes at a house where nobody's home.

That fashionable swing-seat they've got in there hanging from the ceiling in the living room will be slowly turning this way and that by itself in the dark.

Ironic. He's a sap. She'll never even know he was here, will she?

(True enough. She never knew.

And then what happened next, well, it happened next, and history, that other word for irony, went its own foul witty way, sang its own foul witty ditty, and the girl was the one who died young in this story.

Riddled. Woodworm. All through him.)

Then the old man confined in the bed in the tree, Daniel, is a boy on a train that's passing through deep spruce woods. He is thin and small, sixteen summers old but he thinks he's a man. It's summer again, he is on the continent, they are all on the continent, things are a little uneasy on the continent. Something's going to happen. It is already happening. Everybody knows. But everybody is pretending it's not happening.

All the people on the train can see from his clothes that he's not from here. But he can speak the language, though none of the strangers round him on the train knows he can, because they don't know who he is, or who she is, his sister next to him, they don't know the first thing about them.

The people round them are talking about the necessity of developing a scientific and legal means of gauging exactly who's what.

There is a professor at the institute, the man sitting across from him says to a woman. And this professor is engaged in inventing a modern tool to record, quite scientifically, certain physical statistics.

Oh? the woman says.

She nods.

Noses, ears, the spaces between, the man across from Daniel says.

He is flirting with that woman.

The measurement of parts of the body, most especially of the features of the head area, can tell you quite succinctly everything you need to know. Eye colour, hair colour, the sizing of foreheads. It's been done before, but never so expertly, never so exactly. It's a case in the first place of measuring and collating. But a slightly more complex case, in the long run, of the sifting of the collected statistics.

The boy smiles at his little sister.

She lives here all the time.

She is assiduously reading her book. He nudges her. She looks up from it. He winks.

She speaks it as her first language. She knows the flirting is the thinnest layer. She knows exactly what they're saying. She turns the page in her book, glances at him then at the people opposite over the top of it.

I hear them. But am I going to let it stop me reading?

She says this in English to her brother. She makes a face at him. Then she glances her whole self back down into the book.

Out in the train corridor, when the boy Daniel goes to relieve himself, there's a capped and booted man blocking the way. His front is all pockets and straps. His arms are stretched in a leisurely way from one side to the other of the passage through to the toilet and the other carriages. He is swaying with the movement of this train as it moves through the spruce woods and farmland almost as if he's a working part of its mechanical structure.

Can the sheer breadth of someone's chest be insidious?

Oh yes it can.

Lazy, sure, he smiles at the boy, the smile of a soldier in repose. He lifts one arm higher so the boy can pass under. As Daniel does, the soldier's arm comes down just far enough to brush, with the material of his shirt, the hair on the top of his head.

Hopla, the soldier says.

Boy on a train.

Blink of an eye.

Old man in a bed.

The old man in the bed is confined.

Wooden overcoat

(y).

Cut this tree I'm living in down. Hollow its trunk out.

Make me all over again, with what you scooped out of its insides.

Slide the new me back inside the old trunk.

Burn me. Burn the tree. Spread the ashes, for
luck, where you want next year's crops to grow.
Birth me all over again
Burn me and the tree
Next summer's sun
Midwinter guarantee

It is still July. Elisabeth goes to her mother's medical practice in the middle of town. She waits in the queue of people. When she gets to the front she tells the receptionist that the GP her mother is registered with is at this practice, that she herself isn't registered with a GP here but that she's been feeling unwell so she'd like to talk to a doctor, probably not urgent, but something does feel wrong.

The receptionist looks Elisabeth's mother up on the computer. She tells Elisabeth that her mother isn't listed at this surgery.

Yes she is, Elisabeth says. She definitely is.

The receptionist clicks on another file and then goes to the back of the room and opens a drawer in a filing cabinet. She takes out a piece of paper, reads it, then puts it back in and shuts the drawer. She comes back and sits down.

She tells Elisabeth she's afraid that her mother is no longer listed on the patient list.

My mother definitely doesn't know that, Elisabeth says. She thinks she's a patient here. Why would you take her off the list?

The receptionist says that this is confidential information and that she's not permitted to tell Elisabeth anything about any patient other than Elisabeth herself.

Well, can I register and see someone anyway? Elisabeth says. I feel pretty rough. I'd really like to talk to someone.

The receptionist asks her if she has any ID.

Elisabeth shows the receptionist her library card for the university.

Valid until my job goes, at least, she says, now the universities are all going to lose 16 per cent of our funding.

The receptionist smiles a patient smile. (A smile especially for patients.)

I'm afraid we need something with a current address and preferably also with a photograph, she says.

Elisabeth shows her her passport.

This passport is expired, the receptionist says.

I know, Elisabeth says. I'm in the middle of renewing it.

I'm afraid we can't accept an expired ID, the receptionist says. Have you got a driving licence?

Elisabeth tells the receptionist she doesn't drive.

What about a utility bill? the receptionist says.

What, on me? Elisabeth says. Right now?

The receptionist says that it's a good idea always to carry a utility bill around with you in case someone needs to be able to verify your ID.

What about all the people who pay their bills online and don't get paper bills any more? Elisabeth says.

The receptionist looks longingly at a ringing phone on the left of her desk. Still with her eyes on the ringing phone she tells Elisabeth it's perfectly easy to print a bill out on a standard inkjet.

Elisabeth says she's staying at her mother's, that it's sixty miles away, and that her mother doesn't have a printer.

The receptionist actually looks angry that Elisabeth's mother might not have a printer. She talks about catchment areas and registration of patients. Elisabeth realizes she's suggesting that now that her mother lives outside the catchment area Elisabeth has no business being here in this building.

It's also perfectly easy to mock up a bill and print it out. To pretend to be a person, Elisabeth says. And what about all the people doing scams? How does having your name on a piece of printed-out paper make you who you are?

She tells the receptionist about the scammer

calling him or her self Anna Pavlova, for whom NatWest bank statements have been regularly arriving for the past three years at her own flat, even though she's notified NatWest about it repeatedly and knows for sure no one called Anna Pavlova has lived there for at least a decade, having lived there herself that long.

So what does a piece of paper prove, exactly, in the end? Elisabeth says.

The receptionist looks at her and her face is stony. She asks if Elisabeth will excuse her for a moment. She answers the phone.

She gestures to Elisabeth to step back away from the desk while she takes this call. Then to make it even clearer she puts her hand over the receiver and says, if I could just ask you to let me accord this caller the requisite privacy.

There is a small queue of people forming behind Elisabeth all waiting to check in with this receptionist.

Elisabeth goes to the Post Office instead.

Today the Post Office is near empty, except for the queue waiting to use the self-service machines. Elisabeth takes a ticket. 39. Numbers 28 and 29 are apparently being served, though there's no one at the counter at all, on either the Post Office side or the customer side.

Ten minutes later a woman comes through the door at the back. She shouts the numbers 30 and 31.

No one responds. So she forwards the lit machine through the 30s, calling out the numbers as she does.

Elisabeth comes to the counter and gives the woman her passport envelope and the new photobooth shots, in which her face is definitely the right size (she has measured it). She shows her the receipt proving she paid the £9.75 Check & Send fee last week.

When are you planning to travel? the woman says.

Elisabeth shrugs. Nothing planned, she says.

The woman looks at the photographs.

There's a problem, I'm afraid, the woman says.

What? Elisabeth says.

This piece of hair here should be off the face, she says.

It *is* off the face, Elisabeth says. That's my forehead. It's not even touching the face.

It should be right back off the face, the woman says.

If I took a picture of myself with it not where it is, Elisabeth says, I wouldn't truly look like me. What would be the point of a passport photo that didn't actually look like me?

I'd say that's touching the eyes, the woman says.

The woman pushes her chair back and takes the photo sheet round to the counter where Travel Cash is issued. She shows it to a man there. The man comes back to the counter with her.

There may be a problem with your photograph,

he says, in that my colleague thinks the hair is touching the face in it.

In any case, the hair is irrelevant, the woman says. Your eyes are too small.

Oh God, Elisabeth says.

The man goes back to his Travel Cash counter. The woman is sliding the pictures of Elisabeth up and down inside a transparent plastic chart with markings and measurements in different boxes printed all over it.

Your eyes don't sit with the permissible regularity inside the shaded area, she says. This doesn't line up. This should be in the middle and, as you can see, it's at the side of your nose. I'm afraid these photographs don't meet the necessary stipulation. If you go to Snappy Snaps rather than to a booth –

That's exactly what the man I saw here last week said, Elisabeth says. What is it with this Post Office and its relationship with Snappy Snaps? Does someone's brother work at Snappy Snaps?

So you were advised to go to Snappy Snaps already but you chose not to go, the woman says.

Elisabeth laughs. She can't not; the woman looks so very stern about her not having gone to Snappy Snaps.

The woman lifts the chart and shows her again her own face with a shaded box over it.

I'm afraid it's a no, the woman says.

Look, Elisabeth says. Just send these photos to

the Passport Office. I'll take the risk. I think they'll be okay.

The woman looks wounded.

If they don't accept them, Elisabeth says, I'll come back in and see you again soon and tell you you were quite right and I was wrong, my hair was wrong and my eyes were in totally the wrong place.

No, because if you submit this through Check & Send today, this will be the last time this office will have anything to do with this application, the woman says. Once the application goes in, it's the Passport Office who'll be in touch with you about your unmet specifications.

Right, Elisabeth says. Thank you. Send them. I'll take my chances. And will you do me a favour?

The woman looks very alarmed.

Will you say hello to your colleague who works here who's got the seafood intolerance? Tell him the woman with the wrong size of head sends her best wishes and hopes he is well.

That description? the woman says. Forgive me, but. Could be anybody. One of thousands.

She writes in ballpoint on Elisabeth's receipt: *customer choosing to send photos at own risk.*

Elisabeth stands outside the Post Office. She feels better. It's cool, rainy.

She'll go and buy a book from that second-hand shop.

Then she'll go to see Daniel.

It takes a fragment of a fragment of a second for Elisabeth's data to go into the computer. Then the receptionist gives her back her scanned ID.

Daniel is asleep. A care assistant, a different one today, is swishing round the room with a mop that smells of pine cleaner.

Elisabeth wonders what's going to happen to all the care assistants. She realizes she hasn't so far encountered a single care assistant here who isn't from somewhere else in the world. That morning on the radio she'd heard a spokesperson say, *but it's not just that we've been rhetorically and practically encouraging the opposite of integration for* <u>*immigrants*</u> *to this country. It's that we've been rhetorically and practically encouraging* <u>*ourselves*</u> *not to integrate. We've been doing this as a matter of self-policing since Thatcher taught us to be selfish and not just to think but to believe that there's no such thing as society.*

Then the other spokesperson in the dialogue said, *well, you would say that. Get over it. Grow up. Your time's over. Democracy. You lost.*

It is like democracy is a bottle someone can threaten to smash and do a bit of damage with. It has become a time of people saying stuff to each other and none of it actually ever becoming dialogue.

It is the end of dialogue.

She tries to think when exactly it changed, how long it's been like this without her noticing.

She sits down next to Daniel. Sleeping Socrates.

How are you doing today, Mr Gluck? she says quietly down by his sleeping ear.

She gets her new/old book out and opens it at its beginning: *My purpose is to tell of bodies which have been transformed into shapes of a different kind. You heavenly powers, since you were responsible for those changes, as for all else, look favourably on my attempts, and spin an unbroken thread of verse, from the earliest beginnings of the world, down to my own times.*

Today Daniel looks like a child, but one with a very old head.

As she watches him sleep she thinks about Anna Pavlova, not the dancer, the scammer, who registered a NatWest bank account at Elisabeth's address.

What kind of scammer names herself – assuming it's a her – after a ballet dancer? Did she really think people working at NatWest wouldn't question someone using the name Anna Pavlova? Or are accounts all set up by machine now and machines don't know how to quantify that stuff?

Then again, what does Elisabeth know? It's possible that it's not that unusual a name. Maybe there are a million and one Anna Pavlovas right now in the world. Maybe Pavlova is the Russian equivalent of Smith.

A cultured scammer. A sensitive scammer. A prima ballerina light on her feet brilliantly expressive prodigiously talented legendary scammer. A sleeping beauty dying swan kind of a scammer.

She remembers her mother believing at some point, way back in the beginning, that Daniel, because he was so thin, so Puck-like and lithe – so much so that even in his eighties he was better at getting up the ladder into their loft space than her mother, then in her forties, was – had once been a ballet dancer, was perhaps a famous dancer grown old.

Which would you choose? Daniel had said once. Should I please her and tell her she's guessed right, and that I'm a recently retired Rambert? Or should I tell her the more mundane truth?

Definitely tell her the lie, Elisabeth said.

But think what will happen if I do, Daniel said.

It'll be brilliant, Elisabeth said. It'll be really funny.

I'll tell you what will happen, Daniel said. This. You and I will know I've lied, but your mother won't. You and I will know something that your mother doesn't. That will make us feel different towards not just your mother, but each other. A wedge will come between us all. You will stop trusting me, and quite right, because I'd be a liar. We'll all be lessened by the lie. So. Do you still choose the ballet? Or will I tell the sorrier truth?

I want the lie, Elisabeth said. She knows loads of things I don't. I want to know some things she doesn't.

The power of the lie, Daniel said. Always seductive to the powerless. But how is my being a retired dancer going to help in any real way with your feelings of powerlessness?

Were you a dancer? Elisabeth said.

That's my secret, Daniel said. I'll never divulge. Not to any human being. Not for any money.

It was a Tuesday in March in 1998. Elisabeth was thirteen. She was out for a walk in the newly light early evening with Daniel, even though her mother had told her she wasn't to.

They walked past the shops, then over to the fields where the inter-school summer sports were held, where the fair went and the circus. Elisabeth had last come to the field just after the circus had left, especially to look at the flat dry place where the circus had had its tent. She liked doing melancholy things like that. But now you couldn't tell that any of these summer things had ever happened. There was just empty field. The sports tracks had faded and gone. The flattened grass, the places that had turned to mud where the crowds had wandered round between the rides and the open-sided trailers full of the driving and shooting games, the ghost circus ring: nothing but grass.

Somehow this wasn't the same as melancholy. It was something else, about how melancholy and nostalgia weren't relevant in the slightest. Things just happened. Then they were over. Time just passed. Partly it felt unpleasant, to think like that, rude even. Partly it felt good. It was kind of a relief.

Past the field there was another field. Then there was the river.

Isn't it a bit too far, to walk as far as the river? Elisabeth said.

She didn't want him to have to go so far if he really was as ancient as her mother kept saying.

Not for me, Daniel said. A mere bagatelle.

A what? Elisabeth said.

A trifle, Daniel said. Not *that* kind of trifle. A mere nothing. Something trifling.

What will we do all the way there and back? Elisabeth said.

We'll play Bagatelle, Daniel said.

Is Bagatelle really a game? Elisabeth said. Or did you just make it up right now on the spot?

I admit, it's a very new game to me too, Daniel said. Want to play?

Depends, Elisabeth said.

How we play is: I tell you the first line of a story, Daniel said.

Okay, Elisabeth said.

116

Then you tell me the story that comes into your head when you hear that first line, Daniel said.

Like, a story that already exists? Elisabeth said. Like Goldilocks and the three bears?

Those poor bears, Daniel said. That bad wicked rude vandal of a girl. Going into their house uninvited and unannounced. Breaking their furniture. Eating their supplies. Spraying her name with spraypaint on the walls of their bedrooms.

She does not spray her name on their walls, Elisabeth said. That's not in the story.

Who says? Daniel said.

The story is from really long ago, probably way before spraypaint existed, Elisabeth said.

Who says? Daniel said. Who says the story isn't happening right now?

I do, Elisabeth said.

Well, you're going to lose at Bagatelle, then, Daniel said, because the whole point of Bagatelle is that you trifle with the stories that people think are set in stone. And no, not *that* kind of trifle –

I know, Elisabeth said. Jeez. Don't demean me.

Demean you? Daniel said. Moi? Now. What kind of story do you want to trifle with? You can choose.

They'd come to a bench at the side of the river; both the fields were far behind them. It was the first time Elisabeth had ever crossed the fields without it seeming like it took a long time.

What's the available choice? Elisabeth said.

Can be anything, Daniel said.

Like truth or lies? That kind of choice?

A bit oppositional, but yes, if you choose, Daniel said.

Can I choose between war and peace? Elisabeth said.

(There was war on the news every day. There were sieges, pictures of bags that had bodies in them. Elisabeth had looked up in the dictionary the word massacre to check what it literally meant. It meant to kill a lot of people with especial violence and cruelty.)

Lucky for you, you've got some choice in the matter, Daniel said.

I choose war, Elisabeth said.

Sure you want war? Daniel said.

Is *sure you want war* the first line of the story? Elisabeth said.

It can be, Daniel said. If that's what you choose.

Who are the characters? Elisabeth said.

You make one up and I'll make one up, Daniel said.

A man with a gun, Elisabeth said.

Okay, Daniel said. And I choose a person who's come in disguise as a tree.

A what? Elisabeth said. No way. You're supposed to say something like another man with another gun.

Why am I? Daniel said.

Because it's war, Elisabeth said.

I have some input into this story too, and I choose a person who's wearing a tree costume, Daniel said.

Why? Elisabeth said.

Ingenuity, Daniel said.

Ingenuity won't win your character this game, Elisabeth said. My character's got a gun.

That's not all you've got and it's not your only responsibility here, Daniel said. You've also got a person with the ability to resemble a tree.

Bullets are faster and stronger than tree costumes and will rip through and obliterate tree costumes, Elisabeth said.

Is that the kind of world you're going to make up? Daniel said.

There is no point in making up a world, Elisabeth said, when there's already a real world. There's just the world, and there's the truth about the world.

You mean, there's the truth, and there's the made-up version of it that we get told about the world, Daniel said.

No. The *world* exists. *Stories* are made up, Elisabeth said.

But no less true for that, Daniel said.

That's ultra-crazy talk, Elisabeth said.

And whoever makes up the story makes up the world, Daniel said. So always try to welcome people into the home of your story. That's my suggestion.

How does making things up welcome people? Elisabeth said.

What I'm suggesting, Daniel said, is, if you're telling a story, always give your characters the same benefit of the doubt you'd welcome when it comes to yourself.

Like being on benefits? Like unemployment benefit? Elisabeth said.

The necessary benefit of the doubt, Daniel said. And always give them a choice – even those characters like a person with nothing but a tree costume between him or her and a man with a gun. By which I mean characters who seem to have no choice at all. Always give them a home.

Why should I? Elisabeth said. You didn't give Goldilocks a home.

Did I stop her for one moment from going into that house with her spraypaint can? Daniel said.

That's because you couldn't, Elisabeth said, because it was already a part of the story that that's what she does every time the story's told – she goes into the bears' house. She has to. Otherwise there's no story. Is there? Except the part with the spraypaint can. The bit just made up by you.

Is my spraypaint can any more made up than the rest of the story? Daniel said.

Yes, Elisabeth said.

Then she thought about it.

Oh! she said. I mean, no.

And if I'm the storyteller I can tell it any way I like, Daniel said. So, it follows. If *you* are –

So how do we ever know what's true? Elisabeth said.

Now you're talking, Daniel said.

And what if, right, Elisabeth said, what if Goldilocks was doing what she was doing because she had no choice? What if she was like seriously upset that the porridge was too hot, and that's what made her go ultra-crazy with the spraypaint can? What if cold porridge always made her feel really upset about something in her past? What if something that had happened in her life had been really terrible and the porridge reminded her of it, and that's why she was so upset that she broke the chair and unmade all the beds?

Or what if she was just a vandal? Daniel said, who went into places and defaced them for no reason other than that's what I, the person in charge of the story, have decided that all Goldilockses are like?

I personally shall be giving her the benefits of the doubt, Elisabeth said.

Now you're ready, Daniel said.

Ready for what? Elisabeth said.

Ready to bagatelle it as it is, Daniel said.

Time-lapse of a million billion flowers opening their heads, of a million billion flowers bowing, closing their heads again, of a million billion new flowers opening instead, of a million billion buds becoming leaves then the leaves falling off and rotting into earth, of a million billion twigs splitting into a million billion brand new buds.

Elisabeth, sitting in Daniel's room in The Maltings Care Providers plc just short of twenty years later, doesn't remember anything of that day or that walk or the dialogue described in that last section. But here, preserved, is the story Daniel actually told, rescued whole from the place in human brain cell storage which keeps intact but filed away the dimensionality of everything we ever experience (including the milder air that March evening, the smell of the new season in the air, the traffic noise in the distance and everything else her senses and her cognition comprehended of the time, the place, her presence in both).

There's no way I can be bothered to think up a story with the tree costume thing in it, Elisabeth said. Because nobody in their right minds could make that story any good.

Is this a challenge to my right mind? Daniel said.

Indubitably, Elisabeth said.

Well then, Daniel said. My right mind will meet your challenge.

Sure you want war? the person dressed as a tree said.

The person dressed as a tree was standing with its branches up in the air like someone with his or her hands up. A man with a gun was pointing the gun at the person dressed as a tree.

Are you threatening me? the man with the gun said.

No, the person dressed as a tree said. You're the one with the gun.

I'm a peaceable person, the man with the gun said. I don't want trouble. That's why I carry this gun. And it's not like I have anything against people like you generally.

What do you mean, people like me? the person dressed as a tree said.

What I said. People dressed in stupid pantomime tree costumes, the man with the gun said.

But why? the person dressed as a tree said.

Think what it'd be like if everyone started wearing tree costumes, the man with the gun said. It'd be like living in a wood. And we don't live in a wood. This town's been a town since long before I was born. If it was good enough for my parents, and my grandparents and my great grandparents.

What about your own costume? the person dressed as a tree said.

(The man with the gun was wearing jeans, a T-shirt and a baseball cap.)

This isn't a costume, the man said. These are my clothes.

Well, these are *my* clothes. But I'm not calling your clothes stupid, the person dressed as a tree said.

Yeah, because you wouldn't dare, the man with the gun said.

He waved his gun.

And anyway, yours *are* stupid clothes, he said. Normal people don't go around wearing tree costumes. At least, they don't round here. God knows what they do in other cities and towns, well, that's up to them. But if you got your way you'd be dressing our kids up as trees, dressing our women up as trees. It's got to be nipped in the bud.

The man with the gun raised it and pointed it. The person dressed as a tree braced him or her self inside the thick cotton. The little grassblades painted round the bottom of the costume shivered round the painted roots. The man looked down the sights of his gun. Then he lowered the gun away from his eyes. He laughed.

See, the funny thing is, he said, it just came into my head that in war films, when they're going to execute someone, they stand them up against trees or posts. So shooting you is a bit like not shooting anyone at all.

He put the gun to his eye. He aimed at the trunk of the tree, at roughly where he guessed the heart of the person inside the costume was.

So. That's me done, Daniel said.

You can't stop there! Elisabeth said. Mr Gluck!

Can't I? Daniel said.

Elisabeth sits in the anodyne room next to Daniel, holding the book open, reading about metamorphoses. Round them, invisible, splayed out across the universe, are all the shot-dead pantomime characters. The Dame is dead. The Ugly Sisters are dead. Cinderella and the Fairy Godmother and Aladdin and the cat with the boots and Dick Whittington, mown down, a panto corncrop, panto massacre, a comedy tragedy, dead, dead, dead.

Only the person dressed as a tree is still standing.

But just as the man with the gun is finally about to shoot, the person dressed as a tree transforms before the gunman's eyes into a real tree, a giant tree, a magnificent golden ash tree towering high above waving its mesmerizing leaves.

No matter how hard the man with the gun shoots at this tree he can't kill it with bullets.

So he kicks its thick trunk. He decides he'll go and buy weedkiller to pour on its roots, or matches and petrol, to burn it down. He turns to go – and that's when he gets kicked in the head by the half of the pantomime horse it's slipped his mind to shoot.

He falls to the ground, dead himself on top of the pantomime fallen. It's a surrealist vision of hell.

What's surrealist, Mr Gluck?

This is. There they lie. The rain falls. The wind blows. The seasons pass and the gun rusts and the brightly coloured costumes dull and rot and the leaves from all the trees round about fall on them, heap over them, cover them, and grass grows round them then starts growing out of them, through them, through ribs and eyeholes, then flowers appear in the grass, and when the costumes and the perishable parts have all rotted away or been eaten clean by creatures happy to have the sustenance, there's nothing left of them, the pantomime innocents or the man with the gun, but bones in grass, bones in flowers, the leafy branches of the ash tree above them. Which is what, in the end, is left of us all, whether we carry a gun while we're here or we don't. So. While we're here. I mean, while we're still here.

Daniel sat on the bench with his eyes closed for a moment. The moment got longer. It became less of a moment, more of a while.

Mr Gluck, Elisabeth said. Mr Gluck?

She jogged his elbow.

Ah. Yes. I was, I was – What was I?

You said the words, while we're here, Elisabeth said. You said it twice. While we're here. Then you stopped speaking.

Did I? Daniel said. While we're here. Well. While we're here, let's just always hold out hope for the person who says it.

Says what, Mr Gluck? Elisabeth said.

Sure you want war? Daniel said.

Elisabeth's mother is much cheerier this week,
thank God. This is because she has received an
email telling her she has been selected to appear on
a TV programme called The Golden Gavel, where
members of the public pit their wits against
celebrities and antiques experts by trawling round
antiques shops on a fixed budget and trying to buy
the thing which in the end will raise the most
money at auction. It's as if the Angel Gabriel has
appeared at the door of her mother's life, kneeled
down, bowed his head and told her: in a shop full
of junk, somewhere among all the thousands and
thousands of abandoned, broken, outdated,
tarnished, sold-on, long-gone and forgotten things,
there is something of much greater worth than
anyone realizes, and the person we have chosen to

trust to unearth it from the dross of time and history is you.

Elisabeth sits at the kitchen table while her mother plays her an old episode of The Golden Gavel to show her what they expect. Meanwhile she thinks about her trip here, most of all about the Spanish couple in the taxi queue at the station.

They'd clearly just arrived here on holiday, their luggage round their feet. The people behind them in the queue shouted at them. What they shouted at them was to go home.

This isn't Europe, they shouted. Go back to Europe.

The people standing in front of the Spanish people in the taxi queue were nice; they tried to defuse it by letting the Spanish people take the next taxi. All the same Elisabeth sensed that what was happening in that one passing incident was a fraction of something volcanic.

This is what shame feels like, she thinks.

Meanwhile on the screen it's still late spring and the junk from the past is worth money. There is a great deal of driving about in old cars from earlier decades. There is a lot of stopping and worrying at the side of the road about the smoke coming out of the bonnets of the old cars.

Elisabeth tries to think of something to say to her mother about The Golden Gavel.

I wonder which make of vintage car you'll get to go in, she says.

No, because the members of the public don't get to, her mother says. It's only the celebrities and experts who get to do that. *They* arrive. *We're* already there at the shop waiting to meet them.

Why don't you get to go in a car? Elisabeth says. That's outrageous.

No point in devoting airtime to people who nobody knows from Adam driving about the place in old cars, her mother says.

Elisabeth notices how truly beautiful the cow parsley is at the sides of the backroads in the footage of The Golden Gavel, which is playing on catch-up, from an episode set in Oxfordshire and Gloucestershire, filmed, her mother tells her, last year. The cow parsley holds itself stately and poisonous in the air while the celebrities (Elisabeth has no idea who they are or why they're celebrities) maunder about. One sings pop songs from the 1970s and talks about when he owned a gold-painted Datsun. The other chats chummily about her days as an extra in Oliver! The vintage cars fume along through England; outside the car windows the passing cow parsley is tall, beaded with rain, strong, green. It is incidental. This incidentality is, Elisabeth finds herself thinking, a profound statement. The cow parsley has a language of its own, one that nobody on the programme or making the programme knows or notices is being spoken.

Elisabeth gets her phone out and makes a note. Maybe there's a lecture in this.

Then she remembers that probably pretty soon she won't have any job to give any lecture in anyway.

She puts her phone down on its lit front on the table. She thinks about the students she taught who graduate this week to all that debt, and now to a future in the past.

The cars on the TV programme draw up outside a warehouse in the countryside. There's a lot of getting out of the cars. At the door of the warehouse the celebrities and the experts meet the two ordinary people, who are wearing matching tracksuits to show that they're the ordinary people. Everyone shakes hands. Then they all set off, the celebrities, the experts and the ordinaries, in different directions round the warehouse.

One of the ordinary members of the public purchases an old till, or what the shop owner calls a vintage cash register, for £30. It doesn't work but its bright white and red buttons bristling off the curved chest of it remind her, the ordinary person says, of the regimental coat her grandfather wore when he was a cinema doorman in the 1960s. Cut to a celebrity who's spotted a cluster of charity boxes in the shapes of little life-sized figures – dogs and children – standing together at the door of the warehouse like a bunch of model villagers from the past, or from a sci-fi vision where past and future crash together. They're the boxes that used to sit outside shops for passers-by to put change into as they left or went into the shops. There is a bright pink girl with a teddybear; a dowdy looking boy mostly painted brown and holding what looks like an old sock; a bright red girl with the words thank-you carved into her chest and a brace on her leg; a spaniel with two puppies, their glass eyes pleading, little boxes round their necks, coin slots in the boxes, alternative coin slots in their heads.

An expert gets really excited. She explains to the camera that the brown clothed boy charity box, a Dr Barnardo's boy, is the most vintage of the set. She points out that the typography on the base the boy is standing on is pre-1960s, and that the little verse written on that base – Please Give, So He May Live – is itself a relic from a different time. Then she gives the camera a nod and a wink and tells it that if it were her she'd go for the spaniel regardless, because things in the shapes of dogs always do well at auction, and the brown clothed boy, though it has vintage status, is less likely to do as well as it ought to, unless the auction is an online one.

What they're not saying, her mother says, and maybe they're not saying it because they don't know it, is that those boxes came about because of real dogs back at the turn of the last century who worked going round places like railway stations with boxes hung round their necks for people to put pennies into. For charity.

Ah, Elisabeth says.

Those dog boxes, like that one there, were modelled on the real live creatures, her mother says. And furthermore. After the real live creatures died they would sometimes be stuffed by taxidermists and then placed back in the station or wherever, whichever public place they'd spent their working lives in. So you'd go to the station and there'd be Nip sitting there, or Rex, or Bob, dead, stuffed, but still with the box round his neck. And that, I'm certain, is where those dog-shaped charity boxes came from.

Elisabeth is faintly perturbed. She realizes this is because she likes to imagine her mother knows nothing much about anything.

Meanwhile the contestants on the screen spill out of the door excited about a set of mugs with Abraham Lincoln's Fiscal Policy printed on their sides. Outside the warehouse, in the green wastelands round about, there's a butterfly on the screen behind the heads of the presenters, small white waverer going from flowerhead to flowerhead.

And in astonishingly good nick, a celebrity is saying.

Hornsea, 1974, her mother says. Collector's dream.

Mid-70s, Yorkshire, the expert who's bought them says. Good clear Hornsea mark from the

American Presidents series on the base, the eagle mark. Hornsea started in 1949 after the war, went into receivership fifteen years ago, thriving in the 70s. Above all it's unusual to see seven of these together like this. A collector's dream.

See? her mother says.

Yes, but you've seen this episode already. So it's no big deal you knowing where they come from, Elisabeth says.

I know that. I meant I'm *learning*, her mother says. I meant I now *know* that that's what they are.

And I'd say that's the lot I'd be most worried about at auction, the first expert says in voiceover while the programme shows pictures of the chipped old charity boxes, one of the ordinary people rocking the red girl with the brace on her leg from side to side to see if there's any money still inside it.

I can't watch any more of this, Elisabeth says.

Why not? her mother says.

I mean I've seen enough, Elisabeth says. I've seen plenty. Thank you. It's very very exciting that you'll be on it.

Then her mother takes the laptop back to show Elisabeth one of the celebrities she'll be on the programme with.

Up comes a photograph of a woman in her sixties. Her mother waves the laptop in the air.

Look! she says. It's amazing, isn't it?

I have absolutely no idea who that is, Elisabeth says.

It's *Johnnie*! her mother says. From *Call Box Kids*!

The woman in her sixties was apparently a person on TV when Elisabeth's mother was a child.

I actually can't believe it, her mother is saying. I can't believe that I'm going to get to meet Johnnie. If only your grandmother was alive. If only I could tell her. If only I could tell my ten year old self. My ten year old self'd die with the excitement. Not just to get to meet. To get to be on a programme. With Johnnie.

Her mother turns the laptop towards her with a YouTube page up.

See? she says.

A girl of about fourteen in a checked shirt and with her hair in a ponytail is dancing a routine in a TV studio made to look like a London street, and the dancer she's dancing with is dressed as a phonebox, so that it literally looks like a public phonebox is dancing with the girl. The phonebox is rather rigid, as dancers go, and the girl has made herself rigid too and is doing steps to match the phonebox's. The girl is bright, warm, likeable, and the dancer inside the phonebox costume is making a pretty good attempt at dancing like a phonebox might. The street stops its business and everybody watches the dance. Then out of the open door of the box comes the receiver, up on its flex like a charmed snake, and the girl takes it, puts it to her head and the dance ends when she says the word: hello?

I actually remember seeing this very episode, Elisabeth's mother says. In our front room. When I was small.

Gosh, Elisabeth says.

Her mother watches it again. Elisabeth skims the day's paper on her phone to catch up on the usual huge changes there've been in the last half hour. She clicks on an article headed Look Into My Eyes: Leave. EU Campaign Consulted TV Hypnotist. She scrolls down and skims the screen. *The Power To Influence. I Can Make You Happy. Hypnotic Gastric Band. Helped produce social media ads. Are you concerned? Are you worried? Isn't it time? Being engrossed in TV broadcasts equally hypnotic. Facts don't work. Connect with people emotionally. Trump.* Her mother starts the forty years ago dance routine up one more time; the jaunty music begins again.

Elisabeth switches her phone off and goes through to the hall to get her coat.

I'm off out for a bit, she says.

Her mother, still in front of the screen, nods and waves without looking. Her eyes are bright with what are probably tears.

But it's a lovely day.

Elisabeth walks through the village, wondering if

those children-shaped charity boxes, since the dogs were modelled on real dogs, were also modelled on real beggars, small ones, child-beggars with callipers, boxes hung round their necks. Then she wonders if there was ever a plan afoot to taxiderm real children and stand them in stations.

As she passes the house with GO and HOME still written across it she sees that underneath this someone has added, in varying bright colours, WE ARE ALREADY HOME THANK YOU and painted a tree next to it and a row of bright red flowers underneath it. There are flowers, lots of real ones, in cellophane and paper, on the pavement outside the house, so it looks a bit like an accident has recently happened there.

She takes a photograph of the painted tree and flowers. Then she walks out of the village across the football pitch and out into the fields, thinking about the cow parsley, the painted flowers. The painting by Pauline Boty comes into her head, the one called With Love to Jean-Paul Belmondo. Maybe there's something in it whether she's got a job or not, something about the use of colour as language, the natural use of colour alongside the aesthetic use, the wild joyful brightness painted on the front of that house in a dire time, alongside the action of a painting like that one by Boty, in which a two-dimensional self is crowned with sensual colour, surrounded by orange and green and red so pure it's like they've come straight out of the tube on to the canvas, and not just by colour but by notional petals, the deep genital looking rose formation all over the hat on the head of the image of Belmondo as if to press him richly under at the same time as raise him richly up.

The cow parsley. The painted flowers. Boty's sheer unadulterated reds in the re-image-ing of the image. Put it together and what have you got? Anything useful?

She stops to make a note on her phone: *abandon and presence*, she writes.

It's the first time she's felt like herself for quite some time.

calm meets energy /
artifice meets natural /
electric energy /
natural livewire /

She looks up. She sees she's only yards from the fence across the common, the other kind of livewire.

The fence has doubled since she last saw it. Unless her eyes are deceiving her, it's now not just one fence but two in parallel.

It's true. Beyond the first layer of fence, about ten feet away from it, with a neat-flattened space in between the two fences, is another identical chainlink fence topped with the same foully frivolous looking razorwire. This other fence is electric-clipped too, and as she walks alongside them both the experience of the diamond-shaped wirework flashing next to her eyes is a bit epileptic.

Elisabeth takes a phone photo of it. Then she takes one or two images of the weed-life reappearing already through the churned-up mud round one of the metal posts.

She looks around. The weed and flower comeback is everywhere.

She follows the fenceline for half a mile or so before a black SUV truck rolling along in the flat space between the layers of fence catches up with her. It passes her and pulls up in front of her. The engine stops. When she draws level with the truck its window slides down. A man leans out. She nods a hello.

Fine day, she says.

You can't walk here, he says.

Yes I can, she says.

She nods to him again and smiles. She keeps walking. She hears the truck start up again behind her. When it draws level the driver keeps the engine dawdling, drives at the same pace as her walking. He leans out of the window.

This is private land, he says.

No it isn't, she says. It's common land. Common land is by definition not private.

She stops. The truck overshoots her. The man puts it into reverse.

Go back to the road, he calls out of the window as he reverses. Where's your car? You need to go back to where you left your car.

I can't do that, Elisabeth says.

Why not? the driver says.

I don't have a car, Elisabeth says.

She starts walking again. The driver revs his engine and drives beyond her. Several yards ahead of her he stops, cuts the engine and opens the truck door. He is standing beside the truck as she comes towards him.

You're in direct contravention, he says.

Of what? Elisabeth says. And whatever you say *I'm* in. Well. It looks from here like you're in prison.

He opens his top pocket and takes out a phone. He holds it up as if to take her picture or start filming her.

She points to the cameras on the fenceposts.

Don't you have enough footage of me already? she says.

Unless you leave the area immediately, he says, you'll be forcibly removed by security.

Are you *not* security, then? she says.

She points at the logo on the pocket he's taken the phone out of. It says SA4A.

And is that an approximation of the word *safer* or is it more like the word *sofa*? she says.

The SA4A man starts typing something on his phone.

This is your third warning, he says. You are now being warned for the last time that action will be taken against you unless you vacate the area immediately. You are unlawfully trespassing.

As opposed to lawfully trespassing? she says.

– still anywhere near the perimeter the next time I pass here –

Perimeter of what? she says.

She looks through at the fenced-off landscape and all she can see is landscape. There are no people. There are no buildings. There is just fence, then landscape.

– lead to legal charges being implemented against you, the man is saying, and may involve you being forcibly detained and your personal information and a sample of your DNA being taken and retained.

Prison for trees. Prison for gorse, for flies, for cabbage whites, for small blues. Oystercatcher detention centre.

What are the fences actually for? she says. Or aren't you allowed to tell me?

The man dead-eyes her. He keys something into his phone, then holds it up to get an image of her. She smiles in a friendly way, like you do when you're having your photo taken. Then she turns and starts walking again along the fenceline. She hears him phone somebody and say something, then get into his SUV and reverse it between the fences. She hears it head off in the opposite direction.

The nettles say nothing. The seeds at the tops of the grass stems say nothing. The little white flowers on the tops of their stalks, she doesn't know what they are but they're saying their fresh nothing.

The buttercups say it merrily. The gorse says it unexpectedly, a bright yellow nothing, smooth and soft and delicate against the mute green nothing of its barbs.

Back then at school a boy was hellbent on making Elisabeth, who was sixteen at this point, laugh. (He was hellbent on just making her, too, ha ha.) He was pretty cool. She liked him. His name was Mark Joseph and he played bass in a band that did anarchic cover versions of old stuff from back at the beginning of the 90s; he was also a computer genius who was ahead of everybody else, and this was back when most people still didn't know what a search engine was and everyone believed that the millennial new year would crash all the world's computers, about which Mark Joseph made a funny spoof and put it online, a photo of a veterinary surgery up the road from the school, caption underneath saying Click Here for Protection Against Millennium Pug.

Now he was following her about in school and trying to find ways of making her laugh.

He kissed her, at the school back gate. It
was nice.

Why don't you love me? he said three weeks later.

I'm already in love, Elisabeth said. It isn't possible
to be in love with more than one person.

A girl at college called Marielle Simi and
Elisabeth, when Elisabeth was eighteen, rolled about
on the floor of Elisabeth's hall of residence room
high on dope and laughing at the funny things that
backing singers sometimes sing in songs. Marielle
Simi played her an old song where the backing
singers have to sing the word onomatopoeia eight
times. Elisabeth played Marielle Simi a Cliff
Richard song in which the backing singers have to
sing the word sheep. They cried with laughter, then
Marielle Simi, who was French, put her arm round
Elisabeth and kissed her. It was nice.

Why? she said, months later. I don't get it. I don't
understand. It's so good.

I just can't lie, Elisabeth said. I love the sex. I love
being with you. It's great. But I have to be truthful.
I can't lie about it.

Who is he? Marielle Simi said. An ex? Is he still
around? Are you still seeing him? Or is it a her? Is it
a woman? Have you been seeing her or him the
whole time you've been seeing me?

It isn't that kind of relationship, Elisabeth said. It
isn't even the least bit physical. It never has been.
But it's love. I can't pretend it isn't.

146

You are using this as denial, Marielle Simi said. You're putting it between yourself and your real feelings so that you don't have to feel.

Elisabeth shrugged.

I feel plenty, she said.

Elisabeth, who was twenty one, met Tom MacFarlane at her graduation. She was graduating in history of art (morning), he was business studies (afternoon). Tom and Elisabeth had been together for six years. He'd moved into her rented flat for five so far of those years. They were thinking of making their relationship permanent. They were talking marriage, mortgage.

One morning when he was putting breakfast things out on the kitchen table Tom asked out of nowhere,

who's Daniel?

Daniel? Elisabeth said.

Daniel, Tom said again.

Do you mean Mr Gluck? she said.

I've no idea, Tom said. Who's Mr Gluck?

Old neighbour of my mother's, Elisabeth said. He lived next door when I was a kid. I haven't seen him for years. Literally years. Ages. Why? Has something happened? Did my mother phone? Has something happened to Daniel?

You said his name in your sleep, Tom said.

Did I? When? Elisabeth said.

Last night. It's not the first time. You quite often say it in your sleep, Tom said.

Elisabeth was fourteen. She and Daniel were walking where the canal met the countryside, where the path peels away and goes off up through to the woods on the curve of the hill. It was suddenly freezing though it was only quite early in autumn. The rain was coming, she could see it when they got to the top of the hill, it was moving across the landscape like someone was shading in the sky with a pencil.

Daniel was out of breath. He didn't usually get this out of breath.

I don't like it when the summer goes and the autumn comes, she said.

Daniel took her by the shoulders and turned her round. He didn't say anything. But all across the landscape down behind them it was still sunlit blue and green.

She looked up at him showing her how the summer was still there.

Nobody spoke like Daniel.

Nobody didn't speak like Daniel.

It was the end of a winter; this one was the winter of 2002–3. Elisabeth was eighteen. It was February. She had gone down to London to march in the protest. Not In Her Name. All across the country people had done the same thing and millions more people had all across the world.

On the Monday after, she wandered through the city; strange to be walking streets where life was going on as normal, traffic and people going their usual backwards and forwards along streets that had had no traffic, had felt like they'd belonged to the two million people from their feet on the pavement all the way up to sky because of something to do with truth, when she'd walked the exact same route only the day before yesterday.

That was the Monday she unearthed an old red hardback catalogue in an art shop on Charing

Cross Road. It was cheap, £3. It was in the reduced books bin.

It was of an exhibition a few years ago. Pauline Boty, 1960s Pop Art painter.

Pauline who?

A female British Pop Art painter?

Really?

This was interesting to Elisabeth, who'd been studying art history as one of her subjects at college and had been having an argument with her tutor, who'd told her that categorically there had never been such a thing as a female British Pop artist, not one of any worth, which is why there were none recorded as more than footnotes in British Pop Art history.

The artist had made collages, paintings, stained glass work and stage sets. She had had quite a life story. She'd not just been a painter, she'd also done theatre and TV work as an actress, had chaperoned Bob Dylan round London before anyone'd heard of Bob Dylan, had been on the radio telling listeners what it was like to be a young woman in the world right then and had nearly been cast in a film in a role that Julie Christie got instead.

She'd had everything ahead of her in swinging London, and then she'd died, at the age of twenty eight, of cancer. She'd gone to the doctor because she was pregnant and they'd spotted the cancer. She'd refused an abortion, which meant she couldn't have radiotherapy; it would hurt the child. She'd given birth and she'd died four months after.

Malignant thymoma is what it said in the list of things under the word Chronology at the back of the catalogue.

It was a sad story, and nothing like the paintings, which were so witty and joyous and full of unexpected colour and juxtapositions that Elisabeth, flicking through the catalogue, realized that she was smiling. The painter's last painting had been of a huge and beautiful female arse, nothing else, framed by a jovial proscenium arch like it was filling the whole stage of a theatre. Underneath, in bright red, was a word in huge and rambunctious looking capitals.

BUM.

Elisabeth laughed out loud.

What a way to go.

The artist's paintings were full of images of people of the time, Elvis, Marilyn, people from politics. There was a photograph of a now-missing painting with the famous image of the woman who caused the Scandal scandal, whose sitting nude and backwards on a designer chair had had something to do with politics at the time.

Then Elisabeth held the catalogue open at a page with a particular painting on it.

It was called Untitled (Sunflower Woman) c.1963.

It was of a woman on a bright blue background.

Her body was a collage of painted images. A man with a machine gun pointing at the person looking at the picture formed her chest. A factory formed her arm and shoulder.

A sunflower filled her torso.

An exploding airship made her crotch.

An owl.

Mountains.

Coloured zigzags.

At the back of the book was a black and white reproduction of a collage. It had a large hand holding a small hand, which was holding the large hand back.

Down at the bottom of the picture there were two ships in a sea and a small boat filled with people.

Elisabeth went to the British Library periodicals room and sat at a table with Vogue, September 1964. *FEATURES 9 Spotlight 92 Paola, paragon of princesses 110 Living doll: Pauline Boty interviewed by Nell Dunn 120 Girls in their married bliss, by Edna O'Brien.* Alongside adverts for the bright red Young Jaeger look-again coat, the Goya Golden Girl Beauty Puff and the bandeau bra and pantie girdle cut like briefs to leave you feeling free all over, was: *Pauline Boty, blonde, brilliant, 26. She has been married for a year and her husband is inordinately proud of her achievements, boasts that she makes a lot of money painting and acting. She has found by experience that she is in a world where female emancipation is a password and not a fact – she is beautiful, therefore she should not be clever.*

The full-page photo, by David Bailey, was a large close-up of Boty's face with a tiny doll's face, the other way up, just behind her.

P.B. *I find that I have a fantasy image. It's that I really like making other people happy, which is probably egotistical, because they think 'What a lovely girl', you know. But it's also that I don't want people to touch me. I don't mean physically particularly, though it's that as well. So I always like to feel that I'm sort of floating by and just occasionally being there, seeing them. I'm very inclined to play a role that someone sets for me, particularly when I first meet people. One of the reasons I married Clive was because he really did accept me as a human being, a person with a mind.*

N.D. *Men think of you just as a pretty girl you mean?*

P.B. *No. They just find it embarrassing when you start talking. Lots of women are intellectually more clever than lots of men. But it's difficult for men to accept the idea.*

N.D. *If you start talking about ideas they just think you're putting it on?*

P.B. Not that you're putting it on. They just find it slightly embarrassing that you're not doing the right thing.

Elisabeth photocopied the pages in the magazine. She took the Pauline Boty exhibition catalogue to college and put it on her tutor's desk.

Oh, right. Boty, the tutor said.

He shook his head.

Tragic story, he said.

Then he said, they're pretty dismissible. Poor paintings. Not very good. She was quite Julie Christie. Very striking girl. There's a film of her, Ken Russell, and she's a bit eccentric in it if I remember rightly, dresses in a top hat, miming along to Shirley Temple, I mean attractive and so on, but pretty execrable.

Where can I find that film? Elisabeth said.

I've absolutely no idea, the tutor said. She was gorgeous. But not a painter of anything more than minor interest. She stole everything of any note in her work from Warhol and Blake.

What about the way she uses images as images? Elisabeth said.

Oh God, everybody and his dog was doing that then, the tutor said.

What about everybody and *her* dog? Elisabeth said.

I'm sorry? the tutor said.

What about this? Elisabeth said.

She opened the catalogue at a page with two paintings reproduced side by side.

One was of a painting of images of ancient and modern men. Above, there was a blue sky with a US airforce plane in it. Below, there was a smudged colour depiction of the shooting of Kennedy in the car in Dallas, between black and white images of Lenin and Einstein. Above the head of the dying president were a matador, a deep red rose, some smiling men in suits, a couple of the Beatles.

The other picture was of a fleshy strip of images superimposed over a blue/green English landscape vista, complete with a little Palladian structure. Inside the superimposed strip were several images of part-naked women in lush and coquettish porn magazine poses. But at the centre of these coy poses was something unadulterated, pure and blatant, a woman's naked body full-frontal, cut off at the head and the knees.

The tutor shook his head.

I'm not seeing anything new here, he said.

He cleared his throat.

There are lots and lots of highly sexualized images throughout Pop Art, he said.

What about the titles? Elisabeth said.

(The titles of the paintings were It's a Man's World I and It's a Man's World II.)

The tutor had gone a ruddy red colour at the face.

Is there, was there, anything else like this being painted by a woman at the time? Elisabeth said.

The tutor shut the catalogue. He cleared his throat again.

Why should we imagine that gender matters here? the tutor said.

That's actually my question too, Elisabeth said. In fact, I came to see you today to change my dissertation title. I'd like to work on the representation of representation in Pauline Boty's work.

You can't, the tutor said.

Why can't I? Elisabeth said.

There's not nearly enough material available on Pauline Boty, the tutor said.

I think there is, Elisabeth said.

There's next to no critical material, he said.

That's one of the reasons I think it'd be a particularly good thing to do, Elisabeth said.

I'm your dissertation supervisor, the tutor said, and I'm telling you, there isn't, and it isn't. You're going off down a rarefied cul-de-sac here. Do I make myself clear?

Then I'd like to apply to be moved to a new supervisor, Elisabeth said. Do I do that with you, or do I go to the Admin office?

A year on from then, Elisabeth went home for the

Easter holidays. It was when her mother was thinking of moving, maybe to the coast. Elisabeth listened to the options and looked at the house details her mother had been sent by estate agents in Norfolk and Suffolk.

After the right amount of time talking about houses had passed, Elisabeth asked after Daniel.

Won't have any help in the house, her mother said. Won't have meals on wheels. Won't let anyone make him a cup of anything or do his washing or change his old bed. The house smells pretty strong, but if anyone goes round there offering anything, offering to help out, he makes you sit down, then makes you a cup of tea himself, won't hear of anyone even doing that for him. Ninety if he's a day. He's not up to it. I had to fish a dead beetle out of the last cup of tea he made me.

I'll just nip round and see him, Elisabeth said.

Oh, hello, Daniel said. Come in. What you reading?

Elisabeth waited for him to make her the cup of tea. Then she got the exhibition catalogue she'd found in London out of her bag and put it on the table.

When I was small, Mr Gluck, she said, I don't know if you remember, but when we went on walks you sometimes described paintings to me, and the thing is, I think I've finally managed to see some of them.

Daniel put his glasses on. He opened the catalogue. He flushed, then he went pale.

Oh yes, he said.

He leafed through the pages. His face lit up. He nodded. He shook his head.

Aren't they fine? he said.

I think they're really brilliant, Elisabeth said. Really outstanding. Also really thematically and technically interesting.

Daniel turned a picture towards her, blue and red abstracts, blacks and golds and pinks in circles and curves.

I remember this one very clearly, he said.

I wondered, Mr Gluck, Elisabeth said. Because of our conversations, and you knowing them so well, the pictures. I mean they've been missing for decades. They've just been rediscovered, really. And no one in the art world knows about them, except, from what I can gather, from people who knew her in person. I went and asked about her at the gallery where they showed these pictures, like seven or eight years back, and I met this woman who knew someone who used to know Boty a bit, and she told me that the woman she knows still sometimes just finds herself in floods of tears, even nearly forty years later, whenever she remembers her friend. So, I was wondering. It struck me. That maybe you knew Boty too.

Well well, he said. Look at that.

158

He was still looking at the blue abstract called Gershwin.

I never knew till now she called it that, he said.

And when you look at the photos of her, Elisabeth said. And she was so incredibly beautiful. And what happened to her in her life is so sad, and then the sad things that happened after her own sad death, to her husband, and then to her daughter, just tragedy after tragedy, so unbearably sad that –

Daniel put one hand up to tell her to stop, then the other, both hands up and flat.

Silence.

He went back to the book on the table between them. He turned the page to the one with the woman made of flames, and the bright yellow abstract opposite it, reds, pinks, blues and whites.

Look at that, he said.

He nodded.

They truly are something, he said.

He turned all the pages, one after the other. Then he shut the book and put it back on the table. He looked up at Elisabeth.

There have been very many men and women in my life whom I hoped might, whom I wanted to, love me, he said. But I only, myself, ever, loved, in that way, just once. And it wasn't a person I fell in love with. No, not a person at all.

He tapped the cover of the book.

It is possible, he said, to be in love not with

someone but with their eyes. I mean, with how eyes that aren't yours let you see where you are, who you are.

Elisabeth nodded as if she understood.

Not a person.

Yes, and the 60s zeitgeist, she said, is –

Daniel, his hand up, stopped her again.

We have to hope, Daniel was saying, that the people who love us and who know us a little bit will in the end have seen us truly. In the end, not much else matters.

But a coldness was shifting all through her body, wiping her into a clarity much like a soapy window by a window cleaner from top to base with a rubber blade.

He nodded, more to the room than to Elisabeth.

It's the only responsibility memory has, he said. But, of course, memory and responsibility are strangers. They're foreign to each other. Memory always goes its own way quite regardless.

Elisabeth will have looked like she was listening, but inside her head there was the high-pitched hiss, the blood going round inside her making itself heard above any and every other thing.

Not a person.
Daniel does not –
Daniel has never –
Daniel has never known –

She drank the tea. She excused herself. She left the book on the table.

He came hobbling after her into the hall holding it out to her as she was unsnibbing the front door.

I left it on purpose, for you, she said. I thought you might like it. I won't need it. I've handed in my dissertation.

He shook his old head.

You keep it, he said.

She heard the door shutting behind her.

It was one of the days of a week in one of the seasons in one of the years, maybe 1949, maybe 1950, 1951, in any case sometime around then.

Christine Keeler, who'd be famous just over a decade later, being one of the witting/unwitting agents of the huge changes in the class and sexual mores of the 1960s, was a small girl out playing down by the river with some of the boys.

They unearthed a metal thing. It will have been round at one end and pointed at the other.

A small bomb will have been about as big as their upper bodies. They knew it was a bomb. So they decided they'd take it home to show to the father of one of the boys. He'd presumably been in the army. He'd know what to do with it.

It was mucky from being buried so they cleaned it up maybe, with wet grass and jumper sleeves, first. Then they took turns carrying it back to their street. A couple of times they dropped it. When they did they ran away like crazy in case it went off.

They got it to the boy's house. The boy's father came out to see what all the kids outside the house wanted.

Oh dear God.

The RAF came. They got everybody out of the houses all up and down the street, then everybody out of the houses in all the streets around the street.

Next day those kids got their names in the local paper.

That story comes from one of the books she wrote about her life. Here's another. When she wasn't yet ten years old, Christine Keeler was sent to live in a convent for a while. One of the bedtime stories the nuns told all the little girls there was about a little boy called Rastus.

Rastus is in love with a little white girl. But the little white girl gets ill, and it looks like she's going to die. Someone tells Rastus that she'll be dead by the time the leaves have fallen off the tree at the front of her house. So Rastus collects up all the shoelaces he can find. Maybe he also unravels his jumper and cuts the unravelled wool into pieces. He's going to need a lot of pieces. He climbs the tree outside the girl's house. He ties the leaves on to the branches.

But one night a really wild wind blows all the leaves off the tree.

(Forty years before Christine Keeler was born, but presumably at a time when a lot of those nuns who apparently told stories like this one to the little girls in their care were growing up or were young adults, Rastus was a name popular in blackface minstrel shows. It became a character-name, a racist shorthand for someone black, in early films, in turn of the century fiction, across all the forms of early media entertainment.

In the States, from the start of the century till the mid-20s, a black figure named Rastus was used to advertise Cream of Wheat breakfast cereal. He wore a chef's hat and jacket in all the photographs of him and in one particular illustration an old and white-bearded black man with a stick stops to look at a picture of Rastus on a poster advertising *Cream of Wheat For Your Breakfast* and the caption underneath reads: *'Ah reckon as how he's de bes' known man in de worl.'*

In the mid-20s, Cream of Wheat replaced the character-name Rastus with the character-name Frank L White, though the illustrations on the posters and in the adverts stayed much the same. Frank L White was a real man whose facial image, in a photograph taken around 1900 when he was a chef in Chicago, became Cream of Wheat's standard advertising image. It's not recorded anywhere whether White was ever paid for the use of his image.

He died in 1938.

It took another seventy years for his grave to be officially marked with a stone.

Back to Christine Keeler.)

There's another story she tells about herself in the couple of books written by her and her ghostwriters.

This one is from another time in her childhood. It's about the day she found a fieldmouse. She brought it home as a pet.

The man she called Dad killed it. He did this by standing on it, presumably as she watched.

Same as all the other times, Daniel is sleeping.

To the people here he is maybe just another shape in a bed they keep serviceably clean. They are still rehydrating him, though they've let Elisabeth know they'll want to talk to her mother about whether to cease rehydrating or not.

I want you, my mother and I both completely want you, especially my mother does, to keep rehydrating him, Elisabeth said when they asked.

The Maltings Care Providers plc are very keen to have a conference with her mother, the receptionist tells her when she arrives.

I'll tell her, Elisabeth says. She'll be in touch.

The receptionist says they'd like to flag up as gently as possible with her mother their concern that payment provision for the accommodation and care package for Mr Gluck at The Maltings

Care Providers plc is shortly going to fall into default.

We'll definitely be in touch about it really really soon, Elisabeth says.

The receptionist goes back to her iPad, on which she's paused a crime serial on catch-up. Elisabeth watches the screen for a moment or two. A woman dressed as a policewoman is being run over by a young man in a car. He runs over her on the road, then he does it again. Then he does it again.

Elisabeth goes to Daniel's room and sits down at the side of the bed.

They are definitely still rehydrating him.

One of his hands has come out from under the covers and gone to his mouth. It has the rehydration needle taped into the back of it and the tube taped along the side of it. (A thin taut string breaks in Elisabeth's chest at seeing the tape and the needle.) Daniel touches, still deep in the sleep, his top lip, but lightly, brushingly, like someone would if he were clearing away breadcrumbs or croissant crumbs. It's as if he's feeling, in the least conspicuous way, to test or to make sure he still has a mouth, or that his fingers can still feel. Then the hand disappears back down inside the covers.

Elisabeth sneaks a look at the chart clipped on to the end of Daniel's bed, the graphs with the temperature and blood pressure readings on them.

The chart says on its first page that Daniel is a hundred and one years old.

Elisabeth laughs to herself.

(Her mother: *How old are you, Mr Gluck?*

Daniel: *Nowhere near as old as I intend to be, Mrs Demand.*)

Today he looks like a Roman senator, his sleeping head noble, his eyes shut and blank as a statue, his eyebrows mere moments of frost.

It is a privilege, to watch someone sleep, Elisabeth tells herself. It is a privilege to be able to witness someone both here and not here. To be included in someone's absence, it is an honour, and it asks quiet. It asks respect.

No. It is awful.

It is fucking awful.

It is awful to be on the literal other side of his eyes.

Mr Gluck, she says.

She says it quiet, confidential, down near his left ear.

Two things. I'm not sure what to do about the money they need you to pay here. I wonder if there's something you'd like me to do about it. And the other thing. They want to know about rehydrating you. Do you want to be rehydrated?

Do you need to go?

Do you want to stay?

Elisabeth stops speaking. She sits up again away from Daniel's sleeping head.

Daniel breathes in. Then he breathes out. Then, for a long time, there's no breath. Then it starts again.

One of the care assistants comes in. She starts wiping at the bedrail then the windowsill with cleaning stuff.

He's quite some gentleman, she says with her back to Elisabeth.

She turns round.

What did he do in his good long life? After the war, I mean.

Elisabeth realizes she has no idea.

He wrote songs, she says. And he helped out a lot with my childhood. When I was little.

We were all amazed, the care assistant says, when he told us about in the war, when they interned them. Him being English really but going in there with his old father the German, even though he could have stayed outside if he'd chosen. And how he tried to get his sister over, but they said no.

In-breath.

Out-breath.

Long pause.

Did he tell you that? Elisabeth says.

The care assistant hums a tune. She wipes the doorhandle, then the edges of the door. She takes a long stick made of white plastic with a white cotton rectangle on the end of it and she wipes the top of the door and round the lampshade.

He's never talked about any of that, not to us, Elisabeth says.

Family for you, the care assistant says. Easier to talk to someone you don't know. He and I had many a chat, before he went off. One day he said a very fair thing. When the state is not kind, he said. We were talking about the vote, it was coming up, I've thought about it a lot, since. Then the people are fodder, he said. Wise man, your grandad. Clever man.

The care assistant smiles at her.

It's a lovely thing you do, coming to read to him. A thoughtful thing.

The care assistant wheels her little trolley out. Elisabeth watches her broad back as she goes, and the way the material of her overall stretches tight across it and under her arms.

I know nothing, nothing really, about anyone.

Maybe nobody does.

In-breath.

Out-breath.

Long pause.

She closes her eyes. Dark.

She opens her eyes again.

She opens her book at random. She starts to read, from where she's opened it, but this time out loud, to Daniel: *His sisters, the nymphs of the spring, mourned for him, and cut off their hair in tribute to their brother. The wood nymphs* mourned him too, and Echo sang her refrain to their lament.

The pyre, the tossing torches, and the bier, were now being prepared, but his body was nowhere to be found. Instead of his corpse, they discovered a flower with a circle of white petals round a yellow centre.

I'm thirteen years old in that one, her mother was saying. Seaside holiday. We went every year. That's my mother. My father.

The next door neighbour was in their front room.

It was just after Elisabeth had told him she had a sister. Now she was worried the neighbour would give the game away and ask her mother where the other daughter was.

So far he hadn't said anything about it.

He was looking at the family photographs of her mother on the wall in the front room.

Now those, he was saying, are completely fantastic.

Her mother hadn't just made coffee, she'd made it in the good mugs.

Forgive me, Mrs Demand, the neighbour said. I mean, the photos are lovely. But the tin signs. The real thing.

173

The what, Mr Gluck? her mother said.

She put the mugs on the table and came over to have a look.

Call me Daniel, please, the neighbour said.

He pointed at the picture.

Oh, her mother said. Those. Yes.

There were hoardings advertising ice lollies in one of the old photographs, behind her mother as a child. This was what they were talking about.

6d, her mother said. I was still a very small child when decimalization came in. But I remember the heavy pennies. The half crowns.

She was speaking in a slightly too loud way. The neighbour, Daniel, didn't seem to notice or mind.

Look at that wedge of dark pink on the bright pink, Daniel said. Look at the blue, the way the shadow deepens there where the colour changes.

Yes, her mother said. Zoom. Fab.

Daniel sat down beside the cat.

What's her name? he said to Elisabeth.

Barbra, Elisabeth said. After the singer.

The singer her mother loves, her mother said.

Daniel winked at Elisabeth and said, but quietly, down towards her like it was a secret so her mother, who'd gone to the CD shelf now and was going through the CDs, wouldn't hear, as if he didn't want her to know,

after the singer who once, believe it or not, sang a song I wrote the words for, in concert. I was very handsomely paid. But she never recorded it. I'd be a trillionaire, had she. Rich enough to time-travel.

Can you sing? Elisabeth said.

Not at all, Daniel said.

Would you actually *like* to time-travel? she said. If you could, I mean, and time travel was a real thing?

Very much indeed, Daniel said.

Why? Elisabeth said.

Time travel *is* real, Daniel said. We do it all the time. Moment to moment, minute to minute.

He opened his eyes wide at Elisabeth. Then he put his hand in his pocket, took out a twenty pence piece, held it in front of Barbra the cat. He did something with his other hand and the coin disappeared! He made it disappear!

The song about love being an easy chair filled the room. Barbra the cat was still looking in disbelief at Daniel's empty hand. She put both paws up, held the hand, put her nose into it to look for the missing coin. Her cat face was full of amazement.

See how it's deep in our animal nature, Daniel said. Not to see what's happening right in front of our eyes.

October's a blink of the eye. The apples weighing down the tree a minute ago are gone and the tree's leaves are yellow and thinning. A frost has snapped millions of trees all across the country into brightness. The ones that aren't evergreen are a combination of beautiful and tawdry, red orange gold the leaves, then brown, and down.

The days are unexpectedly mild. It doesn't feel that far from summer, not really, if it weren't for the underbite of the day, the lacy creep of the dark and the damp at its edges, the plants calm in the folding themselves away, the beads of the condensation on the webstrings hung between things.

On the warm days it feels wrong, so many leaves falling.

But the nights are cool to cold.

177

The spiders in the sheds and the houses are guarding their egg sacs in the roof corners.

The eggs for the coming year's butterflies are tucked on the undersides of the grassblades, dotting the dead looking stalks on the wasteland, camouflaged invisible on the scrubby looking bushes and twigs.

3

Here's an old story so new that it's still in the middle of happening, writing itself right now with no knowledge of where or how it'll end. An old man is sleeping in a bed in a care facility on his back with his head pillow-propped. His heart is beating and his blood's going round his body, he's breathing in then out, he is asleep and awake and he's nothing but a torn leaf scrap on the surface of a running brook, green veins and leaf-stuff, water and current, Daniel Gluck taking leaf of his senses at last, his tongue a broad green leaf, leaves growing through the sockets of his eyes, leaves thrustling (very good word for it) out of his ears, leaves tendrilling down through the caves of his nostrils and out and round till he's swathed in foliage, leafskin, relief.

And here he is now, sitting next to his little sister!

But his little sister's name escapes him for the moment. This is surprising. It's one of the words he's held dear his whole life. Never mind. Here she is next to him. He turns his head and she's there. It's unbearably lovely to see her! She's sitting next to the painter, the one that turned him copiously down, well, that's life, he can even smell the scent the painter wore, Oh! de London, bright, sweet, woody, when he first knew her, then she got older and more serious and it was Rive Gauche, he can smell it too.

They're both, his sister and the painter, ignoring him. Nothing new there. They're conversing with a man he doesn't recognize, young, long hair, earnest looking, wearing old clothes from the past or maybe from a heaped-up pile of old costumes below a stage in a theatre; the man straightens a wide cuff at his wrist, he is speaking about how he likes a stubble field *better than the chilly green of the spring*, he says. His sister and the painter are agreeing with him and Daniel finds himself becoming a bit jealous, *stubble-plain looks warm*, the young man turns to the painter, *in the same way some pictures look warm*, the painter nods, *without my eyes*, she says, bright and glittering the pieces of her voice, *I don't exist*.

He tries to get his little sister's attention.

He nudges her elbow.

She ignores him.

But there's something he's been waiting to say to his little sister, he's wanted to for more than sixty years, since he thought it, and every time he's thought it again since, he's wished she were alive even just for half a minute. How interesting she'll find it. (He wants her to be impressed, too, that he's thought it at all.) Kandinsky, he says. Paul Klee, I'm sure. They're making the first pictures ever made of it. A whole new landscape painting. They're picturing the view from the inside of the eye, but precisely when the migraine is happening to it!

His little sister is prone to migraines.

I mean, all the bright yellow, the pink and black triangles pulsating along the curves and the lines.

His little sister sighs.

Now he is sitting on the windowsill of her room. She is twelve. He's seventeen, much older than she is. So why does he feel so junior? His little sister is brilliant. She is at her desk deep in a book, half-opened books all over her desk, all over the floor and the bed. She likes to read, she reads all the time, and she prefers to be reading several things at once, she says it gives endless perspective and dimension. They've been at each other's throats all summer long. He and his father are off back tomorrow, school, England, where he also doesn't quite belong. He is trying to be nice. She is ignoring him. The nicer he is, the more she despises him. This being despised by her is new. Last year and all the years before it he was her hero. Last year she still liked it when he told the jokes, made the coins vanish. This year she rolls her eyes. The city, old as it is, is also somehow new and strange. Nothing's different, but everything is. It's scented by the same old trees. It is summer-jovial. But this year its joviality is a kind of open threat.

Yesterday she caught him in tears in his room. She opened the door. He ordered her away. She didn't go. She stood in the doorway instead. What's wrong? she said. Are you scared? He told her no. He told her a blatant lie. He told her he had been thinking about Mozart and how young and broken he'd been when he died, and how light the music, and that this had moved him to tears. I see, she said in the doorway. She knew perfectly well he was lying. Not that Mozart isn't capable of making him cry, and often does, with the high sweet notes which feel, though he'd never say such an unsayable out loud thing to anyone, let alone his little sister, like tiny orgasms. But truly? It wasn't what was making him cry right then. Come on, summer brother (it's what she's taken to calling him, like he's not always her brother, he's just her brother in the summer), she said drumming her fingers on the wood of the door panelling. That's nothing to cry about.

Today she looks up from the desk and feigns surprise that he's still here.

I'm just going, he says.

But he stays sitting there on the windowsill.

Well, if you're going to sit there emanating such melancholy, she says, can you make yourself more useful? Instead of sick?

Sick? he says.

Transit gloria mundi, she says. Ha ha.

She is unbearable. He hates her.

Don't just sit there like an unstrung puppet, she says. Be here. Do something. Tell me something.

Tell you what? he says.

I don't know, she says. I don't care. Anything. Tell me what you're reading.

Oh, I'm reading so many things, he says.

She knows he's reading nothing. She's the one who reads, not him.

Tell me something from one of the many things you're reading, she says.

She is trying to humiliate him, first for feeling, second for not reading like she does.

But there's a story they were made to read, school, French lessons. That'll do.

I've actually been reading, he says, the world-renowned story of the ancient old man who happens to be in possession of a magic goatskin. But being so old, nearly as old as legend itself, he's going to die soon –

Because human beings can't be legends, being mortal, she says.

Uh huh, he says.

She laughs.

And he wants to pass on the magic goatskin to someone else, he says.

Why does he? she says.

His mind goes blank. He has no idea why.

So the magic won't get wasted, he says. So, uh, so that –

Where did he get the magic goatskin in the first place? she says.

He has no idea. He wasn't really listening in the class.

Was there once a magic goat? she says. On the ledges of a cliff? One that could jump any height and any angle and still land on its delicate little hoofs? Or did it have to be skinned and then the skin became magic *after* the sacrifice, because of the sacrifice?

She doesn't even know the story and she's made up a better one than the one he's trying to remember.

Well? she says.

The magic goatskin, he says, was, well, it was the cover on one of the ancient old man's oldest most powerful books of magic, and therefore had been saturated in magic for hundreds and hundreds of years. So he removed the skin from it precisely, in fact, so that he could pass it on.

Why doesn't he *therefore* pass on *precisely in fact* the whole book? his little sister says.

She's turned at her desk towards him, her face half mockery, half affection.

I don't know, he says. All I know is that he decided to pass it on. So he, uh, finds a young man to pass it on to.

Why a young man? his little sister says. Why doesn't he choose a young woman?

Look, he says. I'm just telling you what I read. And the old man said to the young man, here. Have this magic goatskin. Treat it with respect. It is very very powerful. What you do to get it to work is, you put your hand on it, and you make a wish. And then your wish comes true. But what he didn't tell the young man was that every time you wish on the magic goatskin, the magic goatskin gets smaller, it shrinks in size, in a small way or a big way, depending on how small or how vast the wish you wish on it is. And so the young man wished, and his wish came true, and he did it again and his wish came true. And he went through his life full of good fortune wishing on the magic goatskin. But the day came when the magic goatskin had shrunk so small it was smaller than the palm of his hand. So he wished for it to be bigger, and when he did it grew bigger, bigger, bigger, every bit as big as the world, and when it reached the size of the world it disappeared, thin air.

His little sister rolls her eyes.

And that's when the young man, now a slightly

older man, though not as old, I don't think, as the original ancient old man, died, he says.

His little sister sighs.

Is that it? she says.

Well, there's other bits of it that I haven't remembered, he says. But yes, that's the gist of it.

Fine, she says.

She comes over to the window and kisses him on the cheek.

Thank you very much for telling me the story of the magic foreskin, she says.

He doesn't hear what she's said until a moment after she's said it. When he does he blushes to the roots of his hair. His whole body blushes. She sees him redden and she smiles.

Because I'm not meant to say that word, am I? she says. Even though that's what the story's really about. Even though hundreds of years of disguise are meant to keep me away from what the world's stories are really all about. Well, foreskin. Foreskin foreskin foreskin.

She dances round the room shouting the word he could hardly say in her presence out loud himself.

She is mad.

But she is uncannily right about that story.

She is brilliant.

She is a whole new level of the word true.

She is dangerous and shining.

She comes over to the window and pushes it

wider. She shouts into the street, into the sky (in English, though, thank God), *foreskins come and foreskins go! But Mozart lasts forever!* Then she skips back over to her seat at the desk, picks up the book she is reading and starts back into the middle of it again like nothing has happened.

He waits a moment then glances out and down to the street. A lady with a little dog has stopped and is standing there looking up, hand shielding her eyes; apart from that the street continues as ever, with no idea that his little sister is *that* mad, *that* brave, *that* clever, *that* wild and *that* calm, and that he now knows for sure that when she grows up she's going to be a great force in the world, an important thinker, a changer of things, someone to be reckoned with.

Summer brother.

Old man in a bed in a care facility.

Little sister.

Never more than twenty, twenty one.

There are no pictures left of her. The photos at their mother's house? long burnt, lost, gone, street litter.

But he has some pages, still, of the letters from when she was nursing their mother. She is eighteen. The clever forward-slope of her.

It's a question of how we regard our situations, dearest Dani, how we look and see where we are, and how we choose, if we can, when we are seeing

undeceivedly, not to despair and, at the same time,
how best to act. Hope is exactly that, that's all it is,
a matter of how we deal with the negative acts
towards human beings by other human beings in
the world, remembering that they and we are all
human, that nothing human is alien to us, the foul
and the fair, and that most important of all we're
here for a mere blink of the eyes, that's all. But in
that Augenblick there's either a benign wink or a
willing blindness, and we have to know we're
equally capable of both, and to be ready to be
above and beyond the foul even when we're up to
our eyes in it. So it's important – and here I
acknowledge directly the kind and charming and
mournful soul of my dear brother whom I know
so well – not to waste the time, our time, when
we have it.

Dearest Dani.

What has he done with the time?

A few trivial rhymes.

There was nothing else for it, really.

Plus, he ate well, when the rhymes brought in the money.

Autumn mellow. Autumn yellow. He can remember every word of that stupid song. But he can't remember,

dear God, he can't.

Excuse me, dear God, can I trouble you to remind me of my little sister's name?

Not that he thinks there's a God. In fact he knows there isn't. But just in case there's such a thing:

Please, remind me, her name, again.

Sorry, the silence says. Can't help you.

Who's that?

(Silence.)

Who's there?

(Silence.)

God?

Not exactly.

Well, who?

Where do I start? I'm the butterfly antenna. I'm the chemicals that paint's made of. I'm the person dead at the water's edge. I'm the water. I'm the edge. I'm skin cells. I'm the smell of disinfectant. I'm that thing they rub against your mouth to moisten it, can you feel it? I'm soft. I'm hard. I'm glass. I'm sand. I'm a yellow plastic bottle. I'm all the plastics in the seas and in the guts of all the fishes. I'm the fishes. I'm the seas. I'm the molluscs in the seas. I'm the flattened-out old beer can. I'm the shopping trolley in the canal. I'm the note on the stave, the bird on the line. I'm the stave. I'm the line. I'm spiders. I'm seeds. I'm water. I'm heat. I'm the cotton of the sheet. I'm the tube that's in your side. I'm your urine in the tube. I'm your side. I'm your other side. I'm your other. I'm the coughing through the wall. I'm the cough. I'm the wall. I'm mucus. I'm the bronchial tubes. I'm inside. I'm outside. I'm traffic. I'm pollution. I'm a fall of horseshit on a country road a hundred years ago. I'm the surface of that road. I'm what's below. I'm what's above. I'm the fly. I'm the descendant of the fly. I'm the descendant of the descendant of the descendant of the descendant of the descendant of the descendant of the fly. I'm the circle. I'm the square. I'm all the shapes. I'm geometry. I haven't even started with the telling you what I am. I'm everything that makes everything. I'm everything that unmakes everything. I'm fire. I'm flood. I'm pestilence. I'm the ink, the paper, the grass, the tree, the leaves, the leaf, the greenness in the leaf. I'm the vein in the leaf. I'm the voice that tells no story.

(Snorts.) There's no such thing.

Begging your pardon. There is. It's me.

Leaf, did you say?

I did say leaf, yes.

You? the leaf?

Are you deaf? I'm the leaf.

Just one lone single leaf, are you?

No. To be more exact. As I've already said. As I've already made clear. I'm all the leaves.

You're all the leaves.

Yes.

So, have you fallen? Are you still waiting to fall? In the autumn? In the summer if it's stormy?

Well, by definition –

And by *all the leaves* you mean, you're last year's leaves?

I –

And next year's leaves?

Yes, I –

You're all the old long-gone leaves of all the years? And all the leaves to come?

Yes, yes. Obviously. Christ almighty. I'm the leaves. I'm all the leaves. Okay?

And the falling thing? Yes or no?

Of course. It's what leaves do.

Then you can't trick me, whoever you are. You don't fool me for a minute.

(Silence.)

There's always, there'll always be, more story. That's what story is.

(Silence.)

It's the never-ending leaf-fall.

(Silence.)

Isn't it? Aren't you?

(Silence.)

Now that the actual autumn isn't far off, it's better weather. Up to now it has been fly-fetid, heavy-clouded, cool and autumnal all summer, pretty much since the first time Elisabeth went to the Post Office to do the Check & Send thing with her passport form.

It's now that her new passport arrives in the post.

Her hair must have passed the test after all. The placing of her eyes must also have passed the test.

She shows the new passport to her mother. Her mother points to the words European Union at the top of the cover of the passport and makes a sad face. Then she flicks through it.

What are all these drawings? she says. This passport has been illustrated like a Ladybird book.

A Ladybird book on acid, Elisabeth says.

I don't want a new passport if it's going to look

like this, her mother says. And all these men, all through it. Where are all the women? Oh, here's one. Is that Gracie Fields? Architecture? But who on earth? and is that *it*? Is this woman wearing the funny hat the only woman in the whole thing? Oh no. Here's another one, but sort of folded-in at the centre of a page, like an afterthought. And here's another couple, on the same page as the Scottish pipers, both ethnic stereotype dancers. Performing arts. Well, that's Scotland and women *and* a brace of continents all well and truly in their place.

She hands it back to Elisabeth.

If I'd seen this ridiculous thing that passes for a passport before the referendum, she says, I'd have known to be ready well ahead of time for what was so clearly on its way.

Elisabeth tucks the new passport beside the mirror in the bedroom her mother's made for her at the back of the house. Then she pulls on her coat to go to the bus stop.

Don't forget, her mother shouts through. Supper. I need you here by six. Zoe's coming.

Zoe is the person who was a BBC child actor when her mother was small, whom her mother met filming the episode of The Golden Gavel two weeks ago and with whom her mother is now firm friends. Zoe has been invited over to watch the opening of the Scottish Parliament, which her mother saved on her TV box at the start of the month and has already insisted on showing to Elisabeth. Her mother, who'd seen it several times already herself, was in tears from the start, from when the man doing the voiceover mentioned the words carved on the mace.

Wisdom. Justice. Compassion. Integrity.

It's the word integrity, her mother said. It does it every time. I hear it and I see in my head the faces of the liars.

Elisabeth grimaced. Every morning she wakes up feeling cheated of something. The next thing she thinks about, when she does, is the number of people waking up feeling cheated of something all over the country, no matter what they voted.

Uh huh, she said.

I'm still looking at properties up there, her mother said. I'm not leaving the EU.

It is all right for her mother. Her mother has had her life.

Rule Britannia, a bunch of thugs had been sing-shouting in the street at the weekend past Elisabeth's flat. Britannia rules the waves. First we'll get the Poles. And then we'll get the Muslims. Then we'll get the gyppos, then the gays. *You lot are on the run and we're coming after you*, a right-wing spokesman had shouted at a female MP on a panel on Radio 4 earlier that same Saturday. The chair of the panel didn't berate, or comment on, or even acknowledge the threat the man had just made.

Instead, he gave the last word to the Tory MP on the panel, who used what was the final thirty seconds of the programme to talk about the *real and disturbing cause for concern* – not the blatant threat just made on the air by one person to another – of *immigration*. Elisabeth had been listening to the programme in the bath. She'd switched the radio off after it and wondered if she'd be able to listen to Radio 4 in any innocence ever again. Her ears had undergone a sea-change. Or the world had.

> *But doth suffer a sea-change*
> *Into something rich and –*

Rich and what? she thought.

Rich and poor.

She rubbed the condensation off the mirror, stood in the echo of herself just standing in a bathroom. She looked at her blurred reflection.

Hi, Elisabeth had said down the phone to her mother next morning. It's me. At least, I think it is.

I know exactly what you mean, her mother said.

Can I come and stay at yours for a bit? I want to get some work done and to be a bit closer to, uh, home.

Her mother laughed and told her she could have the back room for as long as she needed.

Meanwhile Zoe, the 1960s child star, was also coming, to have Scotland played to her.

Zoe and I bonded over a silver sovereign holder,

her mother'd told her. I don't know if you know what they are, do you? They look like little fob-watches when they're closed, I've seen one or two on the TV antiques markets. There was one on top of a cabinet and Zoe picked it up and opened it and said oh what a pity, someone's taken all the clockwork out of it. And I said no, it's probably a sovereign holder. And she said blimey, is that the size of sovereignty? Old money, after all? Might have known. The original £1 coin. Soon to be worth 60p. We both laughed so loud we spoiled a take in the next room.

I want you to meet her, her mother says again now. She's cheered me up no end.

I won't forget, Elisabeth says.

She forgets as soon as she's through the door.

Time and time again. Even in the increased sleep period, with his head on a pillow and his eyes closed, hardly here, he does it, what he's always been able to do.

Endlessly charming, Daniel. Charmed life. How does he do it?

She'd brought the chair from the corridor. She'd shut the door to the room. She'd opened the book she bought today. She'd started to read, from the beginning, quite quietly, out loud. *It was the best of times, it was the worst of times, it was the age of wisdom, it was the age of foolishness, it was the epoch of belief, it was the epoch of incredulity, it was the season of Light, it was the season of Darkness, it was the spring of hope, it was the winter of despair, we had everything before us, we had nothing before us.* The words had acted like a charm. They'd released it all, in seconds. They'd made everything happening stand just far enough away.

It was nothing less than magic.

Who needs a passport?

Who am I? Where am I? What am I?

I'm reading.

Daniel lies there asleep like a person in a fairytale. She holds the opened book at its beginning in her hands. She says nothing at all out loud.

There was a time, she says inside her head, when I was very small and my mother banned me from seeing you, and I did what she'd asked but only for three days. By the morning of the third day I knew for the first time that one day I would die. So I blatantly ignored her. I went against her instructions. There was nothing she could do about it. It was only three days, and I prided myself on your not noticing or knowing about it at the time.

But I want to apologize for not being here these last years. It's ten years, all in. I'm really sorry. There wasn't anything I could do about it. I was hopelessly hurt, about something stupid.

Of course, it's possible that you didn't notice that absence either.

Myself, I thought about you the whole time. Even when I wasn't thinking about you, I thought about you.

Silence from Elisabeth, except for the sound of her breathing.

Silence from Daniel, except for the sound of his.

Not long after this, she falls asleep on the upright chair with her head leaning against the wall. She sits in the whited-out place in her dream.

The whited-out place this time is her flat.

To be truthful, it isn't *her* flat and she knows this in the dream; she's got used to the idea now that she'll probably never be able to buy a house. It's no big deal, no one can these days except people who're loaded, or whose parents die, or whose parents are loaded. But never mind. She has a lease. She has a lease on a white-walled flat in a dream. She can hear the people next door's TV through the wall. It is one of the ways you know you've got neighbours.

Someone knocks at the door. It'll be Daniel.

But it isn't. It's a girl. She has a face as blank as a piece of paper, blank as a blank screen. Elisabeth begins to panic. A blank screen means the computer is failing and all the knowledge is disappearing. There'll be no way she'll be able to access her workfiles. There'll be no way of knowing what's going on in the world right now. There'll be no way of getting in contact with anyone. There'll be no way she'll be able to do anything ever again.

The girl ignores Elisabeth. She sits down in the doorway so that Elisabeth can't shut the door. She gets out a book. She must be Miranda, from The

Tempest. Miranda from The Tempest is reading Brave New World.

She looks up from her book as if she's just realized Elisabeth is there too.

I've come to bring you news of our father, she says.

Earlier today their father, according to the blank-faced girl, had gone to buy a new laptop.

A present for you, the girl (Elisabeth's sister) says. But then this happened.

Then Elisabeth sees, like she's watching a film, what happened next.

On the way to John Lewis a man (her father?) stops at the window of Cash Converters to look in and see if anything there is cheaper. A woman stops and looks in the window too. Are you looking at the laptops? she says. Yes, Elisabeth's father says. The thing is, the woman says, I'm about to go into that shop and sell them my new laptop, and as I say, it's brand new. I've got a new job in America and I now don't need this new laptop. But if you're looking to buy a laptop, I can sell it to you instead of to Cash Converters and at a very good price for a brand new laptop.

Elisabeth's father goes with the woman to a car park where she opens the boot of a car and unzips a holdall in the boot. She takes out a brand new laptop. Elisabeth, in the dream, can smell how new it is.

£600 cash, the woman says, does that sound fair? Yes, Elisabeth's father says. That sounds very fair. I'll go and get the money from a cash machine.

I'll come with you, the woman says putting the laptop back into the holdall and shutting the boot.

They go to a cash machine. He gets the money out. They go back to the car. He gives the woman the money. The woman opens the boot, takes the holdall out and hands it to him. She shuts the boot of the car and she drives away.

Then our father opened the bag, the girl with the blank face says. And there was nothing in that bag but onions. Onions and potatoes. Here.

She hands Elisabeth a holdall. Elisabeth opens it. It's full of potatoes and onions.

Thank you, Elisabeth says. Thank him for me.

She looks over to where the cooker should be. But there's nothing at all in the white-painted room.

Never mind, she thinks. When Daniel comes, he'll know a way of making something with these.

That's where she wakes up.

She remembers the dream for a fraction of a second, then she remembers where she is and she forgets the dream.

She stretches on the chair, her arms and shoulders, her legs.

So this is what sleeping with Daniel is like.

She smiles to herself.

(She's often wondered.)

It was a standard sort of Wednesday in April in 1996. Elisabeth was eleven. She was wearing new rollerblades. When you put your weight on them coloured lights lit up and flashed at the heels. You couldn't see this yourself unless it was dark outside and you put all the lights out in your bedroom or drew the blind and pressed down on them with your hands.

Daniel was at the front gate.

I'm going to the theatre, he said. The outdoor theatre. Want to come too?

He told her it was a play about civilization, colonization and imperialism.

It sounds a bit boring, she said.

Trust me, Daniel said.

So she went, and it wasn't boring, it was really good, about a father and a daughter. It was also about fairness and unfairness, and people getting hypnotized on an island and hatching plots against each other to see who could take control of the island, and some characters were meant to be the slaves and other characters got to be freed. But mostly it was about a girl whose father, a magician, was sorting out her future for her. In the end the daughter could have been in it a bit more than she was, but all the same it was still really good; in the end Elisabeth was nearly crying when the grown-old father stepped forward without his magic cloak and stick and asked the people in the audience to clap because if they didn't he'd be trapped forever in the play on the fake island with its cardboard scenery. If they hadn't, it was really very much as if he *might* still be stuck there in the open air theatre standing in the dark all night.

It was also quite exciting to be able, just by clapping your hands, to free someone from something.

She rollerbladed home in front of Daniel so Daniel would be able to see the lights light up.

When she was in bed that night she remembered her feet and the pavement passing so fast beneath them and thought how strange it was that she could remember totally useless details about things like cracks in a pavement more clearly than she could recall anything about her own father.

The next day at breakfast she said to her mother,

I couldn't sleep last night.

Oh dear, her mother said. Well, you'll sleep tonight instead.

I couldn't sleep for a reason, Elisabeth said.

Uh huh? her mother said.

Her mother was reading the paper.

I couldn't sleep, Elisabeth said, because I realized I can't remember a single thing about what my father's face looks like.

Well, you're lucky, her mother said from behind the paper.

She turned the page, folded it against another page, shook the paper into shape again and put it back up in the air between them.

Elisabeth strapped her rollerblades on, laced them up and went round to Daniel's house. Daniel was in the back garden. Elisabeth rollerbladed down the path.

Oh hello, Daniel said. It's you. What you reading?

I couldn't get to sleep last night, she said.

Wait, Daniel said. First of all, tell me. What are you reading?

Clockwork, she said. It's really good. I told you about it yesterday. The one about people making up the story but then the story becomes true and starts to happen and is really terrible.

I remember, Daniel said. They stop the bad thing happening by singing a song.

Yes, Elisabeth said.

If only life were so simple, Daniel said.

That's what I'm saying, Elisabeth said. I couldn't sleep.

Because of the book? Daniel said.

Elisabeth told him about the pavement, her feet, her father's face. Daniel looked grave. He sat down on the lawn. He patted the place on the grass next to him.

It's all right to forget, you know, he said. It's good to. In fact, we have to forget things sometimes. Forgetting it is important. We do it on purpose. It means we get a bit of a rest. Are you listening? We have to forget. Or we'd never sleep ever again.

Elisabeth was crying now like a much younger child cries. Crying came out of her like weather.

Daniel put his hand flat against her back.

What I do when it distresses me that there's something I can't remember, is. Are you listening?

Yes, Elisabeth said through the crying.

I imagine that whatever it is I've forgotten is folded close to me, like a sleeping bird.

What kind of bird? Elisabeth said.

A wild bird, Daniel said. Any kind. You'll know what kind when it happens. Then, what I do is, I just hold it there, without holding it too tight, and I let it sleep. And that's that.

Then he asked her if it was true that the

rollerskates with the lights on the backs of them only worked on roads, and if it was true that the lights in the backs of them didn't come on at all if you rollerskated on grass.

Elisabeth stopped crying.

They're called rollerblades, she said.

Rollerblades, Daniel said. Right. Well?

And you can't rollerblade on grass, she said.

Can't you? Daniel said. How very disappointing truth is sometimes. Can't we try?

There'd be no point, she said.

Can't we try anyway? he said. We might disprove the general consensus.

Okay, Elisabeth said.

She got up. She wiped her face on her sleeve.

Recalled to life, Elisabeth says. Hunger, want and nothing. The whole city's in a storm at sea and that's just the beginning. Savagery's coming. Heads are going to roll.

Elisabeth is in the hall hanging her coat up. Her mother has just introduced her to her new friend Zoe and asked Elisabeth how far through A Tale of Two Cities they are today.

Who's Mr Gluck? her mother's new friend Zoe says.

Mr Gluck is a jolly old gay man who used to be our neighbour years back, her mother says. She was very fond of him, he befriended her as a child. She was a difficult child. Pity me. A very difficult child to read.

No he isn't. Yes I was and still am. And no I wasn't. In that order, Elisabeth says.

See? her mother says.

I like a difficult read myself, Zoe says.

She smiles at Elisabeth with genuine friendliness. She is in her sixties maybe. She is handsome and unfussily stylish. She is now apparently a pretty well-known psychoanalyst. (Elisabeth had laughed when her mother told her this, at last you're seeing someone after all the years you've needed to, she'd said.) She bears a fleeting ghost of a resemblance to that girl dancing with the phonebox in the film back then; the girl-ghost is a technicolor shimmer somewhere still about her person. Her older self is warm, bright like an apple still high up in a tree after all the others have been picked. Meanwhile Elisabeth's mother is making an effort, wearing make-up and a set of brand new looking linen clothes like the ones they sell in the expensive shop in the village.

And you've kept in touch all these years, Zoe says.

We'd lost touch, actually, her mother says, till a neighbour tracked me down on the net and let me know he'd packed up his house, sold his old Barbara Hepworth piece of holy stone –

Maquette, Elisabeth says.

Oh my goodness, Zoe says. He's got taste.

– and signed himself into a care home, her mother says. And I happened to tell Elisabeth, who'd been out here to see me a total of, I kid you not, once, in a total of, I kid you not, six years, I told her on the phone, I said oh by the way, old

Mr Gluck. He's in this place called The Maltings apparently not far from here. And I kid you not. She's been here every week, all this summer. Twice, sometimes. And now she's living here for a while. Nice having a daughter again. So far, anyway.

Thanks, Elisabeth says.

And now I'm looking forward to a bit of fine-tuned attention myself in my later years, her mother says. All those books I've never read, Middlemarch, Moby-Dick, War and Peace. Not that I'll be able to do my later years quite like Mr Gluck has. He's a hundred and ten by now.

He's a what? Zoe says.

She always gets his age completely wrong. He's only a hundred and one, Elisabeth says.

Zoe shakes her head.

Only, she says. Blimey. Seventy five'll do. Anything after that, bonus. Well. I'm saying that now. Who knows what I'll say if I get to seventy five?

He used to set up a projector and a screen in his back garden on summer nights, her mother says, and show her old films, I'd look out the window, it'd be a starry night and they'd be sitting in a little box of light. That was back in the years when we still had summers. When we still had seasons, not just the monoseason we have now. And do you remember the time he threw his watch into the river –

Canal, Elisabeth says.

– and told you it was a time and motion study? her mother says.

What a fine friendship, Zoe says. And you go and see him every week? And read to him?

I love him, Elisabeth says.

Zoe nods.

Her mother rolls her eyes.

He's pretty much comatose, she says in a more hushed voice. I'm afraid. He won't.

He isn't comatose, Elisabeth says.

When she says it she feels the edge of anger on her own voice. She calms her voice down and speaks again.

He's just sleeping, she says, but for very long times. He's not comatose. He's resting. It'll have tired him out, packing up his house, all his things.

She sees her mother shake her head at her new friend.

Me, I'll be throwing it all away, Zoe says. Canal, river, wherever's nearest. Or giving it away. No point keeping any of it.

Elisabeth goes through to the sunroom and lies flat out on the sofa. She'd forgotten the film nights, Chaplin getting a job at the circus as an assistant then pressing by mistake the button he's been told not to press on the magician's table and the ducks and the doves and the piglets coming flying out of all the hidden compartments.

So I stood in the hall and phoned the number

every week, I was desperate, her mother is saying through in the kitchen, 01 811 8055, I still remember it off by heart, it meant I hardly ever saw the programme, I was always in the hall. But once I'd had the idea, I thought it was so funny, I thought I was the height of wit. So, every week. Then one week I actually got through. And the switchboard girl, they used to sit at the back of the studio and take the calls and write the swaps down, she came on the phone and she said the magic words Multi-Coloured Swap Shop, and I said it, I'm Wendy Parfitt and I'd like to swap my kingdom for a horse, and they put it up on the screen and showed it as one of their top ten swaps, Wendy Parfitt, OFFERS kingdom, WANTS horse.

I once met him, Noel, her friend says. Well, thirty seconds. Very exciting. In the staff canteen.

Our whole life, her mother is saying. My whole life, as a child. The night after our father's funeral, our mother – I suppose she didn't know what else to do – switching on the TV, and we all sat there, her too, watching The Waltons, as if it'd make things better, make everything be normal again.

All as mysterious to me, all as exciting, as comforting, as it was to you, her mother's friend is saying. Even though I was meant to be being such a part of it. And now all anyone wants to know is whether there was any abuse. Did anyone ever do anything they shouldn't have to us. The people who ask, they're *longing* to ask, not just that, they're longing to hear something bad, they want it to have gone wrong, they always seem disappointed when I say no, when I say that it was a great time, that I loved working, I loved above all being a working actress, I loved it too that I got given the most fantastic clothes, that I taught myself to smoke in the back of the car that picked me up for work and took me home from work – and if I say *that*, the thing about cigarettes, the eyebrows go up and it's like *that*'s an abuse of innocence, the urge I had to be my older self. The urge we all have to be older, to not be the child any more.

Elisabeth wakes up. She sits up.

It's getting dark outside.

She looks at her phone. It's near nine.

She can hear the low murmur of conversation across the hall. They've moved to the sitting room. They must have had supper without her.

They're talking about a particular room they went into in one of the shops on the Golden Gavel shoot. Her mother has told her about this room. It was huge, the room, her mother told her, with nothing in it but thousands of old sherry glasses piled inside each other.

Like entering what you think is going to be history and finding endless sad fragility, Zoe says. One kick. Disaster. Careful where you tread. And all the old dial-phones.

The ceramic dogs, her mother says.

The inkwells. (Zoe.)

The engraved silver matchboxes, Anchor and Lion hallmark, Birmingham, turn of the century. (Her mother.)

You're pretty good at that stuff. (Zoe.)

I watch a lot of TV. (Her mother.)

Got to get out more. (Zoe.)

The butter churn. (Her mother.) The wall-mounted coffee grinder. (Zoe.) The Poole pottery. The Clarice Cliff fakes. The tinplate Japanese robots. (Elisabeth can no longer tell now whose voice is whose.) The Pelham Puppets, remember them, still in their boxes. The clocks. The war medals. The engraved crystal. The nests of tables. The tiles. The decanters. The cabinets. The apprentice pieces. The plant-stands. The old books of photographs. The sheet music. The paintings. And paintings. And paintings.

All across the country all the things from the past stacked on the shelves in the shops and the barns and the warehouses, piled into display units and on top of display units, spilling up stairs from the cellars of the shops, down stairs from the attic rooms of the shops, like a huge national orchestra biding its time, the bows held just above the strings, all the fabrics muted, all the objects holding still and silent till the shops empty of people, till the alarms play their electronic beeps at the doors, till the keys turn in the locks in the thousands of shops and barns and warehouses all across the country.

Then, when darkness falls, the symphony. Oh. Oh, that's a beautiful idea. The symphony of the sold and the discarded. The symphony of all the lives that had these things in them once. The symphony of worth and worthlessness. The Clarice Cliff fakes would be flutey. The brown furniture would be bass, low. The photographs in the old damp-stained albums would be whispery through their tracing paper. The silver would be pure. The wickerwork would be reedy. The porcelains? They'd have voices that sound like they might break any minute. The wood things would be tenor. Yes, but would the real things sound any different from the reproduction things?

The women start to laugh.

Elisabeth can smell smoke.

No. She can smell dope.

She lies back down on the sofa and listens to them laughing about the number of times they spoiled the set-up of shots on their filming of The Golden Gavel by laughing in the wrong places or not saying the right thing. She gathers, from what they say, that there was quite a fuss caused by her mother's stubbornness, refusing to say the hello to the person who owned the antiques shop they were filming in as if they were just meeting for the first time, when truthfully they'd met an hour beforehand and she'd done the take already five times. *Hello again!* she said every time. *Cut!* the production team yelled.

I just couldn't do it, her mother says. It was so stupidly false. I was hopeless.

You were. And it gave me such hope, the new friend says.

Elisabeth smiles. That's nice.

She sits up. She goes through to the kitchen. The supper things are all still out on the table waiting to be cooked.

She goes through to the sitting room instead and the room is fuggy with dope. Her mother's new friend Zoe is sitting on the chaise longue and her mother is sitting in her new friend's lap. They've got their arms round each other like the famous Rodin statue, in the middle of the kiss.

Ah, Elisabeth says.

Zoe opens her eyes.

Uh-oh. Caught, she says.

Elisabeth watches her mother struggle to retain not just her composure but any balance at all on her new friend's knee.

She winks at her mother's new friend through the dope smoke.

She's been waiting for you since she was ten years old, Elisabeth says. I'll make supper, shall I?

It was a sunny Friday evening more than a decade ago, in the spring of 2004. Elisabeth was nearly twenty. She was staying in. She was watching Alfie, a film meant to have an appearance by Pauline Boty in it. The film starred Michael Caine as a philanderer. It had been a very groundbreaking film at the time because Caine as Alfie spoke so frankly, straight to camera, and about sexual adventuring.

Quite early on in the film Michael Caine walks along a bright sunny 1960s London street and knocks on the glass of a window saying Prompt Service Within, to get the attention of a young woman in the window.

It's her.

She turns, looks delighted and beckons him in. As he goes through the door he switches the open sign to closed and follows her to the back. Then he takes her in his arms and kisses her, and then slips behind the clothes-rack for a comedy quick one three seconds long with her.

It was definitely Pauline Boty.

It was filmed the year before she died.

Her name wasn't in the credits.

I was having a beautiful little life, and I couldn't see it, the Michael Caine voiceover said. *There was this manageress of a dry-cleaner's*. He went into the shop, behind the clothes with the girl, then a few moments later came out the other side saying, *and I was getting a suit cleaned in the bargain*.

According to what Elisabeth had read about her life, Boty was already pregnant in these shots.

She was wearing a bright blue top. Her hair was the colour of corn.

But you can't write that in a dissertation. You can't write, *she made it look like a blast*. You can't write, *she looked like she'd be really good fun, like she was full of energy*, or *energy comes off her in waves*. You can't write, even though it's a lot more like the language expected, *though she's in that film for less than twenty seconds she adds something crucial and crucially female about pleasure to its critique of the contemporary new and liberated ethos, which was indeed what she was also doing with her aesthetic*.

Blah.

Elisabeth opened the Boty catalogue again and

flicked through it. The wild bright colours came off the pages at her as she did.

She stopped on one of the long-lost pictures, the one of Christine Keeler on the chair. Keeler had slept with two men, one had been Secretary of State for War in the government in London, one had been a Russian diplomat, and it was about blatant lying in Parliament, then about who had most power and who owned information about nuclear weapons – except that it soon, ostensibly at least, became about something else altogether, about who owned Keeler, who farmed her out, and who did or didn't make money out of it.

The Boty picture, Scandal 63, had been missing since the year it was painted. There were only photographs of it. In the finished version, Boty had painted Keeler on her Danish chair surrounded by abstracts, though some of the abstracts looked more figurative: that, there on the left, arguably, was a tragedy mask; that down there was a woman having what looked like an orgasm. Above Keeler on the chair, on something resembling a dark balcony, Boty had painted, a bit like decapitated heads on a city wall, the heads and shoulders of four men, two black men and two white men. In an earlier version, which you could see half of in a picture with Boty herself in it, you got a sense of the size of the picture, big enough to come up quite far past Boty's waist. In this earlier version Boty didn't use the famous image of Keeler in the chair. She changed her mind for the later version, and did.

Elisabeth wrote in pencil on a page of her foolscap pad: *art like this examines and makes possible a reassessment of the outer appearances of things by transforming them into something other than themselves. An <u>image of an image</u> means the image can be seen with new objectivity, with liberation from the original.*

Dissertation blah.

She looked at the photograph of Boty standing beside Scandal 63. She took the book over to the window to see the photographs in what was left of the daylight.

No one knew who'd commissioned this painting.

No one knew where it was now, if it was still anywhere, if it still existed.

She looked again at how the mask, the gargoyle tragedy face, formed and unformed itself at the side of the picture.

Elisabeth had tried to read up about the Scandal scandal so she could think about and write about this picture. She'd read everything she could find online and everything in the library: some cultural books about the 1960s, a couple of books by Keeler, a copy of the Denning Report on the Scandal scandal. She hadn't known that proximity to lies, even just reading about them, could make you feel so ill. The whole thing was a bit like being made to watch something as innocent as Alfie through a gimp mask and a lot of painful S&M gear you'd never agreed to wear in the first place.

In her head whenever she thought of the true-life story round the Scandal scandal, one tiny detail in the story barbed into her like a fishhook.

An art historian called Blunt, who'd soon have his own sex/intelligence scandal to deal with, had turned up, in the middle of the Scandal trial in 1963, at an art gallery in London where there was an exhibition of portraiture. It was the work of Stephen Ward, who'd become the villain or the fall guy of the scandal at the time and who'd shortly be dead in what looked to be suicide. Ward had done portraits of rich and famous people of the time, aristocracy, royalty, political royalty, and many of them were on show here. Blunt had handed over a massive amount of cash and bought them all, everything in the gallery, outright.

He'd apparently taken them away and, the books and articles said, had them destroyed.

How had he destroyed them? Had he set them alight in some well-to-do hearth? Had he doused them in petrol in an isolated country house garden?

What Elisabeth imagined was that there was a hole dug deep in a stubbly harvested cornfield somewhere in the middle of nowhere by a tractor-sized digger, properly deep, deep enough for a couple of bodies. A small team of people stood round the rim of the hole and tossed into it portrait after portrait, making a mass grave of portraits, a pile-up of VIPs.

Then she imagined the small team of people dragging and shoving a freshly slaughtered horse or cow off the back of a lorry into the digger's mouth. She imagined the digger mechanically positioning the horse or cow carcass above the hole with the portraits in it, then the driver pushing the lever and the carcass dropping into the hole. She imagined the digger shunting the field's earth over the art and the carcass and filling the hole. She imagined the treads of the digger flattening the mound, and the people dusting their clothes down, washing the earth off their hands and cleaning it out of their nails when they got back to somewhere with water.

The horse or the cow was an extra flourish. If Elisabeth were a painter it'd be how she'd have signified the rot.

Sometimes she imagined the Boty Scandal 63 painting in there too, the carcass falling on to it, the weight of it splitting the picture's wooden stretcher. She imagined Blunt coming up the stairs of the house Boty's studio was in, his pockets full of banknotes, him not deigning to touch the banister with the filth of the pre-war years, the war years and the post-war decade still deep in its wooden ridges.

But you can't write any of that in a dissertation.

Look, she'd been doodling in the margin. There were swirls and waves and spirals.

She looked back at what she'd actually written down. *Art like this examines and makes possible a reassessment of the outer appearances of things.*

She laughed.

She took her pencil, rubbed out the capital A with the rubber on its tip, made it the lower case word *art*, then added a completely new word right at the front of the sentence so the sentence began

Arty art

Portrait in words of our next door neighbour

Our Next door neighbour to our new house we have moved to is the most elegant neighbour I have so far had. He is not old. My mother will not let me ask him the questions about being a neighbour that I am meant to be asking him for the portrait in words project we are meat to do. She says I am not allowed to bother him. She has said that she will buy us a new video player and the Beauty and The Beast video if I make up I am asking him the questions in stead of ask them in real life. To be honest I would rather not have the video or video player I would rather ask him them, what it is like to have new neighbuors and is it the same for him. Here are the questions I would ask him 1 what is it like to have neighbours 2 what is it like to be a neighbour 3 what it is like to be meant to be old but

231

not to be 4 why his house is full of pictures why they are not like the pictures we have in our house and lastly 5 why there is music playing when ever you walk close to the front door of our next door neighbour.

Next morning in 2016, the little TV up on the shelf in the kitchen is on but with the sound turned down; it must have been on, lighting and darking the kitchen by itself, all night.

Elisabeth is the only person up so far. She fills the coffeepot with water and puts it on the ring and as she turns the cooker on she sees on the screen two young twenty-somethings shopping separately in a supermarket advert suddenly simultaneously dropping the products in their hands, a loaf of bread, a couple of packets of pasta, and finding themselves in each other's arms as if by magic, then waltzing in amazement that they know how to waltz. In the next aisle a small child catches the carton of eggs his parents have just let slip. He watches his parents as they spin round and round together by a pyramid of cheeses. Near the fish counter an old couple, the man holding a tin of something up to his glasses, the woman holding on to the trolley like a zimmer, both look upwards, like they hear something above them. They exchange a knowing look. Then the woman holding the trolley pushes it away, steps backwards unbelievably light and poised on her feet, the man lets his stick fall to the ground, bows low to her and they start waltzing with old-style grace.

Elisabeth runs across to the shelf for the remote but she only gets the sound back on for the final seconds of the ad, where the child who caught the eggs shrugs his shoulders at the camera, the last shot is the sunlit summer supermarket from outside, people dancing in its car park, the warm middle-aged male voiceover saying: *all year round making a song and a dance about you.*

When her mother gets up she finds Elisabeth watching an advert for a supermarket over and over again on the laptop.

What's that burning smell? she says.

She opens the windows, cleans up round the cooker and throws away the singed dishtowel.

It begins with a supermarket car park full of cars heaped with snow, snow falling. Then the song and the dance. Then, as the song ends, the summer supermarket from outside.

Pretty gloomy song for supermarket advertising, her mother says. Then again I can't listen to anything these days without feeling maudlin.

Oh, I don't know, Elisabeth says. You've always been maudlin.

True enough. Over the years I've had a substantial career in maudlin, her mother says taking the computer.

Has her mother been this witty all these years and Elisabeth just hasn't realized?

Mike Ray and the Milky Ways, her mother says.

Never heard of them, Elisabeth says.

Her mother looks it up.

One-hit wonders, 1962, Summer Brother Autumn Sister (Gluck/Klein). Number 19, September 1962, her mother says. Well well. Maybe you're right. Maybe our Mr Gluck did write it after all.

Verse 1:

Snow is falling in the summer / Leaves are falling in the spring / Gone the reasons, gone the seasons / Time has gone and taken everything

Chorus: Summer brother autumn sister / Keeping time through time / Autumn mellow autumn yellow / Give me back a reason to rhyme

Verse 2:

I will find her in the autumn / Autumn kissed her. Autumn mist / Summer brother autumn sister / Autumn's gone so summers don't exist

Chorus x 1
Bridge:

Summer brother autumn sister / Time and time again
are gone / Out of season I will find her / With time's
fallen leaves behind her / Every time I sing this song

Chorus x 2 Ad lib to fade

(© words & music Gluck/Klein)

There is almost nothing else online about *Gluck
songwriter*, or *Gluck lyricist* or *Gluck/Klein
words & music* except links back to this song and
to the supermarket advert. There are lots of those
links. Twenty five thousand, seven hundred and five
people have watched the advert on YouTube.

Were you just playing the Milky Ways? Zoe says
coming through to the living room in Elisabeth's
mother's bathrobe. What's that burning smell?

She goes through to the kitchen whistling the
chorus.

Elisabeth checks for the song on the online
charts. It's doing rather well. She search-engines the
contact details for the supermarket's head office.

What's your second name? she says to Zoe.

Spencer-Barnes, Zoe says. Why?

Elisabeth calls a number on her phone.

Hello, she says. This is Elisabeth Demand, I'm
calling from the Spencer-Barnes Agency, can you

put me through to your marketing department? No, that's fine, answerphone is fine. Thank you. (Pause.) Hello, I'm calling from the Spencer-Barnes Agency, my name is Elisabeth Demand, that's D, e, m, a, n and d, and I'm calling on behalf of my client Mr Daniel Gluck whose copyright via your use in your current campaign of Mr Gluck's 1962 hit song Summer Brother Autumn Sister is being infringed every time your latest television commercial is aired. Obviously if you or your agency partners will be so good as to contact me, which you can do on this number – clearly we'd appreciate your alacrity – and negotiate and then be ready to transfer immediately funds totalling what we agree is legally owed to our client Mr Gluck, then the matter will cease to be problematic for us as far as both our client and the question of infringement law is concerned. I'll wait to hear from you that the situation has been resolved. If I haven't heard within twenty four hours we'll be taking action, and I'd suggest at least blanket suspension of your commercial until this has been taken in hand. Many thanks.

She left her number at the end of the message.

Infringement, her mother says. Alacrity. Via.

Elisabeth shrugs.

Do you think it'll work? her mother says.

Worth a try, Elisabeth says. I bet they think he's long gone.

What about the other people? Zoe says. What about Mike Ray? The Milky Ways?

My only concern is Daniel, Elisabeth says. I mean Mr Gluck.

Your girl's a powerhouse, Zoe says.

Isn't she. But never underestimate the source, her mother says.

The source? Elisabeth says.

Me, her mother says.

That'll be the day, Elisabeth says.

Yet another good old song, Zoe says.

She starts singing it.

It is like magic has happened in my life, Elisabeth's mother whispers to Elisabeth when Zoe's left the room.

Unnatural, Elisabeth says.

Who'd have known, who'd have guessed, it'd be love, at this late stage, that'd see me through? Elisabeth's mother says.

Unhealthy, Elisabeth says. I forbid it. You're not to.

She gives her mother a hug and a kiss.

That's enough, her mother says.

What's this book? Zoe says.

She comes through from the hall.

Who's this artist? she says. These are wonderful.

She sits down at the kitchen table with the old Pauline Boty catalogue open at the painting called 5 4 3 2 1.

One of the people my erudite daughter educates people about, Elisabeth's mother says.

Artist from the 1960s, Elisabeth says. The only British female Pop artist.

Ah, Zoe says. I didn't know there were any.

There were, Elisabeth says.

Victim of abuse, I expect, Zoe says.

She winks at Elisabeth. Elisabeth laughs.

Just the usual humdrum contemporary misogynies, she says.

Committed suicide, Zoe says.

Nope, Elisabeth says.

Went mad, then, Zoe says.

Nope. Just the usual humdrum completely sane occasional depressions, Elisabeth says.

Ah. Died tragically, then, Zoe says.

Well, that's one reading of it, Elisabeth says. My own preferred reading is: free spirit arrives on earth equipped with the skill and the vision capable of blasting the tragic stuff that happens to us all into space, where it dissolves away to nothing whenever you pay any attention to the lifeforce in her pictures.

Oh, that's good, Zoe says. That's very good. All the same. I bet she was ignored.

She was after she died, Elisabeth says.

I bet it goes like this, Zoe says. Ignored. Lost. Rediscovered years later. Then ignored. Lost. Rediscovered again years later. Then ignored. Lost. Rediscovered ad infinitum. Am I right?

Elisabeth laughs out loud.

Have you actually *done* one of my daughter's courses? her mother says.

What's her story, then, this girl? Zoe says.

She's looking at the photograph of Boty young and laughing, not yet twenty, on the inside fold of the catalogue cover.

Her story? Elisabeth says. Got ten minutes?

Autumn. 1963. Scandal 63. Up till last night the most prominent Keeler was right here, centre canvas, shouldering her way into the upper balcony, poised at the midpoint of the upper echelon between Ward and Profumo – at least, one of the Christine images was. Till last night there'd been several Christine images at different points on the canvas. One Christine image was striding along, another was naked, smiling prettily at the foot of the frame, another was in ecstasy down below the feet of the central Christine walking above swinging her handbag. But then last night at the Establishment Lewis was there, he was at the bar.

Lewis took the press photo that had spread like Spanish flu. Iconic. He'd seen what Pauline was working on, he photographed it actually. He'd come to the studio and photographed her holding

Scandal 63 on one side, Ready Steady Go on the other, kind of equivalents, and he saw her come in and he said, want to come up and see my Keelers? and Pauline said I say, what can you possibly mean, I'm a married woman you know, yes please. So they'd gone upstairs to his place above the club and he showed her and Clive the shots under the magnifiers, and she'd looked up close at the original, *the* image. Keeler with her arms up, chin on both her fists, it was splendid.

Then she'd noticed along from it on the contact sheet the slightly different version of the same.

So she said to Lewis, can you maybe make me that one up, please?

It was a good one, looked less coy, more self-protecting. One arm was down. You could see what Keeler looks like when she's thinking.

I'll do Keeler thinking, she thought. Keeler the Thinker.

Then she pointed at the marks on Keeler's leg, quite visible the bruising in the magnification.

Gosh, she said.

Can't see it in the money shot, Lewis said. Papers, too grainy.

So now she was repainting the commission. It would be full of questions now, not statements. It would still look like the image everyone thought they knew, but at the same time *not be* it. Keeler trompe l'oeil. And even an eye that didn't at first

242

notice, even an eye that took the pose for granted, would still know, unconsciously – something not quite as you expect, as you remember, as it's meant to be, can't quite put your finger.

The image and the life: well, she was used to that. There was Pauline and there was the image – feather boa flung about, winking at the camera, it was fun. High in confidence. Low in confidence. Dressed as Marilyn in the college revues, *I wanna be loved by you*. Playing Doris Day, *every body loves my body*. Little-girl song in a grown-woman voice, *daddy wouldn't buy me a bauhaus, I've got a little cat* (gasps at how she made sure they knew cat meant cunt). *Diamonds are a girl's, my armpits are charmpits* (gasps at the word armpits, not a word ever heard out loud). At the Royal College, where girls were so rare they made you stare, where the architects hadn't bothered putting women's toilets in the blueprint, she walked the corridors hearing the whispers as she went by, *rumour is, that one there's actually read Proust*, she put her arm round the boy and said it's true darling *and* Genet *and* de Beauvoir *and* Rimbaud *and* Colette, I've read all the men and the women of French letters, oh and Gertrude Stein as well, don't you know about women and their tender buttons?

The bomb was going to drop. They'd maybe only a few years to live.

A boy asked her, *why do you wear so much*

243

bright red lipstick, all the better to kiss you with she said and jumped out of her chair and came after him, he ran away, he was actually sort of terrified, she chased him out of the college and across the grass and up the pavement till he leapt on the back of a passing bus and she stood holding herself, she was laughing so much. A man, quite an old one, a very nice one, had made her laugh like that too by crawling towards her on his hands and knees across the room kissing the floor between him and her as he did; he was the songwriter, came to the flat, she called him Gershwin for fun. He asked her, looking at her Belmondo with the hat, *who's he*? Film star, French, she said, that picture's all heart-throb versus cunt-throb don't you think? and poor old Gershwin blushed all the way to his tips – ears, toes, everywhere he had a tip blushing, sweet older chap he couldn't help it, he was from another time. Well, they almost all were. Even the people meant to be from *now* were really from *then*. He was in the studio the other day, looked at 5 4 3 2 1, *what does it say*? he'd said and he'd read it out loud. *Oh for a fu–. Oh. Ah. I see. How very, ah, Shakespearianly put.* Well, if you're Gershwin, she said, I'm the Wimbledon Bard-o. Get it? *Oh yes,* he said, *Bard, Bardot. How apt.*

He liked her a lot.

Oh well.

Couldn't be helped.

Imagine if pictures in a gallery weren't just pictures but were actually sort of alive.

Imagine if time could be kind of suspended, rather than us be suspended in it.

She had no idea sometimes, to be honest, what she was trying to do. To be vital, she supposed.

Low in confidence, only sixteen, when a tutor suggested to her *stained glass isn't just for churches, it can be for anywhere. It doesn't have to be for holy things, it can be for anything.* High in confidence leaving the little corner on The Only Blonde In The World just the bare canvas like a corner of the painting had come away by itself, trompe l'oeil like you could peel them off and know that's what they were, images. Marilyn all dazzling, hurrying by in Some Like It Hot, cutting through abstraction with her brightness. Could you paint the female orgasm? It *was* Marilyn. It was coloured circles, lovely, lovely, and everything was exciting, TV was exciting, radio was exciting, London was exciting, full of exciting people from all over the world, and theatre was exciting, an empty fairground was exciting, cigarette packets were exciting, milk bottle tops were exciting, Greece was exciting, Rome was exciting, a clever woman in a hostel's shower room wearing a man's shirt to sleep in was exciting, Paris – exciting (*I am alone in Paris!! wherever I go I am followed or asked to take coffee etc. etc. otherwise Paris is*

marvellous, the painting – no words possible).
High in confidence, art could be anything, beer
cans were a new kind of folk art, film stars a new
mythology, nostalgia of NOW. It was exciting
when she worked out the photographers taking the
photos of *her* couldn't cut her *art* out of their
pictures if she posed as *part* of her art.

(Wrong.

Blast.

They still managed to cut round her and slice the
art out and away, leaving the breast and the thigh
bits, of course.)

Get my paintbrushes into the shot, will
you, Mike?

She was wearing a hat, a shirt and her
underwear, mimicking as closely as she could Celia
in the portrait, except she'd taken her jeans off to
be sure they'd keep both her and the picture in the
picture. But Lewis and Michael were great boys,
she kind of liked them immensely. They let her tell
them how to set up the shots and mostly they did as
she asked. Happy to pose nude. I like nakedness. I
mean who doesn't, to be honest? I'm a person. I'm
an intelligent nakedness. An intellectual body. I'm a
bodily intelligence. Art's full of nudes and I'm a
thinking, choosing nude. I'm the artist as nude. I'm
the nude as artist.

A great many men don't understand a woman
full of joy, even more don't understand paintings

full of joy by a woman. It's really all based on sex the whole thing, look, the bananas and fountains and that huge mouth and the hand, well, they're all phallic symbols. *Well, anyway*, they say, *I'm a man, and being a man is lots better than being a woman.*

She saw the notice pinned to the side of the building, bright yellow, saying in different coloured letters CRAZY COTTAGE then underneath in blue the bigger letters BRIGITTE'S BIKINI then small in faded black COME IN & SEE then a little THE on the side then huge in red SEX KITTEN. Take my photo looking at this, please, Mike, she said. She came right up to the side of the building as if she were coming round its corner and simply sort of reading the sign because that's what she was, a girl reading the world.

But love was terribly important. She didn't mean romantic love. Generalized sort of love. Enjoying oneself was terribly important. Sex could be as varied as being alive could be varied. Passion always sounded to her like something without humour in it. A passionate moment for her –

I can remember once sitting opposite my brother and feeling so much love for him that it was almost as though I was knitted to him.

This lovely feeling (she'd say to the writer interviewing her for a book) lasted for, say, half an hour. But she'd married her husband because he *liked* women, he knew they weren't *things*, or something you didn't quite know about. He accepted me intellectually, which men find very difficult.

High in confidence. Low in confidence. Her mother was out in her father's English rose garden pruning the roses; her mother made the dresses and made the meals. Out in the Carshalton garden with the pruning shears her mother said it way before James Brown, *it's a man's world*, moving the mark on the sherry bottle so her father wouldn't notice, her mother, Veronica, banned back in the day from taking a place at the Slade by her own father, grieving for that place all her secateur life, working on Pauline's father to let her, Wimbledon Art School. It was her mother took her to America on the QE2, her mother listening to Maria Callas at full volume (when her father was out), shouting at the radio news (in the kitchen when her father wasn't in the kitchen), her mother who fell ill, Pauline was eleven, endless X-rays for everyone, scans, her mother who was going to die. The family went to chaos, it was good the chaos, except for the depressions. No, it was formative. Lost a lung, her mother, but she was kind of perfectly all right, she was keeping a scrapbook of the cuttings from the papers. PAULINE PAINTS POPS. And ALL MY OWN WORK. (That was the headline on Pauline hanging an abstract in the London Labour Party Trades Union Congress Headquarters.) *Actresses*

*often have tiny brains. Painters often have huge
beards. Imagine a brainy actress who is also a
painter and also a blonde.*

Imagine.

Her father was stern. Her father disapproved.
Her father had very strong reservations. Desirable?
a semi? I daren't say anything or daddy will be
upset. Half Belgian, half Persian, staunch British
conservative, he'd seen the Himalayas and Harrogate
and had chosen accountancy. His father'd been
killed by pirates (true). His mother's family had
been shipbuilders on the Euphrates. So the
Norfolk Broads is where he kept his own boat, and
the rules of cricket, the making of tea the way
it should be made were what to measure
life by.

He didn't even want me to work when I left
school.

The fights were sort of huge, often before
breakfast, the stupidest worst time to fight with
him. Her older brothers flinched and shook their
heads. Her brothers had it too, men had it too,
maybe even worse – the brother who wanted to go
to art school, their father made him an accountant.
She got to go eventually, well, after all, not a proper
job, so it was maybe more okay, for a girl, to.

But her brothers, when she was little. *Shut up,
you're only a girl.* Used to want to be a boy. Before,
she used to pull at – you know the sort of skin you

have – to make it sort of longer. Used to think I had an ugly cunt you see, I don't now. Free and easy.

Made me what I am.

The ideal woman, a kind of faithful slave, who administers without a word of complaint and certainly no payment, who speaks only when spoken to and is a jolly good chap. But a revolution is on the way, all over the country young girls are starting and shaking and if they terrify you they mean to is what she'd soon be saying out loud on the radio herself, you know.

One day a group of students was staging a protest outside a building. A BBC man came up with a mike. He chose the pretty girl. She was in a duffel coat strewing rose petals on the paving in front of the building.

What's a pretty girl like you doing at this sort of event?

She told him. This building is a real stinker. We're protesting it. We're mourning the death of architectural beauty.

But I've heard that this building is thought to be very efficient inside, he said.

We are outside, she said.

High in confidence. Low in confidence. Moodswings. Not a cosy girl. Don't come and see me today. Goodbye Cruel World, I'm off to join the circus. That was a pop song, Ken used it in his film when he followed her and three of the boys about and showed their lives, their work, their day. She filmed a dream instead, a real recurring dream (her final year dissertation was dreams) and after that film by Ken, in came all the dream jobs, the acting offers, 1963, dream of a year, *anus* mirabilis ha ha ha. All the things that had happened were the kind of thing, she supposed, that if they were ever to do one of those timelines of your life, born 6 March 1938, died whenever, would look sort of marvellous on a timeline. Grabowski show, radio work, married Clive, dancer on Ready Steady Go!, acting at Royal Court (acting was a time thing, though, sort of confidence trick. Painting was the real thing).

And then the future.

All the thirties up to thirty nine sounded great.

Between forty and fifty would be hell.

She hoped she'd never get hard. She'd never want to be too fixed in her ways.

(She'd be sketching and painting right up to her death. She'd sketch, among others, her friends in the band, 19th Nervous Breakdown. Paint it, Black. Her baby'd be in a cot at the foot of the bed. Her pictures after she died? Gone, lost, and the ones that weren't lost, thirty years in silence in her father's attic and an outhouse on her brother's farm, close shaves when it came to trips to the skip. The writer and curator who'd search for them thirty years after and find them in that outhouse? He'd burst into tears when he did.)

There was a circle of roses at the heart of her surname, all round the O in a woven open wreath.

There was a carved mermaid holding up the table.

There was never any money.

There was the brass bed, the paraffin stove.

There was pretending to be off-your-head berserk when the landlord came round hammering at the door to try to get to sleep with you.

There was wearing your coat all day in your room on the cold days.

None of that was life.

Life? was what you worked to catch, the intense happiness of an object slightly set apart from you. Painting? was what you did, alone, and you sat there, and it was your own terrible fight or your own lovely bit, but it was really terribly alone.

To take the moment before something had actually happened, and you didn't know if it was going to be terrible or if it might be very funny, something extraordinary actually happening and yet everybody around it not taking any notice at all.

She pasted. She cut. She painted. She concentrated.

In her dream, she slapped the past in its face.

Telling her schoolfriend Beryl, they were both sixteen, I'm going to be an artist.

Women don't get to be that, Beryl said.

I will. A serious artist. I want to be a painter.

It is yet another day, weather, time, news, stuff happening all across the country/countries, etc. Elisabeth goes for a walk in the village. Almost nobody is about. The few people out cutting things back in their gardens scowl at her or ignore her.

She steps to one side to make room on the narrow pavement and says hello to an old lady she passes.

The old lady nods, doesn't smile, walks past, imperious.

She comes to the spraypainted house. Either the people who were living here have moved or they've repainted the front of their house this bright seaside blue. It's like nothing's ever happened, unless you know to look a little more closely to make out the outline of the word HOME under the layer of blue.

When she gets back to her mother's the front

door is wide open. Her mother's friend Zoe comes out of it at a gallop. She almost collides with Elisabeth. In the near-miss she catches her up in her arms and swings her round in something like a Scottish country dance move, then skips backwards away from her down the path.

You'll never believe what your mother's gone and done, Zoe says.

She is laughing so much that Elisabeth can't not laugh too.

She got herself arrested. She threw a barometer at the fence, Zoe says.

What? Elisabeth says.

You know, Zoe says. Thing that measures pressure.

I know what a barometer is, Elisabeth says.

We were in the next village along, in the antiques place, you know it? Your mother took me there to show off how much she knows about antiques. And she saw a barometer she liked, so she bought it, cost a fair bit too. And we were on our way back in the car and the radio was on, and the news story came on about our new government cutting their funding for the houses where the kids who arrive here as asylum seekers have been staying, and the report said those kids are now going to be dumped in the same high-security places they put everybody. And your mother lost it. She started shouting about how those places are worse than jail, everyone under guard, bars on the windows, not fit for anybody, doubly not fit for kids. And then the next news story on the radio was the scrapping of the Minister for Refugees. She made me stop the car. She left the car door hanging open and she ran off up a path. So I got out and locked the car up and I followed her, and when I found her, well, I heard her before I saw her, she was shouting at men in a van at the fence, I mean fences, and she was shaking the barometer in the air at them and then I swear she threw it at the fence! And the fence gave this great cracking sound, a flash came off it, and the men went crazy because she'd shorted their fence. I couldn't help it. I yelled too. I yelled that's the way Wendy! That's the spirit!

Zoe tells Elisabeth that her mother'd been held for an hour, got off with a caution and is right now at the antiques yard down the road at the junction, stockpiling more stuff to throw at the fence, that her mother's new plan is that every day she's going to go and get herself arrested (and here she imitates Elisabeth's mother perfectly) *bombarding that fence with people's histories and with the artefacts of less cruel and more philanthropic times.*

She sent me home to bring the car, Zoe says. She's going to load it up with junk missiles. Oh, and I mustn't forget. They phoned for you on the house phone. Ten minutes ago.

Who did? Elisabeth says.

The hospital. Not hospital, the care place. Care providers.

Her mother's friend sees her face change. She stops being flippant immediately.

They said to tell you, she says. Your grandfather's been asking for you.

This time, the woman at reception doesn't even glance up. She is watching someone get garrotted on Game of Thrones on her iPad.

But then she says, still without looking up,

he's eaten a good lunch today, enough for like three people. Well, older people. We told him you'd be delighted he'd woken up and he said, please let my granddaughter know I'm looking forward to seeing her.

Elisabeth walks down the corridor, comes to his door and looks in.

He is asleep again.

She gets the chair from the corridor. She puts it beside the bed. She sits down. She gets out A Tale of Two Cities.

She closes her eyes. When she opens them

again his eyes are open. He is looking straight at her.

Hello again, Mr Gluck, she says.

Oh, hello, he says. Thought it'd be you. Good. Nice to see you. What you reading?

November again. It's more winter than autumn. That's not mist. It's fog.

The sycamore seeds hit the glass in the wind like – no, not like anything else, like sycamore seeds hitting window glass.

There've been a couple of windy nights. The leaves are stuck to the ground with the wet. The ones on the paving are yellow and rotting, wanwood, leafmeal. One is so stuck that when it eventually peels away, its leafshape left behind, shadow of a leaf, will last on the pavement till next spring.

The furniture in the garden is rusting. They've forgotten to put it away for the winter.

The trees are revealing their structures. There's the catch of fire in the air. All the souls are out

259

marauding. But there are roses, there are still roses. In the damp and the cold, on a bush that looks done, there's a wide-open rose, still.

Look at the colour of it.

I'm deeply indebted to everyone who's written about Pauline Boty but above all to the seminal work of Sue Tate and to her two volumes, Pauline Boty: Pop Artist and Woman (2013) and, as Sue Watling, with David Alan Mellor, Pauline Boty: The Only Blonde in the World (1998); and also to the interview with Boty by Nell Dunn in Vogue, September 1964, the full-length version of which is published in Nell Dunn's Talking to Women (1965). The stories about Christine Keeler which feature briefly in the novel can be found in Nothing But . . ., by Christine Keeler with Sandy Fawkes (1983), and Secrets and Lies, by Christine Keeler with Douglas Thompson (2012). I'm also fortunate to have been able to read a typescript of Sybille Bedford's as yet unpublished account of Stephen Ward's trial in 1963, The Worst We Can Do: A Concise Account of the Trial of Dr Stephen Ward, some of whose details of the trial (the court transcriptions of which still haven't been released into the public domain) have slipped into this novel.

Thank you, Simon, Anna, Hermione, Lesley B., Lesley L., Ellie, Sarah, and everyone at Hamish Hamilton.

Thank you, Andrew and Tracy
and everyone at Wylie's.

Thank you, Bridget Smith, Kate Thomson,
Neil MacPherson and Rachel Gatiss.

Thank you, Xandra. Thank you, Mary.

Thank you, Jackie.

Thank you, Sarah.

THE ACCIDENTAL

Filled with Ali Smith's trademark wordplay and inventive storytelling, *The Accidental* is the dizzyingly entertaining, wickedly humorous story of a mysterious stranger whose sudden appearance during a family's summer holiday transforms four variously unhappy people. Each of the Smarts—parents Eve and Michael, son Magnus, and daughter Astrid—encounter Amber in his or her own solipsistic way, but somehow her presence allows them to see their lives (and their life together) in a new light. Smith's narrative freedom and exhilarating facility with language propel the novel to its startling, wonderfully enigmatic conclusion.

Fiction

THE BOOK LOVER

The Book Lover is a treasure trove of what Ali Smith has loved over the course of her reading life: in her twenties, as a teenager, as a child. Full of pieces from amazing writers such as Sylvia Plath, Muriel Spark, Grace Paley, and Margaret Atwood, it also has a wonderful selection of lesser-known authors such as Clarice Lispector, a Brazilian genius who's far too underpublished, and Joseph Roth. From surprising figures like Beryl the Peril, Billie Holiday, and Lee Miller to unusual selections from the most prominent writers in history, *The Book Lover* is an intimate, personal anthology that gives readers a glimpse of how writers develop their craft—by reading other writers.

Fiction

THE FIRST PERSON AND OTHER STORIES

From the Whitbread Award–winning author of *The Accidental* and *Hotel World* comes this stunning collection of stories set in a world of everyday dislocation, where people nevertheless find connection, mystery, and love. These tales are of ordinary but poignant beauty: at the pub, strangers regale each other with memories of Christmases past; lovers share tales over dinner about how they met their former lovers and each other; a woman tells a story to her fourteen-year-old self. As Smith explores the subtle links between what we know and what we feel, she creates an exuberant, masterly collection that is packed full of ideas, humor, nuance, and compassion. Ali Smith and the short story are made for each other.

Fiction

PUBLIC LIBRARY AND OTHER STORIES

Why are books so very powerful? What do the books we've read over our lives—our own personal libraries—make of us? What does the unraveling of our tradition of public libraries, so hard-won but now in jeopardy, say about us? The stories in Ali Smith's new collection are about what we do with books and what they do with us: how they travel with us; how they shock us, change us, challenge us, banish time while making us older, wiser, and ageless all at once; how they remind us to pay attention to the world we make. Woven between the stories are conversations with writers and readers reflecting on the essential role that libraries have played in their lives. At a time when public libraries around the world face threats of cuts and closures, this collection stands as a work of literary activism—and as a wonderful read from one of our finest authors.

Fiction

HOTEL WORLD

Five people: four are living; three are strangers; two are sisters; one, a teenage hotel chambermaid, has fallen to her death in a dumbwaiter. But her spirit lingers in the world, straining to recall things she never knew. And one night, all five women find themselves in the smooth plush environs of the Global Hotel, where the intersection of their very different fates makes up this playful, defiant, and richly inventive novel. Forget room service: this is a riotous elegy, a deadpan celebration of colliding worlds, and a spirited defense of love. Blending incisive wit with surprising compassion, *Hotel World* is a wonderfully invigorating, life-affirming book.

Fiction

HOW TO BE BOTH

Passionate, compassionate, vitally inventive, and scrupulously playful, Ali Smith's novels are like nothing else. Borrowing from painting's fresco technique to make an original literary double-take, *How to be both* is a novel all about art's versatility. It's a fast-moving, genre-bending conversation among forms, times, truths, and fictions. There's a Renaissance artist of the 1460s. There's the child of a child of the 1960s. Two tales of love and injustice twist into a singular yarn where time gets timeless, knowing gets mysterious, fictional gets real—and all life's givens get given a second chance.

Fiction

ALSO AVAILABLE

There but for the
The whole story and other stories